CW00937688

Reclaiming Byzantium

Reclaiming Byzantium

Russia, Turkey and the Archaeological Claim to the Middle East in the 19th Century

Pınar Üre

I.B.TAURIS

LONDON • NEW YORK • OXFORD • NEW DELHI • SYDNEY

I.B. TAURIS
Bloomsbury Publishing Plc
50 Bedford Square, London, WC1B 3DP, UK
1385 Broadway, New York, NY 10018, USA

BLOOMSBURY, I.B. TAURIS and the I.B. Tauris logo are trademarks of
Bloomsbury Publishing Plc

First published in Great Britain 2020

Copyright © Pınar Üre, 2020

Pınar Üre has asserted her right under the Copyright, Designs and Patents Act,
1988, to be identified as Author of this work.

For legal purposes the Acknowledgements on p. ix constitute an extension
of this copyright page.

Cover image: Relief depicting a Byzantine two-headed eagle, Ikosifinissis
monastery, near Serres, Greece, 15th century. (© DeAgostini/Getty Images)

All rights reserved. No part of this publication may be reproduced or
transmitted in any form or by any means, electronic or mechanical,
including photocopying, recording, or any information storage or retrieval
system, without prior permission in writing from the publishers.

Bloomsbury Publishing Plc does not have any control over, or responsibility for,
any third-party websites referred to or in this book. All internet addresses given
in this book were correct at the time of going to press. The author and publisher
regret any inconvenience caused if addresses have changed or sites have ceased
to exist, but can accept no responsibility for any such changes.

A catalogue record for this book is available from the British Library.

A catalog record for this book is available from the Library of Congress.

ISBN: HB: 978-1-7883-1012-3
ePDF: 978-1-7883-1746-7
eBook: 978-1-7883-1745-0

Typeset by Newgen KnowledgeWorks Pvt. Ltd., Chennai, India
Printed and bound in Great Britain

To find out more about our authors and books visit www.bloomsbury.com
and sign up for our newsletters.

To Güner, Murat, and Kutay Üre

Contents

Acknowledgements

It would not have been possible to write this book without the help of a number of individuals.

First of all, I would like to thank Prof. Dominic Lieven for his helpfulness and encouragement throughout this study. His supervision provided me with invaluable academic insight and guidance. I would like to extend thanks to my former colleagues at the International History Department at the London School of Economics and Political Science and Istanbul Altınbaş University. I always feel very lucky to be part of such intellectually stimulating and socially supportive communities since the early stages of my academic career.

I owe thanks to the staff of Istanbul Archaeological Museums, especially Havva Koç, for making the marvellous museum library available for me. I also would like to express my gratitude to the staff of the St Petersburg Branch of the Archive of Russian Academy of Sciences.

I would like to thank Prof. Peter Holquist from the University of Pennsylvania and Prof. Hakan Kırımlı from Bilkent University for their valuable academic support since the first years of my academic career. For a young researcher, it is a gift to work with such inpiring historians. I should also thank Prof. Simon Dixon and Prof. Peter Waldron for their constructive suggestions during my PhD defense a few years ago. These suggestions ultimately shaped this book.

I should also extend my gratitude to the editorial team at I.B. Tauris, who eventually made this book a reality and helped make my dream come true.

On a personal note, I would like to thank all the wonderful people I met in Ankara, Istanbul, London, Philadelphia and St Petersburg, who supported me in one way or another during the research and writing phases of this book. I am incredibly lucky to have so many great friends who shared their wisdom with me when I needed it. These friends are too many to name, but they know who they are.

Finally, I cannot find the right words to thank my family. This book could not be written without their love and encouragement. My gratitude to them knows no bounds. It is to them this book is dedicated.

Introduction: Regenerating distant past
Nationalist and Imperialist uses of ancient
history in the 19th century

But no physical object or trace is an autonomous guide to bygone times;
they light up the past only when we already know they belong to it.
Memory and history pin-point only certain things as relics; the rest of what
lies around us seems simply present, suggesting nothing past.[1]

In May 2016, the famous Mariinsky Symphony Orchestra of St. Petersburg organized a classical music concert in the famous Roman theatre of the ancient city of Palmyra, which was recently liberated from the destruction of ISIS, or the so-called Islamic State by the forces of the Russian-backed Syrian president Bashar al-Assad.[2] Before the concert started, Russian president Vladimir Putin addressed the audience through a videoconference and stated that the concert was 'an amazing humanitarian act'.[3] The concert, which was named 'With a Prayer from Palmyra: Music Revives the Ancient Walls', was a celebration (and an obvious PR campaign) of the victory of the Syrian and Russian forces in the Syrian Civil War. The implicit message behind the spectacle was a clash between the 'civilized and uncivilized', and Russia naturally appeared as the redeemer of civilization by saving the ancient monuments of Palmyra from further destruction at the hands of militants.

Russia's relationship with the ruins of Palmyra, or antiquities in the Near East in general, did not start in the 21st century with the Syrian Civil War. In fact, archaeologists of the Russian Empire were conducting studies in Palmyra and in other ancient cities across the Near East already in the late 19th century. Just like it is in contemporary politics, back in the 19th century, ancient history was already a stage for imperial rivalry and great power politics. Hence, the discovery and protection of archaeological artefacts were regarded as signs of imperial prestige and triumph of civilization.

On the Ottoman side, foreign archaeological activities were regarded with suspicion especially in the late 19th century. In an attempt to preserve its vulnerable sovereignty, Ottoman Empire closely monitored foreign archaeological activities on its territories. For the Ottoman Empire, archaeology was also a way of projecting its image as a modern, Westernized empire. For both Russian and Ottoman archaeologists, European scholarship was regarded as an example that should be followed, and a rival at the same time.

The 19th century was marked by the institutionalization of archaeology as a scientific discipline, particularly in Europe.[4] University chairs and museums were established in European capitals. Academics from Britain, France, and later Germany and the United States organized archaeological institutes, societies and schools in the famous centres of the ancient world – primarily Rome, Athens and Cairo.[5] These historical cities became meeting points for archaeologists from different countries, who found the opportunity to share their projects with international academia. The study of the ancient world provided the archaeologists a window through which they could look into the origins of European civilization as they saw it. Modern European empires defined themselves as the spiritual heirs of the ancient civilizations that flourished in the Mediterranean basin and the Near East.[6]

The creation of schools of archaeology in cities such as Cairo and Athens mirrored the political competition between major European powers. The success of archaeological activities was increasingly associated with national and imperial prestige.[7] The political rivalry between Britain and France was replicated by the British Museum and the Louvre, and Germany caught up with them after its political unification in 1871. Antiquities flowing from Egypt and the Near East filled European museums.[8] National museums in the imperial capitals became the visual representations of the territories each empire held under its control, while overseas archaeological institutes became the physical embodiments of their imperial presence in the given territory.

Around the same time, touristic trips to ancient cities and museums gradually became a part of leisure for European upper classes, who wanted to flee modernity into realms of alternative imagination. The first 'Grand Tourists' of the 18th and early 19th centuries were members of the European upper classes, but with the growth of mass tourism in the late 19th century, middle classes joined them.[9] After visiting archaeological sites in Greece, Italy and the Near East, European travellers recorded their observations with the help of photographs, travel diaries, and guidebooks, and recreated the ancient past through a Western lens. The preoccupation of different segments of the society with ancient history meant that re-creation of the past in a modern context was not only an official project initiated by the state, rather, it was simultaneously influenced both from above by the state and from below by individuals.

Intensive European archaeological involvement in other parts of the world implied that modern inhabitants of ancient lands either had lost the glamour of their past or were the descendants of 'barbarians' who destroyed the ancient civilizations under examination. After a long period of ignorance and neglect, it was European archaeologists who were unearthing this glorious past and were therefore the legitimate heirs to the heritage left by ancient civilizations.[10] Therefore, a direct historical line was drawn from the ancient civilizations of the Near East to modern European nations, with European culture standing at the peak of human progress.[11] In an 1853 issue of the *Illustrated Magazine of Art*, an anonymous author professed that 'France and England divide the glory of having rescued from the underground darkness and oblivion of twenty-five centuries, some of the most magnificent remains of the old world'.[12] As Díaz-Andreu Garcia argued, archaeological discourse was useful in legitimizing the assumed inferiority of people inhabiting the regions under European political, economic and cultural control.[13] In fact, archaeology provided a narrative explaining the 'inevitability of certain lands to be conquered and the right of certain people to rule'.[14] Archaeology's links to power politics became even more evident during the First World War, when many archaeologists put their knowledge of local languages, cultures and topography to the use of the intelligence services of their states.[15]

The Russian Empire joined the competition over the ancient world as a latecomer. The choice of location for the first overseas Russian archaeological institute was neither Rome nor Athens – but Istanbul, or Constantinople, or the Russian Tsargrad, the former capital of the Eastern Roman Empire and Orthodox Christianity, a capital for whose possession some Russians longed in the 19th century.[16]

This study will explore Russian archaeological practices in the Ottoman Empire through the prism of a scholarly institution, the Russian Archaeological Institute in Constantinople (*Russkii Arkheologicheskii Institut v Konstantinopole*, hereafter as RAIK), which operated between 1895 and 1914. Established under the administrative structure of the Russian Embassy in Istanbul, the institute occupied a place at the intersection of science and politics. Focusing nearly exclusively on Byzantine and Slavic antiquities in the Ottoman Empire, the activities of the institute reflected the imperial identity of Russia at the turn of the century. As was explicitly expressed by Russian diplomats, bureaucrats and scholars, the establishment of an archaeological institution in the Ottoman capital was regarded as a foreign-policy tool to extend Russia's influence in the Near East, a tool of 'soft power' in modern parlance. At the time of its existence, RAIK contributed significantly to the development of Byzantinology with its numerous excavations and publications. Russian archaeologists had to close down their office with the outbreak of the First World War. The complications that arose with the disintegration of the institute were solved only in the late 1920s between the Soviet Union and Republican Turkey, under completely different political circumstances.

The relationship between ancient monuments, archaeological practice and politics attracted the attention of scholars of history and archaeology in recent years. The subject was covered from a variety of perspectives: scholars questioned how archaeological knowledge was used in the nation-building process in different parts of the world from Southeast Asia to Western Europe, or how knowledge production influenced centre–periphery relations in colonial settings. The development of archaeology in the Ottoman Empire, both as a local Ottoman practice and in terms of foreign archaeological activities on Ottoman territories also received considerable attention. Although there has been a great deal of interest in the political aspects of the archaeological activities by British, French and other Western European nations in the Near East, Russian archaeological activities did not receive the same level of interest.

The archaeological activities of RAIK defy easy categorization: Russian scholarly institutions in the Ottoman Empire cannot be characterized as colonial, as Russia was not a colonial power in this region and the Ottoman Empire, at least theoretically, was an empire of equal status. It cannot be categorized as strictly nationalist, as the focus of its interest went beyond Russia's 'national' borders. Russian archaeological activities in the Ottoman Empire gives insight into the relationship between these two empires, as well as Russian Empire's aspired place in international politics.

When talking about foreign archaeologists in the Ottoman Empire, scholars generally draw a line between European archaeologists who had higher scholarly qualifications and local Ottoman bureaucrats who tried to counter European imperialist discourse by claiming antiquities for the Ottoman state. The unequal political relationship between great powers of Europe and the Ottoman Empire was reflected in the sphere of archaeology, as well. In this dichotomy, it is the European scholars that set the agenda and determine the parameters of scholarship, and Ottomans merely follow them with a desire to prove their equal status. Russian archaeologists were different from their 'more' Western counterparts, and the diplomacy of archaeology between Russia and the Ottoman Empire was distinctive for a number of reasons. As two latecomers to modernization and Europeanization, scholars, bureaucrats and diplomats of both empires regarded such practices as archaeology as an entry ticket to Western civilization. The act of engaging in scholarly activities was regarded as a sign of being a part of the 'civilized' nations. On the other hand, by emphasizing Byzantine, Slavic and Orthodox cultural heritage, Russian archaeological activities in the Ottoman Empire reaffirmed distinct characteristics of Russian imperial identity, and were also closely linked to its foreign-policy priorities.

In his article on the political aspects of archaeology in the 19th century, Bruce Trigger identified three main currents: nationalist, imperialist and colonialist. Nationalist archaeology was employed by the young nation-states in search of ancient ancestors for their newly created regimes. Trigger associated imperialist archaeology with a small number of states that exerted political, economic and cultural influence over large areas of the world.[17] Finally, colonial archaeology was identified with the archaeological activities of – mostly – European archaeologists in the colonial domains of their empires. Nevertheless, none of these categories seem to explain Russian or Ottoman archaeological activities with justice. Actually, the literature on the political aspects of archaeology generally focuses on either colonial archaeology, as was practiced by European archaeologists in European colonial possessions, or nationalist archaeology, as was practiced by native archaeologists in sovereign nation-states in an attempt to legitimize the nation-state rhetoric. However, Russia and the Ottoman Empire, as two cosmopolitan, traditional empires of the pre-First World War period, do not fit in these categories. Russian archaeological activities in the Ottoman Empire and Ottoman reactions to them rather reflect their imperial identities, and how the political programs and imperial visions of the Ottoman Empire and Russia came into conflict with each other.

An ancient site, a monument and an object of archaeological interest may have multiple histories and multiple meanings, depending on the position of the interpreter. An ancient monument is not only a reminder of a bygone past, but it is also a medium for the (re)construction and (re)making of identity through a particular interpretation of history. After all, remembering and interpreting the history of an ancient monument in a specific way, while ignoring other possible readings, is a political choice. Multiple actors with opposed world views may promote their conflicting interests through the symbolism of historical monuments. In other words, the competition over antiquities may be correlated with political competition between different groups.

In his seminal book *Imagined Communities*, Benedict Anderson observed that along with maps and censuses, archaeology has also been an important 'institution of power' that reflected the way in which colonial states imagined the history of their colonial possessions.[18] Archaeological activities and the establishment of national museums helped visualize and classify history into strictly delineated national, geographic and demographic units. Ancient monuments proved to be visible links between particular cultures and lands, stretching from immemorial past to present, providing legitimacy for existing states to rule over territories once inhabited by their assumed predecessors.[19] Anderson's study brought up questions about the spatial dimension of history, and in recent years this particular dimension has been scrutinized with reference to imperial Russian history, as well.[20]

It should be noted that this study does not intend to question the scientific legitimacy of archaeology or put forward epistemological questions about whether archaeological data can or cannot provide objective knowledge. The recreation of the past through archaeological or historical scholarship is not entirely a mental construction but requires data; therefore, even when their analyses is coloured by particular social and political concerns, the scholarship is justifiable as long as it helps us understand the past.[21] Nevertheless, as Trigger pointed out, ideologies influence the questions archaeologists ask or refrain from asking.[22] This study is concerned with questions that Russian archaeologists preferred to ask, the motivations that prompted Russian imperial government to support and fund certain archaeological projects and the symbolic meaning of ancient history in the diplomatic relations between states.

As will be discussed in the following chapters, the relationship between RAIK staff and Russian diplomatic representatives in the Ottoman Empire had a close-knit nature, which implied a convergence of interests between the two groups. The political relevance of archaeological projects were often emphasized both by Russian diplomats and archaeologists who encouraged the establishment of the institute. Of course, not only Russian but also French, British and German scientific communities in the Ottoman Empire were supported by their respective governments and diplomats, since it was easier to secure research permits in a foreign country through diplomatic channels than it was for individual scholars. However, in an autocratic regime like Russia, where the individual autonomy and freedom of scholars were constrained by state authority, scientific projects that diplomats preferred to support indicated the priorities of imperial foreign policy. RAIK's projects reflected Russian imperial identity and underlying ideological tenets of Russian foreign policy at the turn of the century. At the same time, the shortcomings and failures of RAIK shed light on the limits of Russia's political influence abroad.

RAIK came into existence at a time when there was increasing international political competition over the Balkans and the rest of the Ottoman territories. There was pressure both from above and from below: on the one hand, nationalist movements swept through Ottoman territories. On the other hand, European powers worked hard to preserve the international status quo in the face of Ottoman decline. Russia's inevitable rivalry with

European powers, and the necessity to catch up with them in every sphere, including science, appeared frequently as a theme in the discourse of Russian archaeologists and diplomats. In the late 19th century, overseas archaeological institutes were the visual expressions of the political influence of European empires over a given region. The people who supported the establishment of RAIK argued that if other European empires invested in archaeology, then Russia should follow the same path. Archaeological scholarship was regarded as a sign of prestige and civilization, and a tool for extending political influence at the same time.

Selim Deringil defines Ottoman and Russian imperial identity in the 19th century with the term 'borrowed imperialism'. He argues that Ottoman and Russian elites adopted European colonial discourse as regards the periphery of their respective Empires in their attempt to survive in a world where rules were made by the industrial empires of Western Europe.[23] For both Russia and the Ottoman Empire, embracing the imperialist rhetoric borrowed from Europe was a way of establishing their precarious status as 'European'. This imperial self-perception was reflected in the way Russia and the Ottoman Empire responded to the archaeological rivalry among imperial powers in the 19th century. Since archaeological discoveries became a marker of national and imperial prestige, promoting archaeological excavations and exhibiting the findings in their imperial museums were essential for Russians and the Ottomans.

In addition to highlighting Russian imperial identity, RAIK's contacts with the Ottoman Empire and Balkan nations give insight about the political agendas of these governments and Russia's relationship with them. Neither the Ottoman Empire nor Balkan states were merely passive actors in this process. The development of legal frameworks to monitor foreign archaeologists and sensitivity about ownership rights over ancient objects imply that monuments were regarded as symbols of sovereignty by the countries that hosted antiquities. Particularly for the Ottoman Empire, archaeology was a means of asserting its place among European empires. By sponsoring archaeological studies of its own and compelling foreign archaeologists to obey certain regulations, the Ottoman government was in fact indicating that it was on an equal footing with Europeans. As two multi-ethnic and multireligious empires, the 'diplomacy of archaeology' between the Russian and Ottoman Empires defy easy categorizations such as nationalist, imperialist or colonialist archaeology; rather require a multi-faceted analysis.

This study is based on official correspondence between RAIK and Russian diplomats, various ministries, government bodies, and the Ottoman government, as well as personal letters of RAIK members, especially those belonging to the director of the institute, Fyodor Ivanovich Uspenskii (1845–1928). Reports submitted to the Ministry of Public Education, excavation and expedition reports also constitute an important source-base for the study. These materials were gathered mainly from the St Petersburg branch of the Archive of the Russian Academy of Sciences (PFA RAN), Russian State Historical Archives (RGIA) in Russia, Prime Ministerial Ottoman Archives (BOA) in Turkey, and from the Bulletin of the Russian Archaeological Institute in Constantinople (IRAIK).²⁴

The holdings at the Ottoman Archives included correspondence between the Russian Embassy and the Ottoman government offices, most notably Ottoman Ministry of Foreign Affairs and Ministry of Education. The Ottoman Imperial Museum was bureaucratically under the auspices of the Ministry of Education, therefore archival documents about the Imperial Museum are located under the Ministry of Education files. In this book, there are several references to the documents of the Chief Secretary of the Ministry of Education (*Maarif Mektubî Kalemi*, MF. MKT.). The activities of Russian archaeologists were overseen by local officials appointed by the Ministry of the Interior, in addition to the Ottoman Imperial Museum. The documents of various Ministry of the Interior offices are categorized into subgroups under the files of the *Dâhiliye Nezâreti* (The subgroups used in this study include DH. HMŞ., DH. İD., DH. MKT., DH. EUM. MTK.). Because of RAIK's diplomatic links, the Ottoman Ministry of Foreign Affairs was an active participant in the dialogue between Russian archaeologists and the Ottoman government. The references to the documents of the Chief Secretary of the Ministry of Foreign Affairs (*Hariciye Mektubî Kalemi*, HR. MKT.) highlight the exchange between Russian archaeologists and the Ministry. The decrees sanctioned by the Sultan are referred to as *İrade,* and the documents cited as İ. HUS., İ. MMS., İ. MSM., İ. ŞD., İ. TAL represent the sultans' *irades.* Under the Hamidian regime, there was an extensive network of government officials and spies reporting every incident across the Ottoman Empire directly to the Sultan himself. The documents collected at the personal palace of Abdülhamid II are accessible under the title *Yıldız Evrâkı.* The archival documents cited as Y. A. HUS., Y. PRK. ASK. and Y. PRK. BŞK. are parts of this file. Finally, the documents from the office of the Grand Vizier (*Sadaret Mektubî Kalemi*, A. MKT.) and documents from the Archive of the Sublime Porte (*Bab-ı Âli Evrak Odası*, BEO) are widely used in this research.

With regard to the archives in Russia, the bulk of materials concerning the history of RAIK is located at the St Petersburg Branch of the Archive of the Russian Academy of Sciences (PFA RAN).²⁵ This archive hosts the diplomatic correspondence between RAIK and the Russian Embassy in Istanbul and various Russian consulates across the Ottoman Empire, yearly reports of

RAIK submitted to the Ministry of Public Education, personal papers of archaeologists affiliated with the Institute, and visual materials. Specifically, I looked into three *fonds*:[26] *Fond* no. 116 holds documents pertaining to the director of RAIK, Fyodor Ivanovich Uspenskii. Uspenskii's correspondence with diplomats, bureaucrats, Russian and foreign archaeologists, as well as his personal notes can be found within this *fond*. *Fond* no. 127 is entitled 'Russian Archaeological Institute in Constantinople' and holds documents about the establishment of the Institute, its bureaucratic structure, personnel profile, scientific expeditions and the final dissolution. This *fond* also deals with relations of Russian archaeologists with the Ottoman government. The last *fond* I investigated at PFA RAN is *fond* no. 169, which holds materials about RAIK's Trabzon[27] expedition in 1916–17. One of the most politically interesting expeditions of the Institute, the Trabzon expedition coincided with Russian occupation of the city, and gives insight into Russian military and political presence in occupied Ottoman towns during the First World War.

The second most important archive that holds materials on RAIK is Russian State Historical Archive (RGIA). At RGIA, I looked into files dealing specifically with the Russian Archaeological Institute, which were located under *fond* no. 757. Due to RAIK's official links to the Russian Embassy in Istanbul, Archive of Foreign Policy of the Russian Empire (AVPRI) also holds documents concerning the Institute, although at a smaller scale compared to PFA RAN and RGIA.[28] The duration of this research coincided with the closure of AVPRI. Luckily, the documents at PFA RAN and RGIA, both in terms of their quantity and in terms of the value of information they provided, were sufficient to examine the political and bureaucratic context in which RAIK was established and operated.

In addition to these archival sources, I also made use of published primary sources. Without doubt, the most important published source about RAIK was the annual publication of the Institute. From 1896 to 1912 RAIK published an annual journal, *Izvestiia Russkogo Arkheologicheskogo Instituta v Konstantinopole* (Bulletin of the Russian Archaeological Institute in Constantinople) in a total of sixteen volumes. Except for the first two volumes, *Izvestiia* was published in Sofia. In addition to academic articles, *Izvestiia* included yearly reports outlining RAIK's scientific activities, communication with Russian and Ottoman government offices, and budgetary questions. Academic articles in the *Izvestiia* incorporated detailed archaeological information, but also provided interesting observations about local customs, topography and political situation in the expedition area. The entire collection of the *Izvestiia* was available at the Library of the Istanbul Archaeological Museum – once known as the Ottoman Imperial Museum.

Individual archaeologists affiliated with RAIK also produced academic works based on their research in Ottoman territories. Among the most important of them, we can count Uspenskii's magnum opus *Istoriia Vizantiiskoi Imperii* (History of the Byzantine Empire), which was published in 1913 in three volumes, and his *Ocherki iz Istorii Trapezuntskoy Imperii* (Essays on the History of the Trebizond Empire), which was published posthumously. Russian academic journals, most importantly *Vizantiiskii Vremennik* (Byzantine Chronicle) and *Izvestiia Akademii Nauk* (Academy of Sciences Gazette) contain articles relevant to my project. I had the chance to find these sources in the Library of the Academy of Sciences (BAN) in St Petersburg.

In the 20th century, many city and town names in Asia Minor and the Balkans were changed by the newly established nation-states. Throughout the book, place names are indicated as they were officially used in the time period under examination. For instance, Manastır is preferred instead of Bitola, or Üsküp instead of Skopje. Selânik, the official name of the *vilâyet*, is preferred instead of the often-used version Salonica. The full name of RAIK included the word Constantinople, and I maintained the exact translation when referring to the Institute. I also referred to the Orthodox Patriarchate in the city as 'Orthodox Patriarchate of Constantinople', as this is the official title of the institution in question. As for the city itself, I used Constantinople for pre-Ottoman and Istanbul for the Ottoman times. Similarly, I preferred Trebizond for pre-Ottoman and Trabzon for Ottoman era. The contemporary names of cities and towns are given in brackets when they are first mentioned in the text.

As for the transliteration of Russian words, the rules set out by the Library of Congress are followed. All the translations from Russian to English belong to myself.

Since RAIK focused primarily on Byzantine history and archaeology, this book will give special importance to the political aspect of Byzantine studies. Both the Russian and the Ottoman Empires had historical and cultural connections to the Byzantine Empire, although in different ways. Chapter 1 will touch upon the development of academic archaeology and Byzantinology in the Russian Empire. The special place of Byzantinology within Russian historical/archaeological scholarship, and more broadly, the image of Byzantium in Russian thought both at ideological and academic levels will be outlined, because the establishment of RAIK can be more clearly understood as an outcome of these scholarly developments.

Chapter 2 will explain the development of Ottoman archaeology in the face of increasing foreign activities across the Empire and how ancient objects acquired a symbolic meaning in diplomatic relations between the Ottoman

Empire and European powers. The importance attributed to ancient objects in the late 19th century will be analysed within the context of Ottoman modernization. Ottoman perceptions of foreign archaeologists and major foreign archaeological expeditions which prompted a change in Ottoman policies will also be examined. The establishment of the Ottoman Imperial Museum and the antiquities regulations of 1869, 1874, 1884 and 1906 will be explained in detail. The aim of the chapter is to understand Ottoman appreciation of ancient history, and its implications for Ottoman self-perception at the turn of the century. The development of archaeology in the Ottoman Empire is important to understand as the context in which RAIK was established and operated. Finally, this chapter will deal with the interactions between RAIK and Ottoman officials and how Russian archaeologists were perceived by the Ottoman bureaucracy. This chapter will also deal with Ottoman appreciation of Byzantine monuments and Byzantine history.

Chapter 3 will explain the establishment of RAIK and its sister organization, Imperial Orthodox Palestine Society (hereafter as IPPO). Diplomatic and academic efforts for the establishment of an archaeological institute, alternative projects and the ideas behind RAIK will be examined in detail based on the official exchange of letters between various government offices of the Russian Empire. The bureaucrats and diplomats who supported RAIK's establishment and their justifications will be outlined. Most importantly, the positions of the Ministry of Foreign Affairs, Ministry of Public Education, Holy Synod, and the Tsar himself will be explained. Finally, the bureaucratic structure of RAIK, its links to the Russian Embassy in Istanbul and the Russian government will be described. The aim of this chapter is to understand the underlying reasons for the establishment of an overseas Russian archaeological institute. Did the RAIK project reflect the mindset of only a handful of individuals responsible for its creation, or did it indicate the ideological orientation of the Russian government in general? This question will be kept in mind while explaining RAIK's official links to the Russian government.

Chapter 4 will continue with the scholarly activities of RAIK. The focus of RAIK's scholarly interests, its studies on Byzantine and ancient Slavic history will be analysed, keeping in mind the political dimension of Russia's interest in Byzantine and Slavic archaeology. The scientific expeditions of the institute, with a specific focus on expeditions to Bulgaria, the Black Sea littoral, Macedonia, and Istanbul will be explained. There will be discussion about the interactions between RAIK and the Ottoman government, Ottoman perceptions of Russian archaeologists, international political background, and Russian archaeologists' opinions on contemporary political developments.

Chapter 5 takes on from where the previous chapter left off, and continues with RAIK's archaeological studies in the Balkans right before the Balkan Wars. The archaeological activities will be explained in reference to the international political developments of the period. Special attention will be devoted to the Slavic Department established within RAIK in 1911, and what the Department meant for RAIK's mission in the Balkans.

The sixth and last chapter will highlight the fate of RAIK after 1914, and briefly explain the outcomes of the First World War. RAIK's last archaeological expedition, the Trabzon expedition in 1916–17 will be analysed in this chapter. Diplomatic complications, which emerged as a result of RAIK's sudden evacuation of Istanbul were solved in 1929 by an agreement between the two new regimes in both countries, Republican Turkey and the Soviet Union. The developments between 1914 and 1929, and Byzantinology's fall from favour in the Soviet period will be explained in this chapter. The changing attitudes towards Byzantinology from the Russian Empire to the USSR implies that the activities of RAIK reflected Russian imperial identity, an identity that was deemed out of fashion in the Soviet period.

Double-headed eagle flying over Russia: Russian appreciation of the Byzantine heritage

To advance through a Crusade,
To purify the Jordanian waters,
To liberate the Holy Sepulchre,
To return Athens to the Athenians,
The city of Constantine – to Constantine
And re-establish Japheth's Holy Land.[1]

1.1 Fyodor Ivanovich Uspenskii: The making of a Russian Byzantinist

In a speech he delivered in commemoration of the 900th anniversary of the Christianization of Rus' in 1888, Fyodor Uspenskii, who would later be the first and only director of RAIK, argued that even though the medieval Rus' society tried to stand against Byzantine cultural influence, Byzantine culture gradually penetrated into Rus' lands, which altered the political ideals of the latter. With the Christianization of the Rus' in the 10th century, Uspenskii argued that the 'Hellenic genius' of the Byzantine Empire merged with a 'great nation' (*velikii narod*) to the north of the Black Sea.[2]

This last sentence perfectly sums up not only the individual opinion of Fyodor Uspenskii but also indicates why Byzantine studies occupied a very important place in Russian archaeological scholarship since its beginnings in the 18th century. Before embarking on the establishment of RAIK, Uspenskii was already a famed scholar specializing on the relations between the Byzantine Empire and its Slavic neighbours and inhabitants. Uspenskii was born to a priest's family and attended a religious school before entering the Historical-Philological Department of the St Petersburg University.[3] His early religious education might have had influence on his future interest in the history of Orthodoxy. As Vladimir

Ivanovich Lamanskii's (1833–1914) student at Imperial St Petersburg University, Uspenskii was influenced by the Pan-Slavist political views of his professor and mentor.[4] A notable scholar, Lamanskii was renowned for his studies on the sociopolitical history of the Byzantine Empire, as well as Byzantine relations with southern Slavs.[5] While still a student at the Historical – Philological Faculty at St Petersburg University, Uspenskii received a prize from the Slavic Benevolent Committee in 1871 with his article 'The First Slavic Monarchs in the North-West' which was published as a book in 1872.[6] In 1874, Uspenskii defended his thesis 'The Byzantine Author, Nicetas Choniates from Chonae',[7] which was based on important sources from the 12th and 13th centuries. Uspenskii's doctoral dissertation, which was completed in 1879, was entitled 'The Formation of the Second Bulgarian Kingdom', in which Uspenskii shed light on the relations between the Bulgarians, Serbs, the Byzantine Empire and medieval Rus'.[8]

Immediately after completing his degree at St Petersburg University, Uspenskii was appointed to the Imperial Novorossiya University as a lecturer, and brought the St Petersburg tradition of Byzantinology to Odessa.[9] In his lectures, Uspenskii underlined the relevance of studying Byzantine history to understand Russian and broader Slavic history. Uspenskii claimed that the Byzantine Empire undertook an educative (*vospitatel'ny*) role in its relations with its European neighbours in the West (*novoevropeiskie narody*) and Slavic neighbours in the North. He argued that European historians, while expressing gratitude for the positive influence the Byzantine Empire exerted on 'wild hordes' (*dikiia ordy* – with this, probably meaning peoples inhabiting areas north of the Byzantine Empire, notably the Slavs) and transforming them into 'historical nations' (*istoricheskie narody*), they should also not forget the sacrifices the Byzantine Empire made in defence of Europe, making itself the 'bastion of civilization' (*oplot' tsivilizatsii*). Uspenskii argued that 'the new empire in Tsargrad, in the period of a thousand years of its existence, continued, by virtue of its historical mission, the development of ideas and institutions (*poniatiia i uchrezhdeniia*), bequeathed [to it] by Rome, and following the tradition, spiritually educating new peoples'.[10]

In his studies, Uspenskii emphasized the organic links between Russia, the Balkan Slavs and the Byzantine Empire. His arguments implied the antiquity of Russian cultural existence in the region once ruled by the Byzantine Empire. If there had been intensive cultural interactions between Russian and Byzantine civilizations, then it was only natural that Russian culture had penetrated into regions within the Byzantine sphere of influence. This argument further strengthened Russia's position as the legitimate inheritor of the Byzantine tradition. The historical and cultural interactions between Russians and Byzantium legitimized contemporary Russian scientific (in fact, not only scientific, but also political) interest in the history of the Byzantine Empire.

Uspenskii outlined his arguments in a speech at the Odessa Slavic Benevolent Society in 1885, in commemoration of the 1,000th anniversary of St Methodius's death. He argued that the priest brothers St Cyril and St Methodius might have had contacts with Russians in Chersonessos – although this argument was not grounded on any objective evidence. Uspenskii further claimed that Russian cultural existence on the Black Sea coast, especially in Crimea, dated back to as late as the 9th and 10th centuries.[11] By tracing archaeological records in the Black Sea basin, Uspenskii's arguments in fact underlined the antiquity of Russian existence on the Black Sea coast, and implicitly endorsed the legitimacy and even necessity of incorporating these regions to the Russian Empire.

Uspenskii's discussion of the Crusades also revealed how he linked distant history to contemporary political issues. Linking the Crusades to European history, Uspenskii claimed that the Crusades opened the path for the struggle between the East and the West, which continued up to the 20th century under the name of the 'Eastern Question'. He nearly identified the Crusades as the origin of the Eastern Question, and claimed that Russia was 'destined' (*suzhdeno*) to take part in it.[12] Therefore, Uspenskii defined the Eastern Question not only as a political problem, but as a civilizational encounter between what he saw as opposing forces, the East and the West, although how he conceptualized East and West remained blurry.

The theme of 'Eastern Question' appeared often in Uspenskii's writings. In fact, he identified the history of Byzantine studies with the history of the Eastern Question. Uspenskii expressed very openly the view that scientific interests always went hand in hand with political and economic interests. Making comparisons with European nations, especially with France, which he deemed the cradle of Byzantine studies, Uspenskii complained that scientific Byzantinology developed comparatively late in Russia. He argued that while the French, since the Crusades, planted the seeds of scientific Byzantinology through their missionaries, consuls and commercial colonies in the Near East, Russians were too late to embark on a scientific study of the Byzantine Empire, despite the fact that political and religious tendencies brought Russia closer to Byzantine civilization than any other European nation.[13] He argued that the development of Byzantinology as a scientific branch of study in Russia should be analysed within the context of Russia's political and cultural interests and self-perception (*samoopredelenie*).[14]

Uspenskii found it embarrassing that Russian academics lagged behind their European colleagues in a field as intrinsically linked to Russian imperial identity as Byzantine studies. He sadly acknowledged that until the establishment of RAIK, very little was done in the name of Byzantine studies in Russia. There was not a single institution dedicated exclusively to the study of Byzantine history, although Byzantine studies had to be the 'main duty of Russian science', and a national obligation.[15] To overcome this shortcoming, Uspenskii made great efforts to strengthen Byzantine studies in Russian academia throughout his academic career. On several occasions, he expressed dismay at the absence of an institution for Byzantine studies and advocated the necessity of a multi-functional institute of Byzantinology. When he was the head of the Odessa Historical-Philological Society, he worked for the establishment of a Byzantinology department, which was realized in 1892.[16] Two years later, when the prominent academic publication, *Vizantiiskii Vremennik* started to be published, one of the promoters of the journal was Uspenskii.[17] When RAIK was established upon the initiative of Russian diplomats in Istanbul, Uspenskii ardently participated in this project. In many respects, the achievements of the institute were unthinkable without the personal contribution of Uspenskii.

Uspenskii's career path was not an exceptional one in late imperial Russia. In fact, his research interests and his arguments very much fit into an already established Byzantinology tradition in Russian academic circles. Both Uspenskii's alma mater, Imperial St Petersburg University, and the city where Uspenskii received professorship, Odessa, were particularly important centres for the study of Byzantine history.

1.2 The development of archaeology and Byzantine studies in the Russian Empire

The first academic studies of Byzantine history, as well as the first archaeological surveys of Byzantine monuments in Russia date back to the 18th century, to the establishment of the Imperial Academy of Sciences in 1724. In 1804, a chair for the Department of Fine Arts and Archaeology was established at this institution under the Faculty of History and Philology.[18] The establishment of universities in Moscow (1755) and St Petersburg (1724; reconstituted in 1819) were also important cornerstones for the development of Byzantine archaeology in Russia.[19] Rich with ancient Greco-Byzantine monuments, the Black Sea coasts became one of the most preferred destinations for Russian antiquarians and historians after the 18th century.[20]

German scholars played an important role in the development of Russian historical scholarship, including the development of Byzantinology in its early beginnings.[21] Russia's Greek community, inhabiting mostly in southern

Russia, also played an important role in the development of Byzantine studies both as scholars and as benefactors. For instance, wealthy members of the Greek community were instrumental in the establishment of the Odessa Society of History and Antiquities in 1839.[22] Outside of Russia, members of the Russian Ecclesiastical Mission in Jerusalem organized expeditions to holy places of Orthodoxy in Palestine and Syria, many of which were Byzantine-era monuments, as early as 1840s.[23] It should be noted that at this early stage, and well into the late 19th century, the line between history and archaeology was blurry not only in Russia but in other parts of Europe as well. Therefore, it is nearly impossible to draw a line between archaeologists and historians of the Byzantine past. Generally, these subjects were taught in the same departments and regarded as the branches of the same discipline.[24]

The institutions that helped the development of Russian archaeology included museums, universities and the Imperial Academy of Sciences, with the latter focusing more on research.[25] An important centre, the Imperial Russian Archaeological Society was established in St Petersburg in 1851, with special branches dedicated to Russo-Slavic, Oriental, classical, and Byzantine art and archaeology.[26] It was followed by the Moscow Archaeological Society, established in 1864 by Count Aleksey Sergeyevich Uvarov.[27] On the initiative of Count Uvarov, the Moscow Archaeological Society initiated national archaeological congresses. These congresses produced lively debates and theoretical discussions, and more than often pointed to the political importance of Slavic and Orthodox antiquities along the Black Sea coast.[28] In the first Russian Archaeological Congress, organized in Moscow in 1869, the main goal of Russian archaeology was designated as the preservation of ancient Slavic and Orthodox monuments, especially in remote and multicultural regions with a substantial Muslim population such as southern Russia, Transcaucasus and the Volga valley.[29]

The first centralized archaeological institution in the Russian Empire, the Imperial Archaeological Commission (IAK) was established in 1859 under the Ministry of the Imperial Court.[30] IAK was responsible for overseeing all archaeological activities within the Russian Empire.[31] As Austin Jersild reminded, 'If the Geographical Society proposed to make sense of the empire's vast expanse, the Archaeological Commission promised to compose order out of the imperial past.'[32] It should be noted that even though some prominent scientific societies were not placed under imperial tutelage, IAK was. For instance, the Imperial Geographical Society, one of the most important scholarly institutions of the late imperial period, was not placed under the Ministry of the Imperial Court, although the Imperial Hermitage and IAK were attached directly to the Court. The royal support for archaeology might be yet another instance indicating that patronizing art and archaeology was regarded as the insignia of imperial prestige by the House of Romanov.

Other prominent centres of archaeological research in the Russian Empire included the St Petersburg Archaeological Institute, established in 1878, and the Moscow Archaeological Institute, established in 1907 with the intention of training professional archaeologists, some of whom worked on Byzantine artefacts. Both of these institutes were established under the auspices of the Ministry of Public Education.[33] St Petersburg and Moscow Theological Academies also trained a number of scholars in Byzantine studies, although with a more religion-oriented focus.[34]

The active participation of the Orthodox Church in archaeological activities led to the emergence of 'church archaeology', which emphasized the parallel study of written and material artefacts regarding the history of Orthodoxy.[35] In an article he wrote in 1906, N. V. Pokrovskii, a professor at the St Petersburg Theological Academy, argued that church archaeology should be a part of the curriculum in theological academies. After being acquainted with the theoretical aspects of church archaeology and completing their degrees, Pokrovskii recommended that students should spend a year at RAIK to get familiar with the Orthodox monuments in Istanbul, as well as in the Balkans, Syria and Palestine.[36] Pokrovskii pointed to the fact that Orthodoxy was an indispensable part of Russian identity, daily life, political culture and art, especially until Peter the Great. This, he argued, was the reason why Christian antiquities were very important to understand the history of Russia.[37]

The staff of RAIK were academically most influenced by the educational programme of the Imperial St Petersburg University, the alma mater of most of its members. Especially from the 1880s onwards Nikodim Pavlovich Kondakov (1844–1925), a specialist in the history of Byzantine art, and his students taught lectures on classical Greek, Byzantine and Slavic archaeology at this university.[38] From the 1870s to the 1890s, Kondakov undertook scientific expeditions to the different corners of the Russian Empire, especially to Crimea and the Caucasus, and he joined expeditions to the Balkans, Ottoman Macedonia, Greece, Syria, Palestine and the Sinai Peninsula. He also extensively studied Byzantine monuments in Istanbul and participated in the establishment of RAIK.[39] V. G. Vasilevskii (1838–1899) was another important name from St Petersburg University.[40] Under his editorship, the first Russian scholarly journal on Byzantine history, *Vizantiiskii Vremennik* (the Byzantine Herald) was launched in 1893.[41]

It was this academic and institutional background that shaped the intellectual outlook of RAIK's founders. In addition to numerous scholars who visited RAIK as researchers, Director Uspenskii was accompanied by full-time working Byzantinist scholars who were actively involved in RAIK's activities as secretaries. From 1895 to 1914, six scholars served as secretaries at RAIK: P. D. Pogodin (1894–7), B. V. Farmakovskii (1898–1901), R. K. Leper (1901–8), B. A. Panchenko (1901–14), F. I. Shmit (1908–12) and N. L. Okunev (1913–14). All of these scholars were graduates of the Historical-Philological Faculty of the Imperial St Petersburg University, except for Farmakovskii, who was a student of Director Uspenskii and graduated from the Historical-Philological Faculty of the Imperial Novorossiya University in Odessa.[42] The educational background of these scholars point out to the academic influence of these two universities on RAIK. At the same time, by virtue of their common educational background, these people were part of a close-knit network of imperial Russian Byzantinists.

Imperial Russian academics made significant contributions to Byzantine studies, primarily by focusing on the interactions between ancient Slavs, the Byzantine Empire, and the nomadic peoples of the Eurasian steppes. Slavic and Byzantine studies were intrinsically linked in Russian academia.[43] The emphasis on this particular aspect of Byzantine history set Russian scholars apart from their European colleagues. From Vasilevskii to Uspenskii, Russian Byzantinists accepted the paradigm that the customs and traditions of Slavic peoples in the Byzantine periphery gradually penetrated into the Byzantine legal system and administrative codes and only with the ascendance of the Latins after the 11th century the harmony between the Byzantine state and its Slavic inhabitants changed for worse.[44] The argument followed that the Latinized (or Westernized) rulers after the 11th century neglected Slavic peasantry and brought the destruction of the Byzantine Empire. The underlying message of this argument was that feudalism and oppressive policies were not characteristic of the Byzantine Empire, but came from the West with the Latin invasion, very much in line with the Slavophile conception of world history. In addition, this argument hinted at the possibility of peaceful cohabitation of all Orthodox peoples under one banner by setting a historical precedent.

Considering all these institutional developments, the last decades of the 19th century and the early 20th century was the 'golden age' of Russian Byzantine studies. In this period, there was intensive correspondence and exchange of ideas between Russian and foreign scholars.[45] Russian Byzantine studies reached such a respectable status in European academia that Karl Krumbacher, the well-known German Byzantinist scholar, was reported to learn Russian and encourage his students to do the same to follow academic publications by his Russian colleagues.[46]

For sure, it was not only Russians who showed interest in the history of the Byzantine Empire. British and French explorers were the first to record and investigate Byzantine monuments in Anatolia and Istanbul.[47] In the late 19th and early 20th centuries, art historians and archaeologists made systematic and comparative studies of Byzantine remains in the Ottoman Empire. Among such scholars, Charles Texier (1802–1871), Gertrude L. Bell (1868–1926), Josef Strzygowski (1862–1941), Karl Krumbacher (1856–1909), Charles Diehl (1859–1944) and Sir William Ramsay (1851–1939) produced some of the most comprehensive works on Byzantine monuments.[48] Even though Classical Greece received more attention, in the late 19th century Byzantine imagery appeared as an exotic theme for European intellectuals, as it combined elements of Greek civilization, Christianity and the Orient. The development of Byzantine archaeology reflected an attempt to portray Istanbul as a historical extension of the Christian, therefore European civilization, and legitimized European claims over the imperial capital.[49]

Referring to the importance of Istanbul for European politics in the 19th century, the Byzantinist scholar A. A. Spasskii pointed to the correlation between international politics and the development of Byzantinology as a discipline.[50] He explained that the Greek War of Independence and uprisings among Slavic peoples stimulated European curiosity about the history and peoples of the East. Spasskii happily noted that after years of neglect and a biased attitude towards the Byzantine Empire, Europeans, first Germans and the French, then British, Russian and Italian scholars, started to pay more attention to the history of this once-mighty empire.

It does not come as a surprise that Russian Byzantinology developed at a time when Russia started to pursue a more active foreign policy in the Near East. Reciprocally, the development of academic Byzantinology in the late 19th century contributed to increasing numbers of bureaucrats with neo-Byzantinist political sympathies, who believed that Russia embodied the best of Byzantine civilization.[51] Of course, scholars of Byzantine history did not receive orders from the government to coordinate their research with official policy, but the imaginary links between Russia and the Byzantine Empire offered a fascinating example for the staunch monarchists of the era.

1.3 From Russian to Ottoman shores: The attraction of the Black Sea as a repository of Byzantine monuments

Archaeological activities on the Russian coast of the Black Sea offer some parallels with RAIK's activities across the coast, therefore deserves a separate analysis. Already in the early 19th century, there was growing sensitivity among both academics and local administrators regarding the preservation of ancient monuments in southern Russia. The imperial government provided financial support for excavations and archaeological projects in the Black Sea region, especially in Kerch, Chersonessos and Taman.[52] In 1823, archaeologist and historian I. A. Stempkovskii, who made extensive research on the Black Sea coast,[53] presented a note to the Governor General of Novorossiya M. S. Vorontsov entitled 'Ideas Regarding the Study of Antiquities in the Novorossiya Krai'.[54] In this document, Stempkovskii outlined the urgent need to save monuments, which were evidence of the religious, cultural and artistic achievements of ancient peoples. He pointed to the need to establish local museums and scientific societies for effective preservation of antiquities.

Some of the first archaeological museums in the Russian Empire were established in Crimea and across the Black Sea coast in Ukraine, in cities such as Odessa, Kerch, Feodosiya and Nikolaev in the first decades of the 19th century.[55] The emergence of museums in this newly conquered region was first and foremost a result of its rich ancient heritage. However, there was also a political aspect of these archaeological endeavours. Ukraine and Crimea were annexed to Russia only in the late 18th century, and the region was demographically highly multicultural and multireligious.[56] Therefore, proving the antiquity of Slavdom and Orthodoxy in this region, especially vis-à-vis Islam, was a precondition of proving the legitimacy of Russian expansion around the Black Sea coasts. Museums helped the Russian administration visualize its imperial rule in a territory recently incorporated into the Empire.

The establishment of archaeological societies and museums in recently conquered regions with a substantial non-Russian population also reflected a desire to export Russia's 'civilizing mission' to the periphery of the Russian Empire. Archaeology proved to be a useful instrument in creating a legitimate basis for imperial expansion in the newly incorporated regions. The basic tenets of imperial Russian archaeology in two Muslim-populated regions, Crimea and Caucasus, offer valuable insight to understand the possible motivations of Russian archaeologists in the Ottoman Empire. In the North Caucasus, imperial Russian archaeologists searched for traces of classical Greek and Christian past.[57] Scholars were supported and accompanied by military personnel in their archaeological endeavours, and imperial archaeology legitimated the belief that a 'glorious Christian past' was buried underneath the Caucasus waiting to be rescued by the Russian colonial rule.[58]

The IAK also had a specific interest in Black Sea antiquities. Particularly in Crimea, a region that caused a series of wars between Russia and the Ottoman Empire in the 18th century, archaeology assumed a religious and political character. Chersonessos received special interest, because it was believed to be the place where the Kievan Prince Vladimir was baptised.[59] The study of ancient history symbolized the quest for the roots of Russia's religious and imperial identity. Constructing a link between Prince Vladimir and the history of Crimea legitimized the recent Russian conquest of this region and proved the antiquity of Russian and Orthodox culture in geography with a multicultural history. Crimea was designated as a holy place, as the cradle of Russian Christianity.[60] The Crimean War with the Ottomans further catalysed the Christianization of Crimea at the expense of the peninsula's Muslim-Tatar heritage.

Along with Moscow and St Petersburg, Odessa appeared as one of the most important centres of Byzantine archaeology in the Russian Empire as a result of its geographical proximity to Crimea and Greco-Byzantine antiquities along the Black Sea coast.[61] The Odessa Society of History and Antiquity, established in 1839, also accounted for the city's reputation as a centre of archaeological research. The archaeological interests of the Odessa Society mostly concentrated on Byzantine and Orthodox antiquities in southern Russia. Restoring Byzantine monuments and reviving Orthodox imagery in a region with a substantial Muslim population was a political as well as an archaeological project.[62] Through its archaeological studies, the Odessa Society helped prove the antiquity of Orthodoxy vis-à-vis Islam in southern Russia. Odessa's status as a hub for Byzantinist scholars is all the more relevant considering that nearly all archaeologists affiliated with RAIK, including its director Fyodor Uspenskii, were professors at the Novorossiya University in Odessa.

Along with secular experts, the Russian Church adopted modern methods of scientific inquiry for the study of Byzantine archaeology, as the boundary between secular and religious was blurry in the context of Russian imperial archaeology.[63] The articles of Innokentii, the Archbishop of Kherson and Tauride (1848–1857), offer an excellent example of the intersection of religion, politics and archaeology.[64] Especially after the mid-19th century, the Tauride Diocese supported the revival of ancient monasteries and the reconstruction of ancient Byzantine monuments in and around Crimea.[65] In an effort to transform Crimea into a Russian Athos, Innokentii described Byzantine monuments, monasteries and churches around Crimea in detail and offered ways for their preservation. Innokentii suggested that financial resources for the reconstruction and restoration of monuments could be provided by private donors and benevolent societies.[66]

At the background of archaeological descriptions, Innokentii's articles abound with comparisons between the Orthodox faith and Islam. He viewed the restoration of Byzantine churches and monasteries in Crimea as the symbol of the 'resurrection' of Orthodoxy in the region.[67] Marked by a religious and nationalist overtone, Innokentii's discourse linked Russian conquest to the revival of Greco-Byzantine antiquity, and presented Russia as the saviour of the Byzantine heritage. In this sense, Crimean and overall Black Sea archaeology offered a perfect example to the Orthodox Church's active involvement in the production of scientific knowledge and the confluence of science, religion and imperial identity in the Russian Empire.[68] Russian archaeological endeavours in the Ottoman Balkans, Istanbul, and the Turkish Black Sea coasts can be analysed within the context of the same religious, imperial and historical interest.

A letter from the Chief Procurator of the Holy Synod, P. P. Izvolskii to the IAK written in 1908, much after Innokentii, revealed that ancient history had become an attractive subject among the bureaucrats of the Holy Synod and upper ranks of the clergy. In this letter, Izvolskii proposed to organize an expedition to Chersonessos, led by the Tauride Diocese. Izvolskii asked the IAK to make excavations for the benefit of the Orthodox Church, in addition to scientific purposes. For this reason, he requested the appointment of not only an academically competent archaeologist, but also an Orthodox believer to the proposed expedition to Chersonessos.[69]

One thing worthy of mention was the frequent emphasis on Christian, rather than Greek heritage, especially after the mid-19th century. In a sense, especially in Ukraine and Crimea, Byzantine monuments were cleared of their Greek background, and their image was reconstructed only as markers of an Orthodox Christian past. The emphasis on Christian archaeology reflected how religion became an integral part of Russian imperial identity after the mid-19th century.[70] As Kohl and Fawcett reminded, 'State-sponsored nationalistic-oriented events and processes are typically and intimately linked to religion, either directly or by a civil-religion connection, to create an ambiance and semblance of sacredness in what otherwise could have been emotionless secular events and processes.'[71] In the Russian example, the connection between religion and imperial/national identity clearly manifested itself in the politics of archaeology.

The revitalization of Byzantine heritage in Crimea, Ukraine and North Caucasus gives insight about Russian archaeological activities on the other side of the Black Sea shore. The activities of RAIK in the Ottoman Empire in many ways reflected similar motivations and political goals as the activities in Crimea. As in Crimea, Russian archaeological activities in Istanbul primarily focused on Byzantine antiquities. Imperial Russian archaeology around the Black Sea illustrated the connection between religion, national identity and official policy.

Apart from this ideological background, there was also a practical link between Russian archaeological activities in the Ottoman Empire and in southern Russia, especially in Crimea and Ukraine. Members and secretaries

of RAIK, Boris Vladimirovich Farmakovskii (1870–1928) and Roman
Khristianovich Leper (1865–1918) worked with the IAK to undertake studies
in Chersonessos and in Crimea before joining RAIK.[72] Farmakovskii was
especially noted for his studies on artefacts from the Pontic Greek colony in
Olbia, discovered in southern Ukraine.[73] These scholars used their expertise
on both Ottoman and Russian coasts of the Black Sea to present a coherent
picture of Pontic and Byzantine history.

1.4 The image of Byzantium in Russian thought
in the late 19th century

If European visitors were captivated by the charm of Istanbul, the imperial
centre of Orthodoxy was even more fascinating for Russians. As the cradle
of Orthodox Christianity, the Byzantine Empire had everlasting influence
on the evolution of Russian culture and identity. After the conversion of
Vladimir of Kiev to Orthodoxy in 988, mutual interactions with the Byzantine
Empire had a determining role on the evolution of Russian ecclesiastical,
cultural and political development.[74] Different from the Balkan Peninsula,
medieval Rus' did not fall directly under Byzantine political jurisdiction, and
Russian recognition of the universal emperor remained to a great extent a
religious conviction.[75] Russian subordination to Byzantine cultural, political
leadership, and ecclesiastical hierarchy had a symbolic rather than a practical
character.[76] With the downfall of the last Roman emperor, Russian rulers had
the opportunity to take over his role.[77]

After the 15th century, legendary claims were put forward to justify the
links between the Byzantine Empire and Russia, but for practical reasons,
such (mostly forgotten) legends resurfaced under the political conditions of
the 19th century. The 19th-century discovery of an obscure 16th-century text
about the so-called Third Rome theory, written by an abbot named Philatheus
and claiming that Moscow was destined to be the third Rome after the demise
of the Byzantine Empire, is a case in point.[78] With the gradual shift in the
balance of power between the Russian and the Ottoman Empires after the
18th century in Russia's favour, Russian tsars had a practical reason to view
themselves as the protectors of Orthodox peoples living under Ottoman rule.
The changing pattern of international politics explains why the Third Rome
theory was rediscovered and reinterpreted in a new light in the 19th century.

Despite the appropriation of the Byzantine legacy in the sense of assuming
the protector role of Ottoman Christians, Russian perception of Byzantium
was not always positive and not everyone was mesmerized by the possibility
of the restoration of the Byzantine Empire under the aegis of Russia. As Russia

turned its face towards the West, Byzantium came to represent stagnation and everything that made Russia lag behind Western Europe. Especially after the reforms of Peter the Great, 18th- and 19th-century reformers and critics of autocracy blamed Byzantine heritage for Russia's economic and cultural backwardness.[79] Even Catherine the Great's (r. 1762–96) scheme to re-establish the Byzantine Empire, the 'Greek Project' as it was called, was not so much a continuation of the previous Muscovite appropriation of Byzantine symbolism. Catherine's interest in the Greco-Byzantine tradition was rather a reflection of the influence of European neoclassicism on the erudite Empress, an idea that permeated the intellectual tradition of 18th-century Europe.[80] In other words, Byzantine image had a complicated place in Russian intellectual history and Russian appreciation of Byzantium was an 'ambiguous blend of attraction and repulsion' since the medieval times.[81]

Following the Crimean War (1853–6), the conquest of Istanbul and the regeneration of the Slavic-Orthodox world under the protective wings of Russia appeared as common themes in the texts and speeches of intellectuals and bureaucrats who glorified Orthodoxy as the most important pillar of Russian identity. The Slavic component of Russian imperial identity was regarded as inseparable from its Orthodox component. The most famous ideologues of Russian Pan-Slavism, Nikolai Danilevskii (1822–1885) and Rostislav A. Fadeyev (1824–1883) both wrote in the 1860s that future belonged to Slavic and Orthodox peoples, without making a clear separation between the two. These nations, most of whom lived in the Balkans under Ottoman rule, were to be first liberated and then led by Russia.[82] Following its conquest, Istanbul would be a free city and the capital of the future Slavic confederation led by Russia.[83] Another very famous supporter of Russian expansion towards the Ottoman Empire was Fyodor Dostoyevskii (1821–1881), a writer with significant influence on public opinion. Like Danilevskii and Fadeyev, Dostoyevskii identified Orthodoxy with Slavdom. In the treatises he wrote in 1876–7 in the midst of unrest in the Balkans, Dostoyevskii argued that Russia, as the greatest and strongest Orthodox nation, was destined to take the lead and liberate Slavic and Orthodox nations from the Ottoman rule. Different from Danilevskii and Fadeyev, Dostoyevskii rejected the idea that Istanbul should be a free city of the Slavic-Orthodox confederation, as Russia was superior to the rest of the Slavic-Orthodox world. Istanbul's spiritual importance meant that it was far too important to leave either to Greeks or Balkan Slavs. He argued that only Russian possession of the imperial city would bring peace and freedom to the Slavic-Orthodox world.[84]

Pan-Slavists were not interested in resurrecting the Byzantine Empire in the original sense, but they wanted to recreate Byzantium as an empire characterized by Slavic culture. In other words, regenerated Byzantium was detached from its Greek origins and depicted as a uniquely Russian achievement.[85] They linked Russia's cultural achievements not to the Byzantine culture imposed from above, but to the peculiar formulation of the Byzantine legacy by the Russian-Slavic people from below. For sure, the origin of Orthodoxy was Byzantium, but the way in which Orthodoxy was interpreted defined the transformation of the pagan Rus' into 'Holy Russia'. In this regard, Russian Pan-Slavists usurped the Byzantine legacy and reformulated it with an emphasis on Slavic culture. The possible conquest of Istanbul symbolized the fulfilment of a Russian imperial dream.

In any case, whether Russian intellectuals exalted the Byzantine heritage, downplayed its achievements or entertained mixed feelings, the common theme was that they acknowledged Russia's status as the inheritor of the Byzantine legacy.[86] There was nearly a consensus among Russian intellectuals, who otherwise had totally different political opinions, that Russia should actively protect the rights of its Slavic and Orthodox brethren in the Ottoman Empire, a role bequeathed to Russia by Byzantium.[87] Liberals and radicals saw the promise of liberty in the Balkan nations' struggle for independence and hoped a similar spirit of freedom would sweep through Russia. Conservatives and religious thinkers, on the other hand, emphasized Russia's destiny to lead the Orthodox-Slavic world and emancipate its ethnic and religious kinsmen.

Conclusion

Overall, Byzantine studies in the Russian Empire was marked by an ideological undertone, explained by Russia's perception of itself as the legitimate heir to the Byzantine civilization. As A. A. Spasskii proclaimed, 'Byzantine history – it can be said that it is our spiritual past, the assessment and learning of which is the immediate duty of Russian historical scholarship.'[88] Proving the links between Russian culture and the Byzantine Empire with reference to Orthodox-Byzantine antiquities on the Black Sea coasts, in Crimea, and in the Ottoman Empire was not only a scientific enterprise, but had a political aspect to it. The context in which Byzantine archaeology in Russia developed is essential for understanding the establishment of RAIK in 1894, the scope and geographical focus of its scientific interests.

In other words, RAIK was not a unique phenomenon: rather, it was part of an already established intellectual and academic tradition within Russian academia. Civilizations that prospered around the Black Sea constituted an important focus of Russian archaeology since the late 18th century. Interest in Byzantine archaeology did not develop only in secular institutions: theological academies and the Orthodox Church also actively engaged in archaeological projects. Actually, RAIK's studies echoed similar archaeological projects in Crimea and southern Russia. Often, the same scholars participated in archaeological projects on both sides of the Black Sea. The director and mastermind of RAIK, Fyodor Uspenskii was a product of this academic tradition, both in terms of his education and training, and his ideological standpoint.

Archaeology offers a perfect example to show how Russia both was and was not European. Russians adopted museological and archaeological practices from Europe in the 19th century. In addition to its relatively late integration to the rest of Europe, Russian culture was also in some ways different. This difference was well illustrated by Russian archaeologists' concentration on Byzantine archaeology more than classical Greece and Rome. Different from European empires that traced their histories back to the western part of the Roman Empire, Russia identified itself with Eastern Rome, and archaeological interest in the Byzantine Empire reflected this imperial identity. By studying the history of the Byzantine Empire, Russian archaeologists stepped into a mystical world, a world from where Russia received Christianity, its alphabet and the basis of its civilization.

Archaeology in the Ottoman Empire:
Cultural property as a symbol of sovereignty

Starting from the mid-19th century, the number of foreign archaeologists in the Ottoman Empire, either professional scholars or amateur enthusiasts, rose dramatically as a reflection of the increasing institutionalization of archaeology in Europe. The British and the French were the first to discover the ancient wonders of the Sublime Porte in the early 19th century. They were followed by German, American and finally Russian archaeological missions in later decades. At first, Ottoman officials and rulers viewed foreign archaeological involvement with a lack of enthusiasm, if not outright apathy. However, towards the end of the century, this indifference was replaced by a growing concern and mistrust about the intentions of foreign archaeological activities. In their struggle to protect the sovereignty of a disintegrating empire from the encroachments of the great powers of Europe, the founders of the Ottoman Imperial Museum (*Müze-yi Hümâyun*) came to regard cultural property as a symbol of the fragile sovereignty of the Empire and promoted protective measures to regulate and finally prohibit the export of antiquities. Moreover, the establishment of museums and the initiation of native archaeological expeditions in the Ottoman Empire reflected the process of modernization that started in the mid-19th century.[1] Until the last days of the Empire, the policy of archaeological protection was not consistent, and rulers continued to use ancient monuments as gifts and bargaining tools in their dealings with foreign governments. In any case, towards the end of the 19th century, archaeological objects acquired a political significance beyond their historical and aesthetic meaning. Ancient history became an arena where the national programs and visions of different actors came into a symbolic conflict with each other.

In the last decades of the 19th century, classical archaeology shifted its attention from Italy and Greece to Ottoman territories.[2] After the unification of Italy, Italian state institutions regulated archaeological activities on the Italian Peninsula more strictly and initiated a period a nationalization of archaeology. In the early 19th century several Italian states issued edicts outlawing the export of antiquities.[3] Greece followed a similar pattern in the years that followed its independence: the first law prohibiting the export of antiquities outside Greece was promulgated in 1834, shortly after the declaration of independence.[4] Even though these measures were not always effective, nevertheless, they signalled the development of local archaeology in Italy and Greece. Therefore, the number of foreign excavations in these two countries became less frequent in the later part of the 19th century. Governments or private institutions in Europe were more likely to sponsor archaeological projects that would eventually enrich the collections of museums in their capitals.[5] After Italy and Greece started to implement protective policies, the Ottoman Empire, particularly Anatolia and Mesopotamia, remained as the primary source of ancient objects for European museums.

Ottoman relations with major European powers in the 19th century can be examined within the framework of informal imperialism.[6] Informal imperialism is defined as limited political, cultural and economic control exerted over a weak sovereign state by a powerful adversary. As the politically weak power is also sovereign and has its own laws, complete military and political control by the powerful state does not occur, but domination is revealed in terms of political assistance and cultural/economic predominance. In the late 19th century the relationship between the major European powers and the Ottoman Empire followed this pattern.

In the 18th and early 19th centuries most European archaeologists in the Ottoman Empire were amateurs, who wanted ancient objects either for their private collections or for the national museums in their countries. Most excavations were carried out on the Aegean coast, in the ruins of ancient cities such as Troy, Xanthos, Miletus, Ephesus and Halicarnassus. Until the organization of the first antiquities collection in Istanbul in the mid-19th century, Ottoman officials did not have much interest in the protection of artefacts, especially if they were only 'stones'.[7] It was quite common for Ottoman sultans to give ancient monuments to foreign kings and emperors as a sign of mutual friendship. An example was Mahmud II, who gave a large amount of the acropolis reliefs removed from Assos to the French archaeologist M. Raoul-Rochette in 1838 as a sign of his friendship with the French king Louis Philippe I.[8]

Starting from the mid-19th century, amateur adventurers who came to the Ottoman Empire in search of ancient civilizations were gradually replaced by professional archaeologists. Foreign archaeological activities were facilitated by the close collaboration between archaeologists and their respective consuls and ambassadors in Ottoman cities. Actually, in some cases, diplomats personally undertook archaeological excavations. For instance, Charles Newton, who was appointed to Mytilene as consul in 1852, made excavations in Halicarnassus, Didyma and Knidos. Stratford Canning, the British ambassador to the Porte, also played an important role in bringing monuments from the Ottoman Empire to Britain through diplomatic pressure.[9] The Ottoman Empire was not a passive witness to the increasing foreign interest in the ancient heritage of its territories. In fact, the second half of the 19th century saw an increasing attention to the long-neglected ancient heritage of the Sultan's domains. Ottoman suspicions of European archaeological activities grew, especially in the face of increasing European political control over the Empire and domestic turmoil at home.

Ottoman reactions to foreign archaeological activities can be better understood in the light of political developments of the period. For Ottoman society, the 19th century was a period of constant change. The idea that Ottoman institutions were in need of reform appeared in Ottoman thinking in the late 18th century, when the military victories of previous centuries gave way to constant defeats by other major powers. Since it was military failures that stimulated the quest for renovation, reform started first in the military realm during the reign of Selim III (1789–1807).[10] Selim III's reign was followed by that of his cousin Mahmud II (1808–39). As Mahmud II consolidated his authority, he undertook new measures to secure administrative centralization, and he challenged the authority of local notables in the periphery of the Ottoman Empire. During Mahmud II's reign, Westernization for the first time appeared as a formal policy. Mahmud II's policies put an emphasis on the necessity of learning European scientific methods without transplanting its culture.[11] However, once contacts with Europe were established, the penetration of Western cultural influence was inevitable. Students were sent abroad and European-style educational institutions were established at home to create the new type of bureaucrat who was open to change and knew foreign languages, as well as the intricacies of European diplomacy.

These reforms culminated in the famous *Tanzimat* (in Ottoman Turkish, reorganization) period (1839–76). *Tanzimat* refers to a series of top–down modernizing reforms carried out by a new generation of bureaucrats, which restructured the Ottoman Empire and accelerated the process of Westernization.[12] The main ideas of *Tanzimat* were formulated in the *Gülhane-i Hatt-ı Hümâyun* (Edict of the Rose Chamber), which was promulgated in 1839. The edict guaranteed the equality of all Ottoman subjects before the law, regardless of their religion. In this sense, the new administrative and legal structure, as it was envisioned by the reformist bureaucrats, undermined the traditional religious categorization of Ottoman subjects. In addition to that, Ottoman bureaucrats tried to forge a supranational Ottoman identity that transcended ethnic and religious identities, which were bringing the Empire to the edge of disintegration. *Tanzimat* also had significant legal consequences, which proved to be transformative for Ottoman society. With modernization and increasing administrative and bureaucratic centralization, *Tanzimat* bureaucrats tried to standardize and secularize Ottoman law and administration.[13]

The establishment of modern Turkish bureaucracy can be traced back to *Tanzimat*.[14] After this period the bureaucrat became a member of an anonymous network of interactions between various government institutions. The emergence of the bureaucracy as a new social class was one of the most important consequences of the *Tanzimat* reforms. The reforms also had visible repercussions. The Ottoman urban lanscape was transformed with the appearance of an increasing number of buildings in European style as a result of European architectural influence. Reformers also tried to introduce municipal regulations to reorganize major Ottoman cities on European lines.[15]

The new Ottoman interest in ancient monuments can be analysed within the context of this modernization trend.[16] Ussama Makdisi defined Ottoman archaeological interest after *Tanzimat* as 'one more step in the self-incorporation of the Ottoman Empire into a European-dominated modernity'.[17] On the one hand, museum building, as a practice imported from Europe, implied the objective of Westernization on the part of Ottoman bureaucracy.[18] On the other hand, displaying ancient objects from all corners of the vast Empire indicated Ottoman sovereign rights over territories that were still under Ottoman political control. The careful surveillance of foreign archaeologists by local authorities showed the eagerness of the burgeoning bureaucracy to carry out legal regulations and extend central rule to the provinces.

Tanzimat reforms were characterized by an Ottomanist identity beyond ethnic and religious denominations. *Tanzimat* reformers advocated the equality of all ethnic and religious groups within the Ottoman Empire and supported the equality of all citizens before the law.[19] In this regard, Ottomanism of the *Tanzimat* era was an attempt to create a sense of political community which was rooted in territory and sought to integrate the heritage of all cultures that had ever existed on Ottoman territories, regardless of religion and ethnicity. In practice, the Ottomanist identity was mostly embraced by educated upper classes and failed to incorporate wider segments of the Ottoman society. Still, Ottomanist thought had an impact on literary and intellectual trends in the last century of the Ottoman Empire. The Ottomanist idea received a revived support after the Young Turk Revolution of 1908, but lost its appeal after the Balkan Wars of 1912–13. The display of Greco-Roman antiquities in the Ottoman Imperial Museum was an extension of the Ottomanist thought behind *Tanzimat* reforms, because the founders of the Museum were perfect examples to upper classes who were born into the *Tanzimat* mindset.

In fact, Ottoman collection of ancient objects did not start in the 19th century. It is known that historical objects from the Byzantine era were preserved in the gardens of the Topkapı Palace long ago, as early as the 15th century, right after the conquest of Constantinople.[20] Nevertheless, the new interest in antiquity collections that started in the second half of the 19th century was different in character, and was more related to the Empire's attempt at integration with Europe, than a continuation of an old Ottoman tradition. In 1846, Fethi Ahmed Pasha, Field Marshal of the Imperial Arsenal and former ambassador to Vienna and Paris, transformed the church of St Irene, located in the gardens of the royal palace, into a museum under the name *Mecmua-i Âsâr-ı Atîka* (Collection of Ancient Monuments), accompanied by *Mecmua-i Esliha-i Âsâr-ı Atîka* (Collection of Ancient Weapons).[21] St Irene was until then used as a depository to store military artefacts from the early Ottoman period. It is very likely that Fethi Ahmed Pasha was inspired by the museums he visited in Europe during his diplomatic service. During the organization of the antiquities collection, Fethi Ahmed Pasha was supported by Sultan Abdulmecid. It is claimed that on a visit to Yalova, a town on the coast of the Marmara Sea, Abdulmecid saw gilded stones. Upon learning that the Byzantine Emperor Constantine's name was inscripted on them, the Sultan ordered to send these stones to Istanbul. These monuments were eventually sent to St Irene for exhibition by Fethi Ahmed Pasha.[22] The collection at St Irene was divided in two parts: on one side, there were old weapons, jannissary costumes and the armour collection from earlier periods of Ottoman history, artefacts which had already been preserved in St Irene. On the other side, the Hellenistic-Byzantine artefacts were displayed.[23]

Mecmua-i Âsâr-ı Atîka was the first Ottoman attempt at creating a Western-style museum.[24] The objects in the collection were exhibited in a rather disorganized manner, where old Ottoman military paraphernalia lay side by side with ancient Greek and Roman tombs. Still, this institution implied the sovereignty of the Ottoman Empire over vast territories, some of which were only theoretically attached to the imperial centre. In a document dating to 1846, local officials in Tripoli, Libya, were asked to send ancient objects to the collection in İstanbul. In this document, the antiquities collection was defined as a museum organized along the same lines as its counterparts in European countries. The document was accompanied by an order stating that ancient objects were henceforth to be sent to the collection in the imperial capital.[25] Embracing the Greco-Roman heritage as well as the

Ottoman past, the museum also reflected the supranational identity behind *Tanzimat* reforms.

Different from European museums where governments supported the educative role of national museums for their own public, the Ottoman Museum targeted not its own citizens (as the museum was opened to the public only in 1880) but a foreign audience, especially foreign government representatives and aristocrats.[26] Even though the number of local visitors, especially student groups increased towards the end of the 19th century, these figures remained relatively low compared to the number of local visitors in European and American museums.[27] As early as the 1850s, the museum became one of the major destinations where Ottoman officials personally accompanied foreign visitors from various countries including Austria, Prussia, the United States, Britain, France and Russia.[28] The fact that museum visits were mentioned in the documents of the Ministry of Foreign Affairs hinted at the symbolic meaning the Ottoman government assigned to its collection of antiquities. By establishing a European-style museum for a foreign audience, the Ottoman government implied not only the Western orientation of the Empire but also visualized its territorial integrity for the Western visitors by displaying objects from different regions under its control. When the romantic poet Théophile Gautier visited the Ottoman capital, he saw *Mecmua-i Âsâr-ı Atîka* as a sign of progress. Even though Gautier did not find the Ottoman weapon and armour collection interesting for a European visitor, he was quite impressed by the Hellenistic-Byzantine antiquities in *Mecmua-i Âsâr-ı Atîka*. He asserted that the various objects on display, including ancient sculptures, reliefs, inscriptions and tombs, heralded the inception of a Byzantine museum, which could evolve into an interesting collection with the addition of new objects.[29]

Ottoman archaeological projects also reflected a centralizing tendency. In 1857, local authorities in various parts of the Empire were asked to identify ancient monuments in their localities and send them to İstanbul for the reorganization of the museum.[30] By bringing ancient objects and displaying them in the capital, the Ottoman government was stating the authority İstanbul exercised over the rest of the Empire. It is noteworthy that right after the conflict between Maronites and Druzes in Lebanon in 1860, Ottoman officials regulated the access to the Baalbek ruins in the region, as if to reiterate authority over a contested territory.[31]

The relocation of antiquities from periphery to the centre was a means of underlining the distinction between the modern and Europeanized centre and premodern periphery and thus legitimated central authority over provinces. Later in 1898, when Emperor Kaiser Wilhelm II visited the Baalbek ruins, the plaque erected in commemoration of his visit was inscribed in Ottoman

Turkish and German, but not in Arabic, the local language. The tickets to the Baalbek ruins were written in three languages: Ottoman Turkish, the official language of the Empire; French, the lingua franca of foreign tourists; and Arabic, the local tongue; but only on the Arabic ticket was there a warning not to steal anything from the ruins. Therefore, Ottoman archaeologists viewed their task as to save ancient monuments not only from the greed of European archaeologists but also from local inhabitants, whom Ottoman officials thought could easily be exploited by European treasure hunters to pillage the ruins.[32] In fact, the museum-building practice in the Ottoman Empire assumed the impossible task of representing a Eurocentric discourse of modernity while resisting it; glorifying an Ottoman imperial past, while embodying an anti-imperialist soul.[33]

The collections of historical relics were reorganized with the transformation of *Mecmua-i Âsâr-ı Atîka* into a proper museum in 1869 under the administration of the Ministry of Education.[34] The first director of the *Müze-i Hümâyun*, that is, the Imperial Museum, was Edward Goold, a teacher at Galatasaray High School, who also prepared the first catalogue of the museum exhibition in French. Goold served as the director of the Ottoman Imperial Museum from 1869 to 1871. In the same year that *Müze-i Hümâyun* was established, the first antiquities law was promulgated in the Ottoman Empire.[35] Even though this was a very sketchy legal regulation, one of the seven articles in the 1869 act outlawed the transfer of antiquities abroad, without specifying what the term antiquity meant. Antiquities could be sold within the Ottoman Empire, but the Ottoman state had priority to buy ancient objects for its museum. Moreover, the act stated that permission from the Ministry of Education was compulsory for excavation and research. In case a foreign government wanted to remove an ancient object outside the borders of the Ottoman Empire, the Sultan had the responsibility to make the decision.[36] This legal regulation is important as it was the first step towards the standardization of procedures as regards antiquities. At the same time, it showed Ottoman bureaucracy's discomfort at the flow of ancient objects to foreign markets. Apparently, as early as 1869, antiquities acquired a meaning as a sign of sovereignty in the eyes of Ottoman bureaucrats. Nevertheless, the 1869 act still regarded antiquities as the property of the Sultan, not of the Ottoman state.

In 1871, the directorate of the Imperial Museum was abolished by Grand Vizier Mahmud Nedim Pasha, and was reinstated again by Ahmed Vefik Pasha in 1872. During this one-year break, the Austrian painter, Teranzio served in the capacity of custodian of the museum on the basis of a reference provided by the Austrian ambassador, also an antiquities collector, Anton von Prokesch-Osten.[37] The second director of the Imperial Museum,

Philipp Anton Dethier, the headmaster of the Austrian High School, was appointed in 1872 and remained in this office until 1881. Dethier planned the enlargement of the museum and was behind the 1874 antiquities legislation.[38] Even though he envisioned the creation of a school of archaeology affiliated with the Imperial Museum that would train photographers and restorators in addition to archaeologists, this plan was never realized.[39] In 1880, the Ottoman Imperial Museum became a full-fledged museum comparable to museums in European countries. The increasing number of objects could no longer be stored in the existing facilities, and therefore were moved to larger premises known as the Tiled Pavilion (*Çinili Köşk*) in the gardens of the Topkapı Palace. In 1880, the collection was for the first time opened to the public.[40] During Dethier's directorship, the number of objects in the museum nearly quadrupled.[41]

The first instances of conflict between European archaeologists and Ottoman officials arose in the mid-19th century, but suspicions reached a peak with the scandalous excavation in Troy by the German antiquarian Heinrich Schliemann in 1871. Schliemann received a permit from Ottoman authorities on the condition that he would send half of the findings to the Imperial Museum in Istanbul. Nevertheless, he did not comply with this arrangement and smuggled the infamous Priam's Treasure to Athens in 1874. The Ottoman government brought the issue to the Greek courts, but despite the legal decision to give the objects back to the Ottoman government, Schliemann refused to comply.[42] The Ottoman authorities punished those who assisted Schliemann in smuggling ancient objects. At the same time, the Ministry of Education issued an edict to suspend excavations in Troy. Objects that were left behind after the Schliemann expedition were placed in the Ottoman Imperial Museum.[43] The issue became such an international scandal that eventually the Prussian government decided to dissuade amateur individuals from undertaking archaeological excavations abroad.[44]

From the Ottoman perspective, the Schliemann expedition was important because it triggered the enactment of a more extensive regulation about the ownership rights of antiquities compared to the 1869 act. According to the act issued in 1874, archaeological finds were to be equally divided among the landowner, the Ottoman government and the archaeologists undertaking the excavation. This regulation also introduced uniform procedures for archaeological excavations and research. Researchers were required to ask for official permission from the Ministry of Education through local administrative offices. Nevertheless, the regulation also paved the way for the flow of ancient objects to foreign markets. The article outlawing the export of antiquities that existed in the 1869 act was replaced with a new article, which stated that antiquities could be exported with the permission of the Ministry of Education, but the Ottoman government had the privilege to retain the object for the Imperial Museum.[45] The reason for this setback is obscure, but some researchers point to the possible influence of the foreign director of the Imperial Museum, Dethier, who might have acted as an intermediary between foreign archaeologists and the Ottoman Empire.[46]

In terms of the development of a consciousness about the protection of antiquities, there was a mutual interaction between the Ottoman Empire and European powers. While the Ottoman Empire felt threatened by European activities on its territories, Ottoman elites also looked upon Europe as an example for the protection of cultural heritage, and therefore countered European arguments with the very methods taken from Europe. The disagreement over the ownership of antiquities revealed the geopolitical difference between European powers and the Ottoman Empire. European archaeologists argued that antiquities belonged to humanity, rather than a single nation. The prevalent view in Western academia was that there was no serious archaeological and scientific interest in countries that were home to Greco-Roman artefacts, except for seeing ancient objects as a means of profit, therefore antiquities could not be sufficiently protected if they were left to the mercy of local governments.[47] From an Ottoman perspective, defending ownership rights over ancient objects vis-à-vis Europeans was a means of indicating sovereignty. On the other hand, similar to Europeans, Ottomans displayed an imperial attitude with regard to exporting monuments from the periphery to its capital, in an attempt to display the objects but also to protect them from the 'natives', that is, from local people.

Political developments and the change of leadership after the 1870s help to explain increasing Ottoman emphasis on sovereignty. In 1876, pro-reform bureaucrats succeeded in forcing the regime to adopt a constitution. The first brief constitutional experiment came to a halt when Abdülhamid II (r. 1876–1909) suspended parliament in 1878 using the Russo-Ottoman War as an excuse. Abdülhamid II came to the throne when the Ottoman Empire was economically bankrupt, and was politically threatened by imperialism. His reign was marked by a politically intolerant autocratic rule. However, this does not mean that he reversed the modernization of the Empire. On the contrary, Abdülhamid II initiated reforms in administration, education and military organization after the example of Europe. Paradoxically, European ideologies profoundly influenced Ottoman intellectual movements during his rule.[48] Administrative centralization, aimed at by the reforms of Ottoman rulers from Mahmud II to *Tanzimat* elites, was effectively realized by Abdülhamid II.

Ottoman archaeology was institutionalized during the Hamidian regime. Yet, it was not simply Abdülhamid II's persona that was instrumental in this institutionalization. More important was the bureaucracy, which was created as a result of a conscious state project since *Tanzimat*. The bureaucratic elite, who embraced European ideas, were eager to apply these ideas to an Ottoman context. The turning point for Ottoman archaeology came when Osman Hamdi Bey (1842–1910), the 'founding father' of Turkish archaeology, was appointed to the directorship of the Imperial Museum in 1881.

Osman Hamdi Bey was a clear representation of an Ottoman elite with *Tanzimat* upbringing: born into a family of high-ranking officials, his father was a reformist bureaucrat who had served as a diplomat in several European cities as well as assuming ministerial positions. Osman Hamdi went to Paris to study law, where he developed an interest in painting. In Paris, he received lessons from Orientalist painters such as Jean-Léon Gerôme and Gustave Boulanger. Upon his return to İstanbul, Osman Hamdi assumed several positions in the Ministry of Foreign Affairs. In 1882, he established the first Academy of Fine Arts in İstanbul to train Ottoman artists in the European fashion.[49] Yet, Osman Hamdi's vision was not based on an uncritical mimicry of European institutions, but a careful reconciliation of European science, art and techniques with Ottoman national culture.[50]

Osman Hamdi Bey started serving at the Imperial Museum in 1877, when he was one of the eight members of the Museum Commission affiliated with the Ministry of Education.[51] From 1881 until his death in 1910, he remained as the director of the Imperial Museum. Osman Hamdi's brother Halil Ethem (1861–1938) assumed the same post after his brother's death, and continued the policies initiated by Osman Hamdi. Osman Hamdi Bey initiated many changes in terms of archaeology: he introduced European exhibition methods, promoted the publication of a museum journal and undertook the first Ottoman archaeological excavations.[52] His strategy was to enrich the museum collection by unearthing ancient objects with aesthetic qualities. In this sense, the early Ottoman archaeological practice was marked by the art history-oriented approach, embraced by Osman Hamdi Bey and his colleagues.[53] In addition to storing antiquities, Osman Hamdi organized the Ottoman Museum as a scientific institution that actively participated in archaeological scholarship. As Edhem Eldem stated, Osman Hamdi envisioned his role as part of his dream to realize a '*mission civilisatrice*' for his country, as a contribution to the integration of the Ottoman Empire into the Western cultural world.[54]

Osman Hamdi Bey did not have a formal archaeology education. For this reason, he tried to establish close connections with foreign scholars and benefited from their expertise. Most notable among these scholars was

Theodor Reinach (1860–1928), with whom Osman Hamdi Bey organized numerous expeditions and made a number of publications.[55] Yet, probably the most important achievement of Osman Hamdi Bey was that he pushed the Ottoman government to enact more extensive laws for the preservation of antiquities within the imperial borders.

The regulation of 1884 came into being in this context.[56] According to this regulation, all foreign archaeological excavations in the Ottoman Empire were placed under the supervision of the Ministry of Education. For the first time, all ancient objects found within the boundaries of the Ottoman Empire were considered the property of the state, not of the Sultan, and their export was outlawed. The term antiquity was defined in a detailed manner that encompassed the history of all peoples inhabiting the Ottoman Empire. This definition included all scientific, technical, artistic and religious artefacts, movable and immovable, belonging to any culture that inhabited Ottoman territories at any time in history. Destruction of historical artefacts, trading or smuggling them was criminalized. Furthermore, all foreign archaeological expedition teams were required to submit specific maps, delineating their intended area of research clearly, to Ottoman authorities. This was a clear message about complete Ottoman legal, cultural and political claim over all antiquities on its territory. While educated elites like Osman Hamdi Bey were motivated by a concern about the artistic and historical value of artefacts, in the end what prompted the Ottoman government to take a definite stand for archaeological preservation was the threat they felt against their sovereignty. There is no doubt that archaeology is by its very nature linked to territory, and control over territory is the essence of sovereignty. In this sense, archaeology implied a strong link between sovereignty and property rights of the state not only over ancient objects, but also over territories where these objects were found. On a side note, with minor revisions, the 1884 regulation remained in effect well into 1974.[57]

Foreign scholars followed the promulgation of the Ottoman antiquities regulation with dismay, to say the least. The regulation reflected the Ottoman demand to be seen as equals with Europeans, and this demand was met with suspicion. Ernest Renan's (1823–1892) report to the French Ministry of Public Instruction perfectly illustrated European perceptions of Ottoman antiquities regulation. The implicit message in Renan's report was that he did not see the Ottomans fit for a 'European' scientific activity:

> This law, a sad proof of the infantile ideas that are formed among the Turkish government in scientific matters, will be remembered as an ill-fated date in the history of archaeological research … What, in effect, makes these measures particularly disastrous, is the immensity

of the lands to which they apply, since Turkey's pretensions now reach out to regions over which it had previously had only nominal control. The concentration of antiquities in a national museum is conceivable (although it presents serious drawbacks) for a country of modest expanse and possessing, as it were, archaeological unity. Yet, what should one say of a museum housing a jumble of objects originating from Greece, from Asia Minor, from Syria, from Arabia, from Yemen, and from so many other lands over which the Porte believes it can claim some imaginary sovereignty?[58]

Despite European suspicions, the relationship between European scholars and the Ottoman government was not totally confrontational. Osman Hamdi Bey's strict observance of legal regulations did not mean that he was uncooperative with foreign scholars. Aware of the shortcomings of Ottoman archaeology, Osman Hamdi established careful diplomatic relations with foreign scholars. Although restrictions were imposed on foreign archaeologists, the Ottoman government also offered support within legal limits.[59] In fact, there was a mutually beneficial relationship between European museums and the Ottoman Museum, a process of knowledge production that transcended official boundaries.[60]

While regulating and monitoring foreign archaeologists more strictly, the Ottoman government also funded archaeological expeditions by the staff of the Ottoman Imperial Museum. In 1883, the very first professional Ottoman archaeological excavation was carried out by Osman Hamdi Bey in Mount Nemrut in the Harput *Vilâyet*, in the ruins of the Kingdom of Commagene.[61] Right after the Berlin Museum sent Karl Humann (1839–1896) to Nemrut in 1882, the Ottoman government commissioned Osman Hamdi Bey and Oskan Efendi to carry out excavations in the same region, in an attempt to catch up with foreign archaeological activities.[62] However, the most significant excavation in Ottoman history was made in 1887 in the Sidon ruins in Lebanon, which bolstered Osman Hamdi Bey's international reputation as a respectable archaeologist. In the first excavation in Sidon, Osman Hamdi worked with Dimosten Baltacı Bey, while the second excavation was undertaken by Teodor Makridi Bey.[63] Of the eighteen sarcophagi found in the excavations, eleven were brought to Istanbul with the encouragement of Abdülhamid II, which placed the Ottoman Imperial Museum among the notable museums in the world. In 1892, Osman Hamdi Bey published a catalogue of his findings in Sidon with the French archaeologist Theodore Reinach in Paris.[64] In the 1890s, Ottoman archaeologists also started to participate in international congresses. In August 1892, two Ottoman officials, Abdurrahman Süreyya Bey and Kamil Bey were sent to the Lisbon

Archaeology Congress by the government to present photographs of the Imperial Museum collection.[65] In the same year, Ottoman representatives participated in the Moscow Archaeology Congress.[66] By 1894, the entire administrative committee of the Imperial Museum consisted of only Ottoman citizens.[67]

Abdülhamid II was so satisfied with the results of these expeditions that he asked Osman Hamdi Bey to continue his research in Sidon and ordered the construction of a new museum building in Istanbul to store objects brought from Lebanon.[68] Consequently, in 1891, the Ottoman Museum moved to a new building, which was designed by the architect Alexandre Vallaury with a neoclassical facade. Despite Abdülhamid's support for the Imperial Museum, the relationship between the Sultan and Osman Hamdi Bey was not free of friction. For instance, in 1905, Osman Hamdi suspected that his house might be searched by police and transferred some of his personal records to his friend Theodor Wiegand's house for protection. Next year in 1906, when Osman Hamdi was bombarded with over a hundred congratulatory telegrams from abroad for the twenty-fifth anniversary of his museum directorship, Abdülhamid suspected and sent an informer to inquire the reason of his correspondence with foreigners.[69]

It was not easy to find financial resources for archaeological expeditions, therefore Osman Hamdi looked for benefactors who would be supportive of his projects. The principal benefactor was Osman Hamdi's father Edhem Pasha, the Minister of the Interior from 1883 to 1885, who provided financial support for the first expedition.[70] In addition to providing monetary support, Edhem Pasha supported his son with his professional network, as well. In his correspondence with local authorities around the Ottoman Empire about ancient objects in their localities, Osman Hamdi Bey made use of his father's position as the Minister of the Interior.[71] In a note he wrote to the Ministry of Education, Osman Hamdi explained the symbolic importance of museums for the cultural development of a country. Referring to the grandeur of European museums, he expressed his disappointment at the reluctance of the Ministry of Education to provide necessary tools to the Imperial Museum and to elevate it to the same level as its European counterparts.[72] Despite these setbacks, the staff of the Imperial Museum undertook a number of archaeological expeditions around Asia Minor, Ottoman Macedonia, the Greek islands, Syria and Iraq, often in cooperation with foreign scholars.[73]

Since Ottoman archaeological practices started at the nexus of European competition over its ancient heritage, implying Ottoman rights over Greco-Roman antiquities was a message about Ottoman sovereignty over territories contested by European powers. It was also an attempt to incorporate Ottoman history to the broader framework of European history. In a way, classical antiquities in the Imperial Museum represented 'an empire able both to reach into the past to set the stage for its own teleological evolution into modernity and at the same time to translate East for West, and, of course, West for East'.[74] By putting stress on Greco-Roman classical antiquities, which Europeans took as the origin of their civilization and of civilization as a whole, the development of Ottoman archaeology implied a desire to be accepted as a European empire.

Nevertheless, the antiquity regulations by no means prevented the flow of antiquities from the Ottoman Empire to foreign museums. There were numerous cases in which local officials reported smuggling of antiquities abroad, mostly with the help of diplomatic staff. This shortcoming proves that legal regulations did not have universal practical application. For instance, according to a report from 1902, when the Russian fleet, under the command of Admiral Grand Duke Aleksandr Mikhailovich, was cruising on the Black Sea, Russian naval officers carried 'stones with figures' from the Amasra port. The Ministry of the Interior issued a strong warning that such incidents should not be repeated, and reminded that the smuggling of ancient objects was strictly outlawed.[75]

It was not only foreigners who overlooked Ottoman regulations: the Ottoman government itself applied protective measures inconsistently and disregarded its own laws in certain instances.[76] Often, Abdülhamid II and European-educated bureaucrats like Osman Hamdi Bey had different agendas about the fate of ancient objects. While educated members of the bureaucracy had the European notion that ancient artefacts should be protected and kept within national boundaries, Abdülhamid II did not abstain from using cultural property as a political tool in diplomatic negotiations. With the decline of Ottoman political and economic power, Abdülhamid II used gifts to win foreign support, especially of Germany after the 1880s.[77] The historical and aesthetic value of the gift was parallel to the importance ascribed to political alliance with the given power. Abdülhamid II's practice also implied that he regarded ancient objects, and in fact the territories of the Ottoman Empire, as his personal property that could be given as gifts upon his personal initiative. This notion contradicted the state-centred view of the burgeoning bureaucracy, whose ascendancy depended on the development of state as a body autonomous from the persona of the Sultan. In other words, the difference of opinion between the Sultan and bureaucrats was an example of a global pattern in which the state with objective laws replaced a monarch as the source of authority.

By far, the major recipient of ancient objects in the form of 'gifts' was the German Empire, as Kaiser Wilhelm II was Abdülhamid II's closest ally in international politics. There is less evidence about gifts received by Russian statesmen or diplomats. When the Porte allowed the Russian ship *Chornoe More* to anchor in the Black Sea harbour Ereğli in order to remove ancient objects, it was specifically stated that these objects were only some 'stones' with figures on them.[78] In the same year, Abdülhamid II presented seven chests of 'stone' removed from Tedmur ruins (Palmyra) in Syria to Grand Duke Sergei Aleksandrovich, who was known to have a personal interest in history and archaeology.[79]

The growing sensitivity about Ottoman property rights over Hellenistic, Roman and Byzantine antiquities is all the more interesting, considering Abdülhamid's political allegiances. Abdülhamid laid a heavy emphasis on Islam as the uniting factor of the Ottoman Empire, because the loss of European territories changed the demographic structure of the Empire in favour of Muslims. In the Hamidian era, Turco-Islamic art also received attention as national symbols. Nonetheless, in the museums that were established in the last century of the Ottoman Empire, the bulk of attention was always devoted to Greco-Roman antiquities and Islamic objects received only little interest.[80] This was partly related to the fact that Ottoman archaeologists imported archaeological methodology and paradigms from their European colleagues, who prioritized the study of classical archaeology.[81] The Department of Islamic Arts was established within the Ottoman Imperial Museum only in 1889, but a full-scale museum for Islamic arts was established only in 1914. As interest in 'exotic' works of Islamic art was growing in the European market, in 1906 the protective laws were extended to Islamic antiquities as well.[82] However, Islamic antiquities became a matter of serious public discussion only after the Young Turk Revolution of 1908, as the Young Turks removed these objects from their religious context and transformed them into secular objects of national identity.[83] Different from Turco-Islamic antiquities, there was rivalry for the ownership of Greco-Roman heritage between European powers and the Ottoman Empire, a factor that encouraged Ottoman elites to put a special emphasis on the latter in Ottoman museums.

The final legal regulation concerning antiquities was promulgated in 1906.[84] According to this amendment, all objects, regardless of their aesthetic quality, that reflected the art, culture and technology of all civilizations that lived on Ottoman territories throughout history, including Islamic antiquities, were categorized as archaeologically valuable. Therefore, the new definition of antiquity reflected the wide range of cultures that made up parts of Ottoman identity. All archaeological objects were strictly considered as the property of the Ottoman state. Museums were authorized as the sole institutions responsible for the inspection, preservation and exhibition of antiquities. Foreign archaeological societies could make excavations only on condition that they received permission from the Ministry of Education through the administration of the Imperial Ottoman Museum. In 1907, along with Britain, France and Germany, the Ottoman Empire ratified the Convention Respecting the Laws and Customs of War on Land, known as the Hague Convention. This treaty, originally concerned the rules of land warfare, was also the first international treaty that codified the protection of cultural property and prohibited the seizure of historic monuments during wars. Unfortunately, later during the First World War, the treaty fell short of fulfilling its mission.[85]

Even Abdülhamid's closest allies, the Germans faced stronger Ottoman supervision in the early years of the 20th century. By 1905, German excavations in Babylon, Assur and Pergamon were suspended, which made German archaeologists complain about the onerous restrictions posed by Ottoman bureaucracy, and especially about Osman Hamdi Bey's determined attitude as regards the execution of the antiquities law.[86]

In a couple of years, the Ottoman Empire went through a dramatic political change, which was also reflected in the politics of cultural property. In spite of the severe suppression of opposition, various clandestine political organizations were established under the Hamidian regime. The most prominent among them were the Committee of Union and Progress, who are often referred to as the Young Turks. Ideologically, Young Turks included liberal-minded pluralists, Turkish nationalists and materialist positivist intellectuals, though occasionally these conflicting elements could be found within the same person.[87] In 1908, these diverse political groups came together to overthrow Abdülhamid II, and engineered a coup d'état to reinstate the Constitution. After 1908, when the Committee of Union and Progress attained extensive authority in the Ottoman Empire, they carried out a reform program with a focus on centralization and secularization.

The Young Turk period was particularly significant for the development of public opinion in the Ottoman Empire and the flourishing of the press. For the first time, party politics, although many times shadowed by political intrigues and the inexperience of politicians, entered the political scene. Legitimacy for political action was sought in parliamentary procedures, albeit imperfectly.[88] The Committee of Union and Progress intentionally nurtured a sense of populism among people, which replaced the charisma of the Sultan.[89] The state was no longer seen as the Sultan's private domain, but was identified with the Ottoman nation, although there was no agreement on what Ottoman nation meant.

Therefore, the promulgation of the 1906 regulation was only one of the reasons for the strict observance of foreign archaeologists in this period. The major reason was that the Young Turks were more eager to apply Ottoman laws and to prevent the foreign acquisition of Ottoman cultural property than their predecessors. From this time onwards, ancient objects were recognized as the property not of the Sultan but of the Ottoman nation and the 'antiquities question had become a highly sensitive matter of international as well as domestic Turkish politics.'[90] On a side note, the recognition of antiquities as the property of the 'Ottoman nation' further increased the ambiguity behind this term: transferring artefacts from the periphery, for instance, from Arab lands to Istanbul and keeping them out of European hands was an act of imperialism and anti-imperialism at the same time. Offering ancient monuments to foreign governments in the form of gifts, as Abdülhamid II had done various times, was unthinkable under the Young Turk regime. Even though foreign archaeologists continued to make archaeological investigations, the flow of antiquities from the Ottoman Empire slowed down. In 1911, the Ministry of the Interior issued a new order to preclude foreigners from undertaking unauthorized excavations.[91]

Only months before the First World War, the Ministry of the Interior repeated its statement that unauthorized excavations should not be permitted across the Ottoman Empire, those smuggling antiquities should be punished and the objects should be confiscated.[92] Despite these official statements, with the outbreak of the First World War, the Ottoman Empire, especially in Mesopotamia and Anatolia, became an open ground for the smuggling of antiquities. Large chunks of Ottoman territory were occupied by the Allied forces, including the Russians between 1914 and 1918. These occupations resulted in large-scale illicit antiquities trade across the borders. In the years to follow until the establishment of the Republic, Anatolian antiquities flowed to foreign markets in the absence of a government authority. In spite of this, the artefacts in the Ottoman Imperial Museum were protected as a result of the dedicated efforts of the museum staff.[93] After the establishment of the Turkish Republic, some of the archaeological material smuggled during the war was repatriated as a result of insistent government efforts.[94] The Turkish archaeological tradition that started in the 19th century laid the groundwork for archaeological policies in the Republican years.

2.1 Byzantine studies in the Ottoman Empire

The gradually growing Ottoman interest in antiquities was directed mostly towards Greco-Roman heritage, and Byzantine monuments received comparatively less attention. Even though Byzantine monuments were stored in the Imperial Museum, these artefacts were not constructed as parts of an Ottoman 'national' history. Moreover, in the Ottoman Empire, there was yet no institution dedicated to Byzantine studies. The few intellectuals who touched upon Byzantine history in their works were either historians, or intellectuals with a particular interest in antiquities. The first book about Byzantine monuments written by an Ottoman citizen was a short brochure by the Greek Patriarch Constantios I (1770–1859) from 1861.[95] In the 19th century, Ottoman historians, such as Ahmed Midhat Efendi, Mizancı Mehmed Murad, Celal Nuri and Namık Kemal, started to integrate Byzantine history into general histories of the Ottoman Empire, often as a historical background to explain and praise the successes of the Ottoman Empire in comparison to its predecessor.[96]

Actually, right after the conquest of Constantinople by the Ottomans in 1453, Ottoman rulers embraced the heritage of their predecessors and refashioned themselves as the heirs of the Byzantine Empire. The adoption of Byzantine traditions was especially visible in early Ottoman architectural practices, protocols and ceremonial performances.[97] The use of Byzantine symbols was a means of providing a legitimate basis for Ottoman acquisition of imperial power, authority and sovereignty in the 15th century. Mehmed II (r. 1444–6; 1451–81) was known with titles similar to those used by the Byzantine *basileus*. In addition to Ottoman self-perception, post-1453 texts by some Greek scholars show that the Ottomans were viewed as the legitimate heirs to the Byzantine throne by a broader audience.[98] The Greek historians Kritoboulos (1410–1470) and Amiroutzes (1400–1470), both of whom personally witnessed the transformation of imperial power from the Byzantines to the Ottomans, eulogized Mehmed II as the legitimate emperor of the Romans, perhaps with a pragmatic intention to accommodate to the new political reality.

Despite the early Ottoman appropriation of Byzantine legacy, this identity gradually changed and the memory of the Byzantine Empire drifted into the dusty pages of history. Byzantium was once again remembered by Ottoman intellectuals only in the 19th century, in a very different context. In the last decades of the 19th century, Ottoman historians discovered the Turkic identity of the Ottoman Empire. However, different from other Turkic states with nomadic traditions, the Ottoman state transformed itself into an Empire, a cosmopolitan political entity with established political traditions. The imperial character of the Ottoman Empire intrigued intellectuals like Ahmed Midhat Efendi as regards the sources of this imperial tradition, which he found in the Byzantine Empire.[99] Ahmed Midhat noted that the Byzantine Empire had no historical connection to modern Greeks. He added that for the sake of historical coherence, Byzantine history should be treated as part of Ottoman history.[100] The common theme in the works of first Ottoman historians who dealt with Byzantine history was that they based their analyses on Western sources, and therefore adopted the negative European attitudes towards the Byzantine Empire, considering it as a despotic and corrupt political entity. In a period when Ottoman intellectuals were speculating about the reasons of Ottoman decline and looking for remedies to reverse the situation, it was practical to link the decline of the Ottoman Empire to the negative impact exerted by the Byzantines, than blaming it on Islam.[101] It is a curious coincidence that Ottoman intellectuals' criticism of Byzantine despotism and corruption echoed the views of Russian intellectuals, who blamed the Byzantine heritage for Russia's contemporary problems.

The first, and in fact the most comprehensive, book published by an Ottoman Turk exclusively on Byzantine history was Celal Esad Bey's (Celal Esad Arseven) *Constantinople de Byzance a Stamboul* (Constantinople from Byzantine to Istanbul), published in 1909. The preface of this work was written by the noted French Byzantinist Charles Diehl. Written in French, the book obviously targeted a foreign audience. In the preface, Diehl noted that Celal Esad's ardent nationalism, which came to the surface in some parts of the book, might bring smiles to specialists in the West, but he praised Celal Esad for successfully undertaking a comprehensive study on Byzantine monuments in Istanbul.[102] Despite the imperfections of the book, Diehl noted that Celal Esad successfully portrayed Byzantine architecture and completed the study with a description of Ottoman monuments in the city. Until the publication of Celal Esad's book, the study of the Byzantine Empire was monopolized by Greeks, Russians, Germans, the British and the French, and Diehl concluded that it was interesting to see an Ottoman Turk writing about Byzantine art and history.

Celal Esad argued that the separation of Latin and Orthodox churches prevented European archaeologists from taking an active interest in the history of the Byzantine Empire. Therefore, Byzantine monuments remained in the shadow of Greco-Roman antiquities for quite a long time in European academia. Celal Esad critically stated that there had been many academics and specialists in Europe, who scorned Byzantine art and downplayed its influence on the development of Western art. At this point, Celal Esad drew similarities between European perceptions of Byzantine and Turkish art, and pointed out that Turkish artistic development was also subjected to similar prejudices.[103]

Diehl had a point when he said that Celal Esad's analysis of Byzantine history was shaped by a nationalist overtone. Although Celal Esad acknowledged the influence of Byzantine art on European as well as Islamic artistic traditions, he provided a negative picture with regard to Byzantine rulers and society. He contended that internal problems, such as the decadence of morals, and economic problems, which were caused by very high court spending, made the Byzantine Empire vulnerable to foreign exploitation. Eventually, the

Byzantine Empire found itself in the middle of a political debacle in the 13th century.[104]

In his description of the conquest of Constantinople by the Turks, Celal Esad made comparison with the Crusader conquest in the 13th century to portray the Ottomans in a favourable light to his European readers. He stated that after the Turkish conquest, Constantinople was looted, as was the common practice at the time. Celal Esad referred to the pillage of the churches such as Chora and St Jean Baptiste by the Ottomans, but he legitimized the situation by contending that the pillage of the Crusaders far exceeded the pillage of the Turks. Celal Esad argued that apart from looting the city, the Ottomans also respected and in fact embraced the existing civilization they encountered in the imperial city. The adoption of Byzantine civilization was visible at the level of state symbols. Celal Esad claimed that upon the conquest of the city, Mehmed II adopted the crescent as the state emblem, which was actually the sign of the Byzantine Empire, and added a star to it.[105]

Celal Esad acknowledged the impact of Byzantine art on Seljukid, and later Ottoman art. Especially after the conquest of Constantinople in 1453, Turkish architecture was definitely inspired by local traditions.[106] Ottoman exposure to Byzantine architectural tradition was particularly visible in religious architecture, considering the similarities between Byzantine churches and Ottoman mosques. But he also added that in a short time Turkish art acquired a unique character.

Another Ottoman intellectual who compiled a work on Byzantine art and architecture was İhtifalci Mehmed Ziya, who was a member of the Muhâfaza-i Âsâr-i Atîka Encümen-i Dâimîsi (Permanent Committee for the Preservation of Antiquities). His book, *İstanbul ve Boğaziçi: Bizans ve Türk Medeniyetinin Eserleri* (Istanbul and the Bosphorus: The Monuments of Byzantine and Turkish Civilisations), originally published in 1920, was more like a list of Byzantine and Ottoman monuments in Istanbul.[107] In his descriptions of Byzantine-era buildings, Mehmed Ziya drew comparisons with European and Ottoman architecture and concluded that Byzantine monuments had more in common with Ottoman, rather than European architecture. For instance, in his description of the Great Palace of the Byzantine emperors, built during the reign of Constantine the Great in the 4th century, Mehmed Ziya claimed that this palace had more similarities with the Russian Kremlin or Ottoman Topkapı Palace, rather than the Versailles or the Louvre.[108] In an attempt to justify Ottoman conquest, Mehmed Ziya claimed that the Ottomans were not responsible for the destruction of the Great Palace, since it was already in ruins during the Byzantine period.[109]

Mehmed Ziya's analyses included interesting comparisons between European and Byzantine civilizations. He contended that while European people were still in a state of 'nomadism' (*bedevi*; could also be translated as 'barbarity'), the Byzantine Empire flourished with magnificence.[110] Like Celal Esad, Mehmed Ziya also blamed foreigners for the downfall of the Byzantine Empire. He claimed that the Byzantine Empire lost its glamour because of the negative impact of foreigners that penetrated into Byzantine society, which ultimately led to the fall of the Byzantine capital to the Turks in 1453.[111]

The studies by Celal Esad and Mehmed Ziya were unique in the way they handled Byzantine history, and definitely did not reflect overall Ottoman historiography. By examining Byzantine history in a more or less positive light, these two studies offered a rare perspective among Ottoman intellectuals. Not surprisingly, in the late 19th and early 20th centuries, alongside Celal Esad's and Mehmed Ziya's accounts about Byzantine history, there were an even greater number of historical works with nationalist undertones, which portrayed the Byzantine Empire as the bastion of corruption and intrigues. In the last years of the Ottoman Empire, the newly emerging nationalist historiography presented a negative image of the Byzantine Empire. What the studies by Celal Esad and Mehmed Ziya had in common was their appropriation of the Byzantine legacy vis-à-vis European rivals. They both pointed to similarities between Ottoman and Byzantine art, and implied that the major recipient of Byzantine civilization was the Ottoman Empire, not any other European power. In an attempt to legitimize Ottoman destruction of the Byzantine Empire, both intellectuals underlined that Byzantine rule was already in decline, and its ultimate downfall was only a matter of time.

Conclusion

The story of Ottoman archaeology in the 19th century is nearly exclusively the story of one man, Osman Hamdi Bey. Even Osman Hamdi, despite his very central role in initiating local archaeological excavations, did not have a formal academic training, and in fact, he was a self-trained enthusiast. The very first university in the Ottoman Empire was established only in 1900, and the first department of archaeology in Turkey was established only in the 1930s, in the Republican period. Consequently, the Ottoman Empire lacked a community of scholars, let alone academic journals dedicated to archaeology. Osman Hamdi Bey's roles as a bureaucrat and as an archaeologist were very much intertwined, and it was his bureaucratic position that helped him follow his artistic and cultural interests. As an individual, Osman Hamdi pursued his agenda independently and established a pattern for archaeological preservation. Yet, it was his bureaucratic power (and the powerful network he was born into as İbrahim Edhem Pasha's son) that made this individuality possible. In other words, Osman Hamdi's autonomy was a result of his bureaucratic career, rather than his status as an aspiring scholar. Therefore, in the 19th-century Ottoman Empire, it is nearly impossible to clearly mark the line between 'scholar' and state bureaucracy. At least in the case of archaeology, the very same individual combined these two purposes. The growing power of bureaucracy over every field of social and cultural life was emblematic of the post-Tanzimat Ottoman society.

The development of archaeology in the Ottoman Empire was a reflection of various domestic and international trends. On the domestic level, the collection of artefacts in the capital showed the Ottoman government's willingness to project its central authority over the provinces. In this sense, Ottoman Imperial Museum was the cultural expression of centralization policies that characterized 19th-century Ottoman reforms. At the same time, by integrating Greco-Roman history into modern Ottoman identity, the Imperial Museum served as the visual representation of the Ottomanist idea behind the *Tanzimat* reforms that influenced Osman Hamdi Bey and his generation. The patterns of Ottoman archaeology from the *Tanzimat* to the Young Turk period gave clues about the changes in identity politics in the Ottoman Empire throughout the 19th century.

Nonetheless, the Ottoman Imperial Museum failed to present a coherent discourse about the evolution of Ottoman society in a historical perspective. While European museums like the British Museum or the Louvre displayed history in a linear manner – exhibitions progressing from the ancient to the modern and geographically from East to West – the Ottoman Museum did not counter this argument by putting forward its own version of history. In fact, 'Ottoman museums jumped from one autonomous collection to another, each of which displayed a single aspect of the new Ottoman identity but none of which promoted a model of cultural progress with its apogee in Ottoman modernity.'[112] The main aim of Ottoman archaeologists was rather to enrich the museum collections, mostly with objects with aesthetic value from Hellenistic and Roman periods.[113]

On an international level, the development of museum-building in the Ottoman Empire was a reaction against increasing foreign archaeological activity, which was seen as an extension of foreign political influence. What characterized Ottoman attitude to foreign archaeologists was a mixture of mistrust and toleration within the confines of law. Foreign archaeologists were reminded of Ottoman sovereign rights through a set of laws and administrative supervision, although in practice, these laws were selectively and inconsistently applied. Responding to foreign archaeological involvement with local archaeological projects implied a desire to protect the sovereignty of the Empire. Consequently, after the mid-19th century, ancient monuments within the borders of the Ottoman Empire were regarded as state property.

Ottoman elites, including Osman Hamdi Bey, embraced European practices and in fact, countered foreign activities by the very methods they adopted from their European colleagues. Archaeology, as a practice originating from Europe, implied Ottoman Empire's incorporation into the European cultural sphere.[114] By displaying Greco-Roman antiquities in the Ottoman Museum, Ottoman elites symbolically reiterated their right over the territories claimed by European powers. Yet, they did not, neither could they, claim ethnic and cultural continuity with the former residents of their lands.[115]

Both Russian and Ottoman Empires had historical and cultural connections to the Byzantine Empire, although Ottoman and Russian discourses were shaped under different contexts. In reality, the Ottoman Empire took over many cultural and political traits from their Byzantine predecessors, and inherited the very territories ruled by Byzantine emperors. Despite these obvious connections, Byzantine legacy remained invisible for most Ottoman intellectuals in the 19th century, not to mention bureaucrats and policymakers. Only in the last years of the Ottoman Empire, a handful of intellectuals in their pseudo-academic historical works established a link between Ottoman history and the Byzantine Empire. However, the discourse of these intellectuals was also problematic because while appropriating Byzantine legacy, they also had to legitimize its destruction by the Ottomans. Overall, Ottoman attitude to Byzantine heritage was characterized by lack of interest, if not total rejection. On the other hand, Russian tsars perceived of themselves as culturally linked to the Byzantine Empire, as the protector of Orthodox faith, and openly proclaimed this identity. Therefore, it is not surprising that from its earliest beginnings, Byzantine antiquities occupied an important place in the development of archaeological scholarship in the Russian Empire.

3

At the intersection of science and politics: Russian Archaeological Institute in the Ottoman Empire

Among imperial powers competing for archaeological glories on Ottoman territories, Russia was a very interesting case, both because of the – mostly – hostile relations between Russia and the Ottoman Empire, and because of the scope of Russian archaeological interests. Different from other European scholars, Russian archaeologists in the Ottoman Empire focused nearly exclusively on Byzantine and Slavic antiquities. This was partly because their expertise lay in these fields, and partly because they felt more competitive in these areas vis-à-vis their European counterparts. Considering that academic archaeology had a longer history in British, French and German universities than in Russia, it is understandable why Russian archaeologists did not see themselves fit for competition over classical Greco-Roman archaeology. Besides, there was also an ideological justification for Russian interest in Orthodox and Slavic antiquities. Official Russian policy projected an image of Russia as the protector of Orthodox and Slavic peoples of the Ottoman Empire, which was symbolically reiterated by a scientific interest in the archaeological remnants of these civilizations.

Throughout the second half of the 19th century, one of the key themes in European diplomacy was the so-called Eastern Question, in other words, the diplomatic problems posed by the disintegration of the Ottoman Empire. Recent scholarship questions the 19th-century European perception that the Ottoman Empire was on the verge of collapse or that it was the 'sick man of Europe', as Nicholas I dubbed.[1] Rather, scholars try to come up with a more balanced view on the Eastern Question by looking at not only Western European, but also Ottoman and Russian sources and the involvement of the peoples on the borderlands. As archaeological policies partially highlighted, 19th-century Ottoman state was in fact a modernizing one that strengthened its institutions and countered European aspirations on its territories. Neither did Russian policymakers unrealistically tried to grasp Ottoman territories, as 19th-century British statesmen feared. Therefore, many of the underlying assumptions of the Eastern Question paradigm rests on 19th-century European, and particularly British, visions of Russia and the Ottoman Empire and has to be reconsidered.

However, if there was one undisputed outcome of the Eastern Question, it was the fact that gradual Ottoman territorial retreat brought forward multifaceted diplomatic complications, and from time to time these complications drew Russia into open confrontation with other European powers. For strategic as well as historical reasons, the Russian Empire was particularly concerned with the fate of the Straits and the Balkans. Strengthening mutual relations with the Southern Slavs and other Orthodox peoples of the Ottoman Empire constituted one of the most important pillars of Russian foreign policy. In this sense, the academic study of Byzantine antiquities coincided with Russian political interests in the region.

The first semi-scientific Russian society in the Ottoman Empire was the Imperial Orthodox Palestine Society (IPPO). The purpose and activities of this society was much wider than historical scholarship, and archaeology was only one of its many fields of interests. However, the establishment of IPPO is important because this was the first institutional basis for Russian archaeological activities in the Ottoman Empire. Moreover, the bureaucrats and diplomats behind the establishment of IPPO also supported the creation of Russian Archaeological Institute in Constantinople (RAIK) a few years later. The involvement of the same bureaucrats in the creation of overseas societies suggests a pattern in Russian foreign policy in the late imperial period.

3.1 Russians in the Holy Land: Imperial Orthodox Palestine Society

Since the mid-19th century, Palestine was at the forefront of international politics, as the Catholic-Orthodox rivalry heightened in the region. This sectarian rivalry was one of the most important reasons behind the Crimean War (1853–6) and intensified Franco-Russian competition over the Holy Land. Grand Duke Konstantin Nikolayevich (1827–1892), brother of Emperor Alexander II, was one of the many leading Russian statesmen with an interest in Palestinian affairs. Konstantin Nikolayevich, an admiral in the Russian Imperial Navy and one of the most influential 'enlightened bureaucrats' of the 1860s, was known for his reformist and liberal inclinations in domestic affairs.[2] The Grand Duke was also one of the most influential foreign policymakers in the immediate aftermath of the Crimean War.

Different from his liberal tendencies in domestic matters, the Grand Duke supported the expansion of Russian political power in the Near East. Once in office, he was eager to promote Russia's standing in the Holy Land, as well.

In 1857, Grand Duke Konstantin Nikolayevich sent Boris Pavlovich Mansurov (1828-1910), a member of the State Council, to Palestine. Mansurov's mission was to investigate the feasibility of a committee to coordinate cultural and humanitarian activities but especially to represent Russian political interests in this sensitive region.[3] Mansurov was the name behind a new foreign-policy approach in Russian diplomatic circles – he emphasized the importance of extending humanitarian, economic and cultural influence in the Near East in addition to military prowess.[4] Interestingly, nearly thirty years later, the same Boris Mansurov will write another report outlining the necessity of creating a Russian archaeological society in Istanbul, which will be dealt with in detail later in this chapter.

Upon his visit to Palestine, Mansurov wrote down a report outlining the deplorable conditions of local Orthodox population in the region and the Catholic propaganda among them.[5] Pointing to the necessity of providing a shelter for Russian pilgrims visiting the Holy Land, Mansurov argued that it was Russia's responsibility to provide guidance to Russian pilgrims and local Christians. In an additional secret report, Mansurov stated that this society should look apolitical, as if it was only established for charitable purposes, but it should be used as an opportunity to further Russian interests in the region.

The Palestine Committee was established in 1859 under the protection of the Ministry of Foreign Affairs but it became defunct when its patron, Grand Duke Konstantin Nikolayevich was appointed as the viceroy of Poland.[6] However, it became the basis for a more efficient institution, which was established on 21 May 1882 under the name Imperial Orthodox Palestine Society (IPPO). The opening day of IPPO had a specific meaning in Orthodox Christianity as the commemoration day of the Byzantine Empress Helena and her son Emperor Constantine, the first Christian Roman emperor and the founder of Constantinople.[7]

IPPO was established only one year after Tsar Alexander III ascended the throne. Alexander III's reign was marked by a heavy emphasis on Orthodoxy as the main pillar of Russia's domestic and foreign policy. Therefore, it does not come as a surprise that the new Tsar was eager to extend Russia's protective wings to Orthodox believers in the Holy Land. IPPO was established upon the initiative of Vasilii Nikolayevich Khitrovo (1834-1903) based on the example of British and German missions in Palestine. The Society received the backing of the chief procurator of the Holy Synod, Konstantin Pobedonostsev (1827-1907). Khitrovo, who served at the Ministry of Finance and Ministry of Navy and was personally acquainted with the Grand Duke Konstantin Nikolayevich, visited Jerusalem in 1871 and decided to alleviate the situation of local Arab Christians and their clergy, as well as that of Russian pilgrims.[8] Upon his return from Palestine, Khitrovo penned a report, similar to the one written by Mansurov twenty years earlier. Like Mansurov, Khitrovo also noted the miserable conditions of local Christians, strong Protestant and Catholic influence, and Greek control over the Orthodox population.[9] In May 1882 with an imperial decree (also signed by the chief procurator of the Holy Synod) the Society was formally established.[10] In 1889, Alexander III made IPPO an imperial society and recognized it as the leading institution responsible for Palestinian affairs, thus bringing it under imperial protection.

The first president of IPPO was Grand Duke Sergei Alexandrovich, brother of Alexander III and uncle of Nicholas II, and Khitrovo was his assistant. Vice president of the Society was Tertii Ivanovich Filippov (1826–1899), an influential bureaucrat serving as the director of the State Comptroller's Office, whose name will reappear during the establishment of RAIK once again.[11] In the board of members, there were a number of scholars, most of whom were well known for their studies on Byzantine history. They included Vasilii Grigorievich Vasilevskii, an important Byzantinist and editor of *Vizantiiski Vremennik*, archaeologist Mikhail Alekseevich Venevitinov (1844–1901) and historian Akim Alekseevich Olesnitskii (1842–1907), both of whom worked on the history of Christian East.

According to its Charter, the duties of IPPO included coordinating and supporting scientific activities in Palestine, providing charity services to those in need, opening schools and hospitals, and sheltering Russian pilgrims in the Holy Land. Until the outbreak of the First World War, the Society opened nearly a hundred schools in Syria, Lebanon and Palestine.[12] IPPO was also responsible for informing Russian public about the Near East. In fact, it was the first platform that brought Byzantinist scholars together and provided them with a common ground for academic cooperation, even though its geographical scope was limited to Palestine and Syria.[13]

Although it was not specifically an archaeological institute, IPPO hosted a number of archaeological expeditions in Palestine and Syria. Among these expeditions, many were dedicated to the study of Byzantine monuments in this region. Archimandrite Antonin Kapustin, member of the Russian ecclesiastical mission in Jerusalem and of IPPO, was especially noted for his participation in archaeological excavations.[14] Among his most important works was the excavation of the Threshold of the Judgment Gate in 1883, which Kapustin wrongly assumed as the gate by which Jesus passed through on the way to Golgotha. He also unearthed the staircase of an ancient church believed to be built during Constantine the Great's reign.[15] These archaeological discoveries were motivated by the competition between various European learned societies operating in the Holy Land. The discovery of Orthodox antiquities reinstated Russia's symbolic dominance in the sacred places of Christianity.[16] Until 1917, IPPO published its scholarly activities in a journal, the Orthodox Palestine Collection (*Pravoslavny Palestinskii Sbornik*), and also in the annual Bulletin of IPPO (*Soobshcheniia Imperatorskogo Pravoslavnogo Palestinskogo Obshchestva*).

One of the founders of IPPO, Khitrovo argued that Russia had very crucial political interests in the Holy Land by the virtue of being the only heir of the Byzantine Empire. This role necessitated Russia to extend its protective wings not only for Orthodox Slavs but also for all Orthodox peoples, including Orthodox Arabs in Syria and Palestine. Khitrovo was far from being alone in his enthusiasm for Russian expansionism, and he had similar-minded acquaintances in the royal family, bureaucracy and academia; most notably professors I. E. Troitskii, I. I. Sokolov, Grand Duke Sergei Alexandrovich, and the head of the Holy Synod Konstantin Pobedonostsev.[17]

From the start, the activities of IPPO were closely linked to international developments and political rivalries, especially to the power game between Greek and Russian ecclesiastical authorities.[18] Russian diplomats were longing for supplementing Russian political leadership over the Orthodox world with intellectual and religious leadership. However, in order to strengthen Russia's position over the Orthodox Church, they first had to counter the ecclesiastical supremacy of Greeks.

In the last decades of the 19th century Pan-Hellenism and Pan-Slavism appeared as competing tendencies. As rivalry between independent Greece and Balkan nations increased in the Balkans, tensions between Greek and Russian clergy also heightened as a result of the latter's alleged Pan-Slav sympathies. Actually, the Russian establishment's anti-Greek nationalism was not as clear as it looked from outside. In reality, IPPO members were also divided into two groups as Philhellenes and Hellenophobes, and one prevailed over the other at different times. While Mansurov and Filippov represented the former camp, Khitrovo was from the second group.[19] When IPPO was created in 1882, the Greek-Slavic confrontation was mounting in the Balkan Peninsula. Therefore, IPPO was established to counter not only Catholic and Western European but also Greek cultural influence in the Near East by offering an alternative educational program for Orthodox Christians.[20]

Despite all odds, IPPO became a platform that brought Russians and local Christians together as they hoped, most notably with Orthodox Arabs, who wanted to free themselves from Greek influence. In the 1890s, relations between Greeks and Russians in Jerusalem deteriorated so much that

Russians instead intensified their activities in Syria, where the Patriarchate of Antioch offered cooperation to Russians. IPPO proved to be quite effective, considering that by 1914 it supported more than a hundred schools in Syria and Palestine. With the outbreak of the First World War, the Ottoman Empire closed down these schools and they were never reopened. But, with its support for Orthodox Arab population, IPPO (and Russians) made a lasting support to Arab nationalism, particularly by helping diminish the power of Greek clergy in the region.[21] A 1914 article from the journal *Bogoslovskii Vestnik* written by an anonymous writer (or writers) claimed that the 'White Tsar' of Russia was the protector of Orthodox Christians in the Holy Land, who were persecuted by Turks, neglected by Greeks and culturally threatened by Catholic and Protestant propaganda. Thanks to IPPO's educational activities, the article proclaimed, local Orthodox population could counter such existential threats.[22]

Despite the extensive work undertaken by IPPO, there were limits of Russian influence in the Near East. Russian Empire was only one of the many foreign governments operating in this region. In addition to Russian schools, there were many Italian, French and American schools in Palestine and Syria. The French clergy, who were dissatisfied with the anti-clerical policies at home, especially took the lead in terms of the numbers of missionary schools in Near East. Similar to IPPO, the French clergy also combined their educational and religious activities with archaeological studies.[23] European nations also strengthened their positions by establishing scientific or humanitarian societies. Yet, there were some tangible results of Russian presence. As in the Balkans, Russian cultural activities in Palestine and Syria did not bring about Russian dominance in the region, but they led to the strengthening of local national feeling. In the Balkans, Russians helped Serbian and Bulgarian national awakening, and in the Near East they helped Orthodox Arabs develop national consciousness. Even after Russian schools and cultural institutions were closed down, this strengthened sense of national identity remained as a potent force.[24]

On the other hand, we should not assume that Russian imperial diplomats were in total agreement about the ways and methods for extending Russian influence abroad. Despite the eagerness of some diplomats for greater Russian involvement in the Near East, there was a clash within Russian foreign service between these messianic views and that of moderate diplomats who did not want to disturb the recently concluded Franco-Russian alliance and overall European balance of power.[25] Therefore, the limits of Russian influence in the Near East were also determined by a wider power game in Europe.

After the establishment of RAIK in 1894, IPPO ceased its archaeological activities and offered an annual material support to RAIK instead.[26] After this date, IPPO's scholarly activities were concentrated in the publication of primary sources in the *Palestinskii Sbornik*.[27] IPPO and RAIK were different from each other: while RAIK was a specifically archaeological institute, IPPO also undertook theological studies in addition to its archaeological work, and the scope of its interest was much wider. Still, the history of IPPO is relevant to understand the conditions in which RAIK was created. The two institutions also had key resemblances, which make the comparison between them sensible. First of all, different from individual archaeologists and adventurers, both IPPO and RAIK conducted systematic studies through their institutional basis. Second, the same bureaucrats were active in the creation of both institutions and both of them were officially linked to important foreign policymakers. Third, these two overseas institutions shared similar political goals, with RAIK having a more strongly emphasized scientific outlook. Last, and most importantly, both institutions operated on Ottoman territories, in politically unstable regions that were setting to intercommunal conflicts and great power rivalry at the turn of the century.

3.2 The establishment of the Russian Archaeological Institute in Constantinople

The idea of creating a specifically archaeological-historical society in the Ottoman Empire first appeared in the early 1870s, during the diplomatic service of Count Nikolai Pavlovich Ignatiev, who supported active Russian involvement in Balkan affairs.[28] However, it was only in the late 1880s that Russian diplomats finalized their plans for the establishment of an archaeological institute and came into contact with Russian scholars to discuss possible proposals for the structure and academic orientation of the planned institute.

As for the location of the archaeological institute, Istanbul was not the only option on the table. There were also proposals to establish an institute in Athens, which could in fact be easier to implement than an institute in Istanbul. The first project for an Athens-based Russian institute came up in 1879.[29] In the 1880s, Russian universities sent students to Athens, but not having a scientific base of their own, they worked in association with German and the French institutes. After the establishment of RAIK in 1894, the discussions for an institute in Athens continued. In 1900, the Athens institute was nearly established upon the initiative of the Russian minister to Athens, M. K. Onu. Onu's project was approved by the Ministry of Public Education and Ministry of Foreign Affairs, and the government even allocated a certain amount of money for the project. The Greek King George I (r. 1863–1913) promised to give Russian scholars a plot of land as gift for the projected institute. But after Onu's death in 1901, the money inflow decreased. In addition, RAIK's director Fyodor Uspenskii was unwilling to open a branch of RAIK in Athens. Due to a number of bureaucratic and financial obstacles, the project for an Athens institute failed. Another briefly discussed possibility in 1890–1 was the establishment of a Byzantine studies branch within IPPO, but this project was also shelved.[30]

The year 1895, when RAIK started to operate in the Ottoman Empire, was a particularly interesting turning point for Ottoman relations with European powers. The large-scale Armenian massacres of 1895–6 led European diplomats to exert pressure on Abdülhamid II to stop the violence.[31] British prime minister Lord Salisbury considered several options to pressure the Sultan, including the occupation of Hejaz and forcing Abdülhamid II to abdicate. Austrian foreign minister Golucowski suggested a joint European occupation of the Straits. Russia opposed this plan, seeing the possibility of international control over the Straits as a threat to its own dreams of occupying the Bosphorus. Provoked by the possibility of British action, Russian ambassador in Istanbul, Aleksandr Ivanovich Nelidov (1838–1910) suggested Russian occupation of the Bosphorus, which Britain and France opposed. France was uncomfortable about the possibility of either Russian or British ascendance in the Bosphorus. In short, the period immediately after 1895 witnessed heightened international competition over the fate of the Straits, and Russia was an active participant in this struggle.

Macedonia was also stage to heightened political tension at the time RAIK was established. The political conflict in Macedonia was partly linked to a religious one that went back to the schism in the Orthodox Church that started in the 1870s.[32] In 1870, Sultan Abdülaziz issued a firman authorizing the partial autonomy of the Bulgarian Exarchate from the Orthodox Patriarchate of Constantinople. According to this firman, the Bulgarian Exarchate would have ecclesiastical authority in Danubian Bulgaria, and would have the right to extend its authority to districts where at least two-thirds of the Orthodox Christian population agreed to join it. The latter clause led to a 'scramble for dioceses'[33] in Macedonia between the Greek and Bulgarian churches in the coming decades, as rival ethnic claims manifested themselves in religious terms.

The Russian government found itself in a delicate situation in a conflict between its religious brethren – Greeks and Bulgarians. The Greco-Bulgarian conflict sparked the tension between Pan-Orthodoxy and Pan-Slavism in Russia, although these two ideologies also shared a common ground for political action and the boundary between them was not always clear. While some voices from Russian bureaucratic, ecclesiastical and intellectual circles sympathized with the Bulgarians and regarded the Greeks as tools of Western Europe, others embraced a Pan-Orthodox vision according to which Russia should lead all Orthodox believers regardless of their ethnicity.[34] At least in the Exarchate crisis, the Pan-Slavists had the upper hand. Despite mixed messages of the Holy Synod and the Russian government who tried to keep a careful distance with both Greeks and Bulgarians, the eventual Russian support went to Bulgarians. This crisis was an example of the fact that Slavdom and Orthodoxy, the two pillars of Russian imperial identity, did not always overlap, but sometimes diverged and even came into conflict with each other.

The Macedonian Question arose as a hot issue in European diplomacy especially after the San Stefano Treaty of 1878, which was signed at the end of the Russo-Ottoman War of 1877–8. The Great Bulgaria created with San Stefano included most of Ottoman Macedonia and stretched from the Black Sea to the Adriatic. San Stefano was regarded as a concession to Russia by other European powers, and consequently was revised with the Treaty of Berlin in 1878 to restore European balance of power.[35] The Treaty of Berlin reassigned the Ottoman Empire most of the Macedonian territories it lost during the war and approved the establishment of a much smaller autonomous Bulgaria. Russian support for Bulgaria at the expense of Serbian interests in Macedonia estranged Serbian government from their Slavic 'big brother' in the North, and eventually led to a Serbian-Austrian compromise.[36]

Nevertheless, Russo-Bulgarian relations were also not free of tension after the liberation of the latter. In 1885, autonomous Bulgaria under Prince Alexander I annexed Eastern Rumelia despite the protests of European powers. Among other European powers, Russia also opposed the unification, partly because any Bulgarian move could leave Russia in a difficult situation by destroying the status quo among the European powers in the Balkans.[37] Another reason was Russia's uneasy relations with Bulgaria's prince, Alexander I, and political elites, who resented Russian interference in Bulgarian politics. Russia called an ambassadorial conference for the restoration of the status quo, which averted an all-European diplomatic crisis for the time being, but after the 1885 unification, Bulgarian-Russian relations were seriously strained.

The Bulgarian unification movement troubled Serbian King Milan, as he feared that the unified Bulgaria would be disproportionately advantaged in the struggle over Macedonia, and he was prompted to declare war on Bulgaria. The Serbian-Bulgarian War of 1885 ended in Bulgarian victory, and the great powers had to accept Bulgarian union with Eastern Rumelia. However, in 1886, Prince Alexander of Bulgaria was ousted from power after a coup supported by Russia. Alexander's rule was followed by Ferdinand I. Ferdinand's first years on the throne were shaped by the policies of the Prime Minister Stefan Stamboulov, who was an opponent of Russian interference in Bulgarian politics.[38] In fact, Stamboulov's policies echoed the overall resentment among leading Bulgarian nationalists against political plots engineered by Russia. Despite Stamboulov's scepticism against Russia, the newly crowned Prince Ferdinand looked for Russian approval to secure his position. In the early 1890s, the difference between Ferdinand and Stamboulov widened, and in 1894, the Prince accepted Stamboulov's resignation. The period after 1894 was marked by another Russo-Bulgarian rapprochement.

In a nutshell, the timing of RAIK was critical for a number of reasons. It was a period of intense rivalry between European powers over the fate of the Turkish Straits and a period of violent inter-communal conflict between Greeks, Bulgarians and Serbs in Macedonia. In the midst of these international political crises, Russian foreign policy rested on avoiding direct confrontation with other European powers while protecting Russian interests in the Near East and the Balkans. However, despite its cautious attitude, Russian foreign office also attached great importance to forging ties with Orthodox and Slavic nations of the Balkans.

Transnational ethnic solidarity may be fictive and imagined, but the fact that many European politicians, diplomats and intellectuals clung to it in late 19th century is crucial for understanding international politics before 1914.[39] Therefore, any analysis of Russia's Balkan policy at the turn of the century should take into account Pan-Slav and Pan-Orthodox sympathies in addition to more tangible factors, such as economic and geostrategic interests. In other words, Russian foreign policy in the period between 1894 and 1914 was driven by a mixture of *realpolitik* and identity politics. As Lora Gerd argued, from 1880s to the first years of the 20th century, Russian government refrained from alienating other European powers, especially Austria and prioritized the protection of the status quo in the Balkans.[40] This cautious policy restricted its political and military options on the ground. Limited practical action was compensated with cultural involvement underlined by a nationalist ideology. The predominant ideology towards the Balkans and the Near East mixed Byzantine legacy with Slavic nationalism and postulated Russia as the protector of all Orthodox and Slavic peoples. The establishment of RAIK took place within this political context.

The idea to create a scientific community dedicated to the study of the ancient world was born among Russian diplomats against the above-mentioned political background. In 1884, a delegation of Byzantinist scholars, participants of the sixth Archaeological Congress in Odessa, visited Istanbul to inspect Byzantine monuments in the city. Among those visitors were Fyodor Ivanovich Uspenskii, Nikodim Pavlovich Kondakov (1844–1925) and Aleksandr Ivanovich Kirpichnikov (1845–1903). The communication with these scholars convinced Russian diplomats that a scientific society in the Ottoman capital would be useful.[41]

The first project for the establishment of a scholarly institution in the Ottoman capital was outlined in 1887 by the secretary of the Russian Embassy in Istanbul, Pavel Borisovich Mansurov, who was also instrumental in the creation of the Palestine Committee in 1859.[42] The ideas postulated in this proposal echoed the arguments Mansurov made nearly thirty years ago when he explained the necessity of a Russian institution in Palestine. In his proposal, Mansurov pointed to the importance of the Balkan Peninsula for Russian foreign policy and argued that current political affairs inevitably led Russia to a power struggle with the great powers of Europe in the Balkans.[43]

Mansurov stated that it was not only great powers that created obstacles for stronger Russian influence in the region. Referring to the recent history of Greece, Romania, Serbia and most lately Bulgaria, Mansurov observed that there were voices against Russia also within these nations. Therefore, Russia was in a delicate position in the Balkans. He noted, 'Whoever will be our opponent in future, [whoever is] hostile towards us, will find a powerful instrument in the millions of inhabitants of the Balkan Peninsula for their endeavours.'[44] He warned that in the absence of effective Russian cultural involvement, especially the educated segments of Balkan societies could gravitate towards Western culture, and this Western orientation often went hand in hand with mistrust towards Russia. Among lower classes of the Balkan societies, Mansurov observed that there was still sympathy towards Russia. He argued that this sympathy should be strengthened, considering that Russia had a historical mission as the protector of Balkan Christians. Among other reasons, the establishment of a Russian scientific community in the Ottoman Empire was a necessity to counter the expansion of Western European cultural and political influence in a region where the primary role should belong to Russia.

Mansurov had a reason to be concerned about the political allegiances of the Balkan Slavs. Although Balkan intellectuals maintained close relations with Russian intellectual circles, on the whole, they looked up to Paris, London, Berlin and Vienna as much as St Petersburg for intellectual stimulation.[45] Even among Russian intellectuals they mostly followed the radical critics of the Russian government, which paradoxically meant that Russian cultural infiltration in the Balkans had mixed results for Russian foreign policy. The European orientation of Balkan intellectuals would have significant geopolitical implications at the turn of the century.

Among other fields of arts and sciences, Balkan scholars were exposed to European influence in archaeological scholarship, too. As a matter of fact, Russian archaeologists were not free of competition in the area of Balkan archaeology. Although Byzantine and Slavic history received considerably less attention than classical Greco-Roman history in European academia, there were still respectable studies by European scholars in these fields. One scholar, Josef Strzygowski, a professor at the University of Vienna, is worthy of mention at this point – both for his groundbreaking theories and for the political implications of his studies. Born in the Polish borderlands of the Habsburg Empire to a German-speaking family, Strzygowski's political sympathies lay in pan-Germanism, while his academic work was characterized by an anti-classicist approach.[46] Strzygowski particularly made pioneering contributions to the study of Byzantine, Islamic, Armenian and Balkan art and architecture. Overall, he rejected the Eurocentric (or rather Mediterranean-centric) approach of most classicists and downplayed the cultural continuity between classical Greco-Roman civilization and medieval Europe. Instead, Strzygowski emphasized the influence of Near Eastern and North European cultures on late antiquity culture in Europe. This perspective was not very different from the paradigm supported by many Russian Byzantinists, who emphasized the Slavic influence on Roman – or Byzantine – culture.

In a sense, Strzygowski's studies liberated individual national cultures on the periphery of the Habsburg Empire by suggesting a course of cultural and artistic development independent from the imperial Roman – later Holy Roman and Habsburg – influence. Not surprisingly, this approach was welcomed by nationalists on the Habsburg periphery. As a result of his good relations with the Serbian King Peter I, in 1909, Strzygowski was appointed to a jury to decide the design of the mausoleum of Karadjordjevic kings.[47] He was also invited by the Serbian Academy of Sciences for scientific collaboration. Strzygowski's reputation in Serbian academia and his popularity with the Serbian king meant that Russian archaeologists and diplomats had a reason to be concerned about competition with European scholars in the Balkans. Not only in terms of intellectual stimulation but also in terms of scholarship many Balkan intellectuals turned their faces towards Europe as much as towards Russia.

Therefore, the concerns of Russian diplomats about the possibility of losing the spiritual and intellectual leadership in the Balkans was not far from reality. In his proposal about the establishment of a scholarly institute, Mansurov argued that Russia's role in the Balkans should be strengthened not only through military and political means, but more importantly, through science, and particularly through a scientific study of the history of the Orient. He claimed that even though Orthodoxy was definitely the most important spiritual force linking Russia to the Balkan Peninsula, in the late 19th century, 'it [is] dangerous to neglect science, the impact of which unconsciously sprawls to very distant spheres.'[48] Mansurov's project was vaguely defined, and projected the study of Turco-Islamic as well as Byzantino-Christian history. When Mansurov's project was realized ten years later with the establishment of RAIK, the aim of the Institute was more clearly and narrowly defined.

What stood out in Mansurov's proposal was the emphasis he put on the importance of cultural influence, and Russia's weakness in this respect. While other European empires reinforced their military and political capabilities with cultural institutions, Russia, as it appeared in the above proposal, was lagging behind its political rivals in the cultural realm. Mansurov feared that Russia's inadequacy risked leaving the arena to other European powers. At the juncture of science and politics, above all other possible scientific activities, archaeology was seen as a legitimate tool for extending cultural, and eventually political influence. Study of antiquities linked the past with the present, gave a solid basis to contemporary political projects and provided a scientific explanation for Russia's claim to be the protector of Orthodoxy and Slavdom.

Among other prominent statesmen, the Russian ambassador in Istanbul, Aleksandr Ivanovich Nelidov especially promoted the project of creating an archaeological institute in Istanbul.[49] Politically, Nelidov was in favour of expansionist policies towards the Ottoman Empire, which in the end compelled the Foreign Service to send him away from Istanbul. M. S. Anderson defined Nelidov as 'the ambitious and rather unrealistic Russian ambassador', who suggested the seizure of the Bosphorus in 1882, 1892 and 1895, a suggestion that failed in view of strong French and British opposition. Nelidov's ambitious plan was not approved by more pragmatic statesmen in the Russian government, who did not want to alienate European powers.[50] Eventually, Nelidov's passionate support for the Russian seizure of the Bosphorus risked breaking the fragile balance of power between the European empires, which accounted for his appointment to Rome in 1897.[51]

Nelidov developed the initial proposal put forward by Mansurov. In November 1887, Nelidov sent letters to Uspenskii, Kirpichnikov and Kondakov, all Byzantinist professors at the Imperial Novorossiya University, explaining Mansurov's project and asking the scholars to share their opinions on this issue.[52] Nelidov's letters echoed Mansurov's basic premises. The ambassador explained that an idea had arisen in the Russian Embassy in Istanbul about the establishment of a scientific institution in the Ottoman capital that would study ethnographical, archaeological, theological and artistic materials of the Christian East from a scientific perspective. Nelidov argued that such an institute would definitely have political uses. It would prepare suitable ground for Russian influence and help develop self-consciousness among the Orthodox population (*edinovertsy*). Serious and independent study of the history of Orthodox peoples, according to Nelidov, would facilitate their cooperation with Russia, and consequently would strengthen Russia's influence in the Balkans and the Near East. In the same year, Uspenskii, along with Kondakov and Kirpichnikov, started the preparations for the creation of an archaeological community in Istanbul.

Uspenskii, Kondakov and Kirpichnikov were not the only scholars who submitted a proposal to the Russian Embassy. Russian diplomats were also attracted to another proposal submitted by the Eastern Commission of the Imperial Moscow Archaeological Society. The proposal of the Imperial Moscow Archaeological Society abounded with messages that called for Russia's special mission in the Balkans.[53] The scholars from the Moscow Archaeological Society emphasized that there were intangible ties connecting Russia to Ottoman Christians, who viewed Russia as their protector. The history of the Balkan Slavs could be considered part of their own national history for Russians. Similarly, Moscow's status as the third Rome gave Russian scholars the responsibility to learn the history of Orthodox Christianity, which was the basis of Russian culture. The Moscow Society considered Russia so closely connected to Byzantine history that they claimed, 'Monuments from the glorious past of the Byzantine Empire, in many ways, speak about us more eloquently than our own monuments.'[54] Therefore, the establishment of a scholarly institution to study Byzantine antiquities, not in Russia but in the very heart of the Byzantine Empire, would 'strongly influence the spiritual and political life of Eastern Christians'.[55] The proposal acknowledged that European scholarship was ahead of Russia in terms of knowledge of the Orient, which gave European nations greater leverage to have a cultural impact on Eastern peoples. The proposal of the Moscow Archaeological Society called for the establishment of an institute for the study of Slavic, Hellenistic-Byzantine and Islamic antiquities. This proposal was considered impractical because of the range of expertise and the institutional complexity it required. However, the Moscow Archaeological Society and its chairman Countess Praskovya Sergeevna Uvarova (1840–1924) actively supported the creation of RAIK in later years, and her effort was praised by Nelidov.[56]

Uspenskii, Kondakov and Kirpichnikov's proposal was oriented specifically towards Byzantine studies. Uspenskii's expertise in medieval Balkan, Slavic and Byzantine history shaped the academic framework of the projected institute in Istanbul. In their proposal, the Odessa professors emphasized

Russia's educational mission among the Orthodox and Slavic population of the Ottoman Empire (*'edinoplemennye i edinovernye naselenii'*).[57] In fact, before the RAIK project appeared as a possibility, Uspenskii was in constant communication with the governor general of Novorossiya, K. K. Roop, for the establishment of a Byzantine Society in Odessa, within the Imperial Novorossiya University. Roop even contacted Count Delianov, the Minister of Public Education, to request support for the Byzantine Society. However, when RAIK appeared as a serious option, Delianov responded that it would be impossible to get approval from the Ministry of Finance for two institutes with similar missions.[58] In the end, the proposed Byzantine Society in Odessa was shelved on behalf of RAIK.

In a letter he wrote to the governor general of Novorossiya in June 1888, Uspenskii underlined the necessity of Byzantine studies for Russia, and explained the reasons for his desire to create a scientific Byzantine Society and a special journal dedicated to Byzantine studies.[59] Uspenskii pointed out that the influence of the Byzantine Empire on the formation of the Russian state and church structure was indisputable. In addition, he argued that not only history but also contemporary political and moral obligations tied Russia to the Christian East. Uspenskii stated that Russian national interests, and therefore the fate of Russian historical scholarship, lay in the study of the Byzantine Empire and Orthodox Christianity. Uspenskii argued that religious principles strongly promoted Russian influence among Ottoman Christians. This role ascribed an important responsibility to Russia to learn the history of the Byzantine Empire and Orthodoxy, because without knowing their past it was impossible to restore ties with Russia's Slavic and Orthodox brethren in the Ottoman Empire.

According to the project laid down by Kondakov, Uspenskii and Kirpichnikov, the mission of the institute was described as follows:[60]

1. Organization and direction of Russian scholars in the region, who would conduct research about the ancient history of Greece, the Byzantine Empire, and the Near East. These scholars would be responsible to the director of the institute and would submit reports of their studies. The plan also included accommodating interns who studied at the theological seminaries in Russia.
2. Study of monuments, geography, topography, laws, mode of life (*byt'*), epigraphy and art in the region that corresponded to the former realm of the Byzantine Empire.
3. Organization of scientific expeditions and excavations upon the agreement of the Russian ambassador with Turkish and Greek authorities.

Uspenskii's support for the archaeological institute implied that he anticipated a 'war of cultures' between the great powers of Europe in the Near East. Therefore, he considered other European powers as rivals of the Russian Empire in this cultural competition. In his memoirs, Uspenskii argued that future wars over the Near East would be fought through creating spheres of cultural influence.[61] He stated that in Western Europe, university chairs dedicated to the study of Byzantine history had been established long ago and they were ahead of Russia in terms of academic study of Byzantine history. This situation necessitated more effort on the part of Russia to catch up with the rest of Europe. Uspenskii argued that Greek and South Slav academia could not afford to study Byzantine question extensively as a result of their meagre means; therefore the responsibility to explore Byzantine history fell on Russia's shoulders. For all these reasons, Uspenskii underlined the need for a specialized scientific society dedicated to the study of Byzantine art and history. He emphasized that this task should be assumed by Russian scholars not only because Russia had strong historical and geographical links to the Byzantine Empire but also because, through their knowledge of Slavic history, Russian scholars could complete the missing links in the history of Eastern Rome, links that could not be sufficiently understood by Western European scholars.

Uspenskii later pointed out that despite the diplomatic and governmental support he received, some academics and bureaucrats had doubts about the projected Byzantine Institute. He referred to his correspondence with the important Byzantinist scholar V. G. Vasilevskii, who was sceptical about the creation of a specialized Byzantine Institute, at a time when there were already a number of archaeological institutions and societies in Russia.[62] The Ober-Procurator of the Holy Synod, Konstantin Petrovich Pobedonostsev (1827–1907), was another influential figure who expressed negative opinions on the matter. Pobedonostsev had doubts about Russian scientific capacity, arguing that Russia did not have enough academic strength to afford an overseas institute, neither was Istanbul an appropriate location for such a project.[63] Pobedonostsev argued that Istanbul did not have libraries or universities to facilitate scholarly activities, and Russian scholars would be academically isolated in this city.

In November 1888, Ambassador Nelidov sent a letter to the Minister of Public Education, Count Ivan Davydovich Delianov (1818–1898), in which he advocated the establishment of a scientific institution in the Ottoman capital.[64] Nelidov argued that Byzantine history was a very important, if not the most important, source of Russian national consciousness (*grazhdanstvennost'*); therefore, it was necessary for Russian scholars to familiarize themselves with the Byzantine civilization and deepen their knowledge of Byzantine history and culture. A scholarly institute in Istanbul would channel individual scholarly activities through an institutional structure. In recent years, increasing numbers of Russian scholars were visiting the Ottoman Empire for research. However, without coordination, these individual scientific enterprises did not produce fruitful results, particularly due to the lack of scientific facilities, libraries and scholarly societies in Istanbul. This insufficiency caused loss of time and money for researchers. A scholarly institution in Istanbul to coordinate Russian scholarly activities in the region would make a significant contribution to Russian historical scholarship.

Nelidov added that the establishment of a 'Russian scholarly institution in Istanbul would be a bridge between us and significant parts of the local community and would strengthen the feeling of respect and trust of the local community towards Russia.'[65] One common theme in Nelidov's, Mansurov's and Uspenskii's letters was the emphasis on the role of science and scholarship as a way to gain respect among the Orthodox Christian Ottoman population. Comparing their international standing with other European empires, Russian diplomats recognized the importance of 'soft power', as well as military power, and science was seen as a powerful instrument of the former. However, with its autocratic political system and the state's conflict with much of the intelligentsia, it was difficult for Russia to represent a positive example for the Balkan nations. As it will be seen in more detail in Chapter 4, the attempts of Russian diplomats to create a basis for solidarity through an archaeological study of Orthodox and Slavic civilizations did not produce the expected outcomes.

In addition to the Ministry of Public Education, Nelidov also forwarded the project prepared by Kondakov, Kirpichnikov and Uspenskii to the Holy Synod in December 1888 and to the Ministry of Foreign Affairs in February 1889.[66] Despite Pobedonostsev's earlier reservations, it seems that he was persuaded about the usefulness of the project, probably because his advisor in Eastern affairs, Ivan E. Troitskii, was a supporter of the project.[67] Both the Holy Synod and the Ministry of Foreign Affairs expressed their sympathy for the proposed institution. In the same year, a commission, made up of professors from the Imperial St Petersburg University upon the recommendation of the Ministry of Education, was organized to discuss the details regarding the institute. The commission concluded that an annual allotment of 12,000 roubles was necessary to maintain the institute. However, despite their approval of the project, it took a few years to convince the Ministry of Finance about the allocation of resources for an overseas institute. In a letter from 4 July 1889, Uspenskii wrote to Nelidov that the Ministry of Finance refused to allocate the 12,000 roubles that was requested for the project, and asked the Embassy to make a renewed application on behalf of RAIK.[68]

RAIK was designed as a centre for the historical and archaeological study of the Christian East, in particular for the study of Byzantine monuments. The project was also seen as a way of strengthening Russia's influence over Christian peoples of the Ottoman Empire. This political message was explicitly stated nearly in every memorandum and official letter that was penned in the process of RAIK's establishment. A very clear correlation between successful scientific achievements and political influence permeated the discourse of Russian diplomats, bureaucrats and scholars that supported the project. The idea particularly received support from the Holy Synod and the Ministry of Foreign Affairs, but the 12,000 roubles requested for its realization created perplexity on the part of the Ministry of Finance.[69]

From 1889 up to the official approval of the Institute by Emperor Alexander III in 1894, there was a constant exchange of letters between Uspenskii, the Embassy in Istanbul, the Ministry of Public Education and the Ministry of Finance – the first three trying to convince the latter. In December 1890, Delianov wrote to Nelidov that he personally communicated with the Minister of Finance, Ivan Alekseevich Vyshnegradskii (1832–1895), about the annual allocation of 12,000 roubles from the State Treasury starting from 1891. Minister Vyshnegradskii responded that although he sympathized with the establishment of a scholarly institute in Istanbul, considering the current high government spending and budget deficit, it would not be possible to allocate the requested amount from the State Treasury in the coming year.[70] Vyshnegradskii repeated his cautious support in his letter to ambassador Nelidov in January 1891: he noted that he found a scholarly institute in Istanbul useful, especially because this institute would be the centre of scholarly research in the East, as well serving as a political centre. Nevertheless, he explained the difficulty of securing sufficient funds for such a project considering financial difficulties. Rather than totally rejecting the proposal, Vyshnegradskii offered a middle way: he suggested that in the coming year, the project proposed by professors Kondakov, Kirpichnikov and Uspenskii could be discussed in detail and the Ministry of Public Education could bring the subject to the State Council next year.[71] Apparently, the early 1890s was not an appropriate time to be asking for financial support for a costy archaeological institute, given that the famine on the Volga basin seriously restrained financial capabilities of the Russian Empire.[72]

Between 1891 and 1894, the draft charter of the project was reviewed by a number of government bodies. Count Delianov submitted the draft to the director of the Imperial Public Library and Imperial Moscow Archaeological

Society for suggestions. In March 1892, Delianov introduced the project to the State Council, and once again the project was turned down due to financial constraints. The State Council decided to postpone the project until favourable economic conditions, and suggested sending the draft charter to the Imperial Academy of Sciences in the meantime for examination.[73] In 1892, the Imperial Academy of Sciences established a commission to examine the project, which eventually expressed support for the creation of a scholarly institute in Istanbul.

Finally, in 1893, the Ministry of Public Education managed to get verbal approval from the Ministry of Finance and secured the necessary funds for the institute. It seems that the political views of Tertii Ivanovich Filippov, the director of the State Comptroller's Office and vice president of IPPO, played a role in this approval. Filippov regarded RAIK as a political instrument that would provide a scientific basis for Russian claims to assume leadership in the Orthodox world.[74] As one of the most influential conservative bureaucrats of the late imperial age, Filippov was known for his pro-Hellenic and pan-Orthodox views during the Bulgarian schism. After learning about the institute project, Filippov wrote to Nelidov:

> Union with the Byzantine Empire determined our highest mission in the world. With this union, we are a people chosen by God, entrusted with the protection of the true church … Having such a perspective on the importance of Byzantium for us and professing it publicly for decades, can I ever be indifferent to the project you proposed?[75]

In the coming decades, Filippov's support for RAIK proved invaluable, because in addition to securing financial support for the institute, Filippov also put his contacts within the Orthodox Patriarchate of Constantinople at the disposal of Russian archaeologists, thus opening the gates of the libraries and archives of Mount Athos to Russian scholars.[76] As the vice president of IPPO and a member of the St Petersburg branch of the Slavic Committee, Filippov had a wide network of friends in academia and in the Orthodox Church, as well as in bureaucracy.[77] Incidentally, the first secretary of RAIK, P. D. Pogodin was Tertii Filippov's nephew.[78]

On 25 October 1893, the Ministry of Public Education again presented its proposal about the institute to the State Council. In this report, Minister Delianov stated the importance of Byzantine civilization for the development of Russian culture and its consequent significance for Russian historical scholarship. This historical links with the Byzantine Empire made a scholarly institution in Istanbul desirable. Delianov stated that he agreed with the Ministry of Foreign Affairs that a scholarly institution in the Ottoman Empire would strengthen Russia's ties with the local population and contribute to Russia's influence over Orthodox Christians, especially in the Balkans.[79] Delianov also outlined the agreement he reached with the new Minister of Finance, Sergei Witte (1849–1915) on the financial question. The two ministers agreed for the allocation of 6,000 roubles from the 1894 budget, and 12,000 roubles starting from 1895. Therefore, the institute would start to function not in January, but in July 1894. Furthermore, Delianov added that the institute should have an imperial status and should be directly attached to the court.[80] This last proposal meant that Delianov wanted RAIK to come under the Ministry of the Imperial Court, which could be secured only with the approval of Alexander III.

On 4 December 1893, the State Council discussed Delianov's proposal and consulted ministries and government bodies to hear their opinions on the issue. On behalf of the Ministry of the Imperial Court, Count Aleksey Aleksandrovich Bobrinskii (1852–1927), a member of the Imperial Archaeological Commission, expressed negative opinions about the creation of an archaeological institute in Istanbul. First of all, he drew attention to the fact that the project bypassed the Imperial Archaeological Commission, which was the foremost archaeological institution in Russia at the time. Bobrinskii gave the example of the Russian archaeological commission in Rome, which ended up being a short-lived experience. Considering the amount of financial resources the institute in Istanbul required, Bobrinskii argued that if the government had necessary funds, they better should allocate it to the Imperial Archaeological Commission for its work on Byzantine antiquities. Instead of a separate institute in Istanbul, Bobrinskii proposed the strengthening of a Byzantinist Institute in southern Russia.[81] Bobrinskii's ideas reflected his correspondence with the Minister of the Imperial Court, Illarion Ivanovich Vorontsov-Dashkov (1837–1916), who also argued that the planned institute in Istanbul would be unproductive and costly.

Vorontsov-Dashkov argued that it was unlikely that RAIK would achieve fruitful results in Istanbul, especially if it would be established in the proposed form.[82] He argued that the aims and duties of the institute, as well as the responsibilities of its director and secretaries were so extensively defined that they would be impossible to realize. Vorontsov-Dashkov instead suggested the organization of the institute into several specialized departments that would more effectively direct scholars in different fields. He warned that without a sufficient number of experts and material resources, the institution would fall short of becoming a 'bridge between us [Russia] and a significant part of the local population', and could not rightfully carry the flag of Russian science abroad. All in all, instead of establishing a separate institute in

Istanbul, Vorontsov-Dashkov suggested the allocation of the government funds to the Imperial Academy of Sciences or one of the existing societies – like the Odessa Society of History and Antiquities.

In a report submitted to the State Council in February 1894, the Ministry of Public Education responded to criticisms and elucidated the reasons for their insistent support for an institution in Istanbul. Overall, the concerns boiled down to three major themes. From a practical point of view, the variety and extent of the institute's duties were difficult to fulfil considering the insufficiency of its staff and annual budget. From a political perspective, if the mentioned institute proved a failure because of lack of support on the part of the Russian government, it would bring loss of prestige, an undesirable outcome. There were also concerns about whether Istanbul was a proper location – critics pointed to lack of scientific institutions, little local sympathy for scholars and particularly negative attitudes towards Russians in the Ottoman capital.[83] Consequently, there were suggestions to opt for an institute in Athens, where there were already scientific institutions and archaeological societies, and where the Queen was a Russian Grand Duchess. Besides, Russians would be more welcome in the Greek capital.[84] Another option was opening a Byzantine studies branch under one of the existing societies in Russia and allocating the funds in this direction instead of a separate institution.

In response to such criticisms, ambassador Nelidov explained that the idea to create a scholarly institution in Istanbul was born out of practical necessity: every year, increasing numbers of Russian scholars visited the Ottoman Empire for research, but without coordination and unaware of each other's studies, they sometimes worked on the same subject in vain. Being unfamiliar with local conditions, these scholars asked for support from the Embassy, although the Embassy was not capable of providing scientific guidance. This situation required an institution that would serve as a hub for Russian scholars. The task of the institute would be the coordination and guidance of Russian scholars visiting the East, rather than large-scale archaeological research, meaning that the institute could survive on the allocated amount of funds. In short, there were already Russian scholars interested in Byzantine antiquities, but they needed subsidies and on-site guidance. With regard to questions about the suitability of Istanbul, Nelidov argued that if the interests of Russian scientists lay in classical antiquities, then the establishment of an institute in Athens could be discussed as an option. However, considering that Russian scholars were more interested in Byzantine history, Istanbul would be an appropriate choice. He further argued that the institute might find more local support than it was assumed in the Ottoman Empire.[85]

Finally, on 24 February 1894, the State Council formally approved the establishment of RAIK with a unanimous decision.[86] The final resolution of the Council concluded that a separate scientific institution in Istanbul would be preferable. Administratively, the institute would be under the Ministry of Public Education and the Russian Embassy in Istanbul at the same time. To enhance its scientific activities, it should be in constant communication with universities, academies and other institutions in Russia. Finding Nelidov's arguments satisfactory, the State Council deemed that the approval of the Imperial Academy of Sciences was convincing enough to support the project. The resolution explained that there was no need to be concerned about finances: the Russian government would not cease to support RAIK in future years. According to the agreement reached between Delianov and Witte, 6,000 roubles would be allocated to the institute starting from July 1894, and 12,000 roubles would be allocated for coming years. However, responding to Delianov's request to give an imperial status to the institute and placing it under the direct patronage of the Emperor, the State Council was reluctant; stating that only after the institute proved itself could this question be considered again.

It seems that Uspenskii wanted to postpone the establishment of the institute until the necessary funds were secured, or at least until a sufficient amount was secured to create a good library. He was also informed by Nelidov that an earthquake in Istanbul in July 1894 made most houses uninhabitable and it was difficult to find accommodation.[87] However, Delianov wanted to accelerate the process, and wanted the institute to be established no later than 1 July 1894.[88]

Final revisions to the RAIK charter were made by the director of the Imperial Public Library, the Imperial Moscow Archaeological Society, the Imperial Academy of Sciences and ambassador Nelidov. It seems that Uspenskii and Nelidov were not in agreement about the authority of the ambassador over the institute. While Uspenskii expected more autonomy from the Embassy, Nelidov seemed to prefer keeping the institute under his command. In a letter written by the Embassy secretary Mansurov to Uspenskii in 1893, Mansurov explained that Nelidov was offended at Uspenskii's draft charter because the changes Nelidov deemed necessary to place the institute more closely within the administrative structure of the Embassy were left out.[89] Nelidov envisaged the institute as a headquarters affiliated with the Embassy that would provide assistance and guidance to Russian scholars visiting the East. When the State Council finally approved the establishment of the institute, Nelidov's role was authorized as he demanded. The State Council emphasized the ambassador's role in appointing the director, as well as honorary members and fellow researchers of the institute.

When the charter of the institute was officially confirmed, the objectives were defined in a way to embrace the history of ancient Greece, Asia Minor and the territories that had been under Byzantine rule. The charter did not openly refer to the history of the Balkan Peninsula and its Slavic inhabitants, so as not to create suspicions on the part of Ottoman authorities as well as European powers that Russia was trying to expand its sphere of influence among South Slavs under the pretext of archaeological activities. Russian scholars were concerned about persuading both Turks and Europeans in Turkey that RAIK was nothing more than a pure scientific enterprise, because there were suspicions that RAIK was in fact a political club posing as a scientific institution.[90] Uspenskii recalled that in the first years when RAIK was established, Russian scholars had to 'dispel the opinion that originally formed among foreigners that Russia had other than scholarly intentions in establishing what would be in fact a political Slavic club under the name of the Institute.'[91] However, Uspenskii noted that in time RAIK acquired a respectable position among similar institutions in the West, thanks to its archaeological discoveries, publications and the quality of its scholarship.

The charter set out the following points:[92]

1. The Russian Archaeological Institute at the Imperial Embassy in Constantinople (its full name – *Russkii Arkheologicheskii Institut pri Imperatorskom Posol'stve v Konstantinopole*) aimed to guide the on-site scientific activities of Russian scholars working on the history of ancient Greece, Asia Minor and the territories that once constituted the Byzantine Empire, with a particular emphasis on the history of Christian antiquities. Consequently, the institute intended to promote the development of Russian archaeology by studying architectural and literary artefacts in the mentioned territories. Universities, academies and institutes in Russia could send their staff to RAIK for on-site research. The director and secretaries of the institute would provide academic guidance to visiting scholars as regards their area of study. Visiting scholars could also conduct research together with the permanent RAIK staff.

2. The scientific duties of the institute included, in line with the first article, the study of monumental art and antiquities, ancient geography and topography, manuscripts, numismatics, epigraphs, languages, and oral literature of the countries and peoples that constituted the Byzantine Empire (contemporary Greek Kingdom and the Ottoman Empire). In this article, the Balkans, particularly Bulgaria was intentionally excluded from the areas of interest to avoid suspicions on the part of the Ottomans. In practice, as will be seen in the next chapter, the

autonomous Principality of Bulgaria was one of the most frequent destinations of the RAIK staff.

3. The institute would undertake archaeological excavations and organize expeditions in line with special agreements concluded between Russian diplomatic posts in Istanbul and Athens and the Turkish and Greek governments.

4. The institute would publish meeting protocols and annual reports about its activities. The report would be submitted to the Ministry of Public Education, and a copy would be sent to the Imperial Academy of Sciences to be published at the discretion of the Academy.

5. The institute was administratively and academically under the direct control of the Ministry of Public Education. At the same time, because it operated outside Russia, it was dependent on the Russian ambassador in Istanbul and was under his immediate protection. The ambassador also acted in the capacity of honorary chairman of the institute.

6. The institute staff included a director, secretary (the number of secretaries depended on the need and increased in time) and members.

7. The director was entrusted with the administrative, academic and economic management of the institute. He was selected among candidates with a doctoral degree from Russian universities, and with a scholarly reputation in the field in which the institute operates.

8. The director was appointed and dismissed by the Minister of Public Education, who made the decision upon consulting the honorary chairman (the ambassador to Istanbul) and the president of the Academy of Sciences.

9. The responsibilities of the director included the following:

   a. Guiding institute members as regards their scientific projects.
   b. Promoting and supporting visiting scholars from Russian universities, academies and institutes, collaborating with them in archaeological projects.
   c. Organizing archaeological excavations and excursions.
   d. Providing guidance to members to familiarize them with ancient monuments in the locality.
   e. Preparing an annual report about the activities of the institute.
   f. Collecting information about discoveries and scholarly activities with regard to regions that fall within the scope of the institute's interest.
   g. Establishing contacts with consular services, institutions and individuals whose assistance would be useful to the institute.

10. The scientific secretary was the immediate assistant to the director in his responsibilities and acted in accordance with his instructions. He was also responsible for the maintenance of the collection and the library, as well as for office duties.

11. The scientific secretary was selected among candidates, who completed a degree relevant to the institute's scholarly interests. He was appointed by the Minister of Public Education upon the proposal of the director.

12. In the absence of the director, the scientific secretary would act on his behalf.

13. Members of the institute were appointed by the Minister of Public Education upon consulting the Honorary Chairman of the institute. The members would be drawn from the following groups:

    a. Members of scholarly societies in Russia.
    b. Officials at the Russian Embassy in Istanbul and Russian diplomatic mission in Athens.
       In addition, members included the following groups of scholars who visited Istanbul:
    c. Recent graduates of the Historical-Philological, Law, and Oriental Studies Faculties, who were commissioned by the Ministry of Public Education upon the recommendation by their home university.
    d. Recent graduates of the Imperial Academy of Arts who were commissioned by the Academy.

14. All persons referred to in the above articles were required, upon arrival at Istanbul, to present the research instructions provided by their home organizations to the director of RAIK. They also had to submit progress reports to the director about their studies.

15. For visiting scholars sent by academic institutions in Russia to RAIK, the period of their stay in Istanbul or other towns was determined in the instructions provided by their home institution.

16. Throughout their stay at RAIK, candidates from theological academies were responsible to the Holy Synod. During their studies at the institute, they were guided by special programmes provided by the academy of which they were members.

17. When the tenure of visiting scholars expired, they should send reports to their home institutions in Russia about the state of their research.

18. Members could make use of the RAIK library and antiquities collection and upon the approval of the director, could take part in scientific activities and publish their works in the institute publications. When

they travelled in the East, they would receive recommendation letters from the Russian ambassadors in Istanbul and in Athens.

19. During their study at RAIK, expenses of the members were not covered by the institute. However, if the members participated in the archaeological expeditions undertaken by RAIK, the director could assign them an appropriate allowance from the expedition budget.

20. In addition to members explained above, RAIK also had honorary members (*pochetnye chleny*) and associate members (*chleny sotrudnikov*), who were proposed by the director and approved by the Minister of Public Education in consultation with the ambassador to the Porte. Honorary members and associate members would be selected among foreigners who were specialists in relevant subjects.

21. The director could summon non-members as well as members to meetings about expeditions, excavations and other scientific matters.

22. RAIK would hold open lectures and seminars. Foreigners could participate when the lectures and seminars were held in foreign languages.

23. RAIK would have a library and an antiquities collection.

24. RAIK would have a seal with the national emblem and with its full name below.

25. The funds allocated for the institute came from (a) the amount allocated from the State Treasury and (b) other sources.

The director and secretaries of the institute would not retain their former positions at Russian universities, but the charter stipulated that they could enjoy the same benefits and privileges as professors at Russian universities. The 12,000-rouble allowance was distributed as follows: 4,000 roubles and 2,000 roubles, respectively, for the salaries of the director and the secretary (or secretaries); 2,500 roubles for the rent, 100 roubles for the maintenance of the library and the museum, 1,000 roubles for scientific excursions and excavations, and 500 roubles for other expenses. On 23 May 1894, Tsar Alexander III approved the charter of RAIK,[93] and on 11 July 1894, the Tsar appointed Uspenskii as RAIK's director, upon Delianov's proposal.[94] The first scientific secretary of RAIK was P. D. Pogodin, suggested by Minister Delianov and approved by Uspenskii.[95]

According to the charter, archaeological expeditions of RAIK were funded by the government, but the charter left the door open for contributions by private donors. In addition, the Ministry of Public Education and the Holy Synod sent scholars from Russian universities and theological academies to undertake research at RAIK and subsidized them. In the charter, the object of RAIK was defined as coordinating and accommodating Russian scholars conducting historical and archaeological research in Greece, Asia Minor and the territories that fell under Byzantine rule. Despite this broad description, RAIK mainly specialized in Byzantine archaeology and the history of the Orthodox Church, to the extent that the activities of the institute may well be described as church archaeology. Although it was not specified in the charter, the second major theme that appeared frequently in the studies of RAIK was the history and archaeology of the South Slavs – either Bulgarian or Serbian – and their relations with the Byzantine Empire.

A clarification as regards the geographical scope of RAIK's activities should be made at this point. Certainly, within the boundaries of the Ottoman Empire, RAIK was supposed to receive excavation and expedition permits from relevant Ottoman governmental institutions. In the independent Serbian Kingdom, Russian archaeologists asked for permission from Serbian authorities. The situation in Bulgaria was a little complicated. After the Russo-Ottoman War of 1877-8, the Principality of Bulgaria became autonomous from the Ottoman Empire. In 1885, the Principality annexed Eastern Rumelia. Although the Principality – including Eastern Rumelia after the annexation – was theoretically under Ottoman suzerainty until 1908, it had its own constitution and even independent foreign policy. Therefore, within the borders of the autonomous Principality of Bulgaria, Russian archaeologists asked for permission from Bulgarian, not Ottoman, authorities. The rest of Macedonia, which remained part of the Ottoman Empire until the Balkan Wars of 1912-13, was under full Ottoman sovereignty. Consequently, archaeological studies in Macedonia were subject to Ottoman approval.

Fyodor Uspenskii happened to be the first and the only director of RAIK. In order to facilitate their communication with Ottoman authorities, both the Ministry of Public Education and the State Council found it practical to place the institute under the protectorate of the Russian Embassy in Istanbul. Administratively, the ambassador was also the chairman of RAIK. In the course of nearly twenty years of its existence, there were five different Russian ambassadors to the Ottoman Empire, the most active supporter of RAIK being Nelidov, who served in the Ottoman capital between 1894 and 1897.

There was definitely a certain degree of religious and nationalist sensitivity behind the establishment of a Russian archaeological institute in the Ottoman Empire. Both Russian diplomats who proposed the project and bureaucrats at the Ministry of Public Education and other government bodies legitimized RAIK through historical references about Russia's – real or imaginary – links with the Byzantine Empire. In this discourse, Russia emerged as the spiritual heir to the Byzantine heritage. A multifaceted and systematic study of Byzantine history was regarded as a step for the development of Russian national consciousness, and a useful tool for furthering contemporary political interests of the Russian Empire. The establishment of RAIK was also an assertion of Russian primacy when it came to claiming the Byzantine inheritance.

After its authorization by the Tsar in 1894, RAIK's office in Istanbul was officially opened with a religious ceremony on 26 February 1985, with the participation and prayers of Archimandrite Boris.[96] Besides, 26 February was also the birthday of the late Tsar Alexander III, who passed away in the autumn of 1894, shortly after approving the establishment of RAIK. The opening ceremony intentionally coincided with his birthday. In the opening ceremony, both ambassador Nelidov and director Uspenskii delivered speeches emphasizing Russia's political role in the Near East and the importance of learning history to develop a solid foreign policy in the region.[97] Nelidov indicated that studying the history of the Byzantine Empire was the chief responsibility of Russian historical scholarship.[98] He argued that the foreign policy of a great nation should be guided by moral and spiritual principles, and Russia could find these principles in the study of the Byzantine Empire.

After Nelidov, Uspenskii took on the stage to explain the cultural and political significance of the establishment of RAIK. In his talk, the director stated that the second half of the 19th century was significant for the Russian nation for various historical reasons: the 1,000th anniversary of the establishment of the Russian state was celebrated in 1862, and the 900th anniversary of the Christianization of Rus' was celebrated in 1888. Such historical incidents tied Russia closely to the Christian Near East, the former realm of the Byzantine Empire, historically, culturally and politically.[99] Therefore, Uspenskii pointed to a correlation between Russia's contemporary political interests in Asia Minor and the Balkans and its historical ties with the region.

Both Nelidov and Uspenskii legitimized the establishment of RAIK by making reference to European political rivalry over the Near East, which reflected itself in archaeology. Years later, in a report he wrote in 1918 to the Department of Science in the People's Commissariat for Education, Uspenskii outlined the founding principles of RAIK with reference to Europe-wide political competition. He stated that Istanbul stood at the centre of international competition, which made the Russian position in this city all the more important. He lamented that if the Russians were not respected in the East as much as the French, it was because Russia did not try to penetrate Turkey through cultural institutions, that is, schools, religious missions, charitable organizations, commercial and industrial initiatives, in the same manner as the French, British and Germans operated. Uspenskii noted, 'In general, the weakest side of our situation is the insufficiency of our cultural initiatives in Tsargrad, in which we are far behind our competitors.'[100] Only one institution, he claimed, RAIK was an exception to this shortcoming. However, Uspenskii noted, even in this unique institution, which acquired a respectable reputation among German and French scholars, Russia could not fully make use of its position because of financial difficulties.

Even though financially and politically it was expedient to have the support of the Russian Embassy, Director Fyodor Uspenskii was by no means willing to surrender his professional autonomy to his political superiors in the diplomatic service. Uspenskii noted that until 1897 the Ottoman government did not recognize RAIK as a separate institution. Until then, there was not a special agreement with the Turkish government, stipulating RAIK as an institution independent of the Russian Embassy and having the right to communicate with the Turkish government separately. In the first years the Ottoman government referred to RAIK staff as Embassy officials, and the institute was regarded as an inherent part of the Russian Embassy. Even after its authorization by the Ottoman government, RAIK had to communicate with the Turkish government through the Embassy every time they needed a permit to carry out excavations or other scholarly activities. Uspenskii seemed to be uncomfortable about his dependence on diplomats. He stated, 'our scientific institution had to endure the burden of depending on coincidental circumstances and other people's failures or reluctance.' The dependence on the Embassy meant that RAIK would be vulnerable to political relations between the two empires. Especially when they launched large-scale projects, RAIK would be sent from one Ottoman Ministry to another, and the future of its studies would remain insecure. Uspenskii considered diplomatic interference offensive: 'Eliminating direct, sometimes humiliating … interference in purely scientific work, legalizing our institution in Turkey by a special agreement with the Ottoman government remains a matter of the future. Without that, we cannot expect reliable, permanent success; we cannot set out plans that require long-term systematic work.'[101]

Despite some opposition and reservation in the process of its establishment, after 1894 there was constant Russian governmental support for RAIK. To ensure constant scholar mobility between Russia and Istanbul, on 12 February 1901, Uspenskii requested the allocation of scholarships for young scholars wishing to undertake research at RAIK from the Ministry of Public Education.[102] Following the example of the German Archaeological Institute in Rome and the French School in Athens, the Ministry of Public Education agreed to grant scholarships every year to two scholars for a duration of two years.

There were also personal channels of communication between some RAIK staff and Russian bureaucrats: As was previously expressed, the first RAIK secretary Pogodin was Tertii Filippov's nephew, whereas another institute secretary, F. I. Shmit was involved in RAIK's activities because he tutored ambassador Nelidov's son in Rome and it was Nelidov who encouraged him to join RAIK and change the path of his career towards Byzantinology.[103]

There was especially a very close cooperation between RAIK and the Holy Synod. In 1901, Uspenskii requested the Holy Synod to send scholars from theological academies to Istanbul. In September 1902, the Holy Synod agreed upon a resolution to send one scholar every year for a yearly term to study at RAIK. After 1902, scholars from theological academies visited RAIK on a more regular basis than scholars from Russian universities. This constant flow of scholars made the Holy Synod one of the most active supporters of RAIK. In addition to its academic and bureaucratic links with the Holy Synod and the Ministry of Public Education, RAIK was also administratively connected to the Ministry of Foreign Affairs through the Embassy in Istanbul. These links with three major governmental institutions made it safe to argue that RAIK was a governmental project, reflecting the ideology of the bureaucracy in the last decades of the Russian Empire.

Alexander III could not survive long enough to appreciate the activities of the institute he approved in 1894, but his successor Nicholas II showed a personal interest in the activities of RAIK, which was manifested by his private donations to acquire antiquities several times.[104] Actually, the last Tsar of the Russian Empire had been a history enthusiast since his childhood. Among the subjects Nicholas II was privately tutored when he was a young Grand Duke, he was attracted to history the most. He was also an honorary member of the Imperial Historical Society from the age of sixteen.[105] Uspenskii's direct communication with Nicholas II implies the Emperor's personal support for RAIK. In his notes from September 1897, Uspenskii recounted that he appeared before the Emperor to request a raise in RAIK's budget. Uspenskii justified his demand by explaining that RAIK was a 'tool for Russia's cultural influence over the East, among Slavs and Greeks.'[106] Nicholas II agreed with this argument, saying, '[t]his is very much desirable.' However, Uspenskii added, with such modest means, it was difficult to fulfil this historical responsibility. The Emperor agreed to make a raise in RAIK's budget, and also praised the achievements of Uspenskii as the director of RAIK.

Despite its constant financial shortcomings, RAIK managed to become a hub for Russian scholars visiting the Ottoman Empire. In 1895, immediately after its establishment, the institute established links with Russian consulates around the Ottoman Empire, as well as with Greek, Serbian and Bulgarian diplomats. A large number of diplomats, Russian as well as foreign, were accepted as honorary members. As soon as RAIK was established, letters were sent to Russian diplomatic missions around the Ottoman Empire and diplomats in independent Balkan nations, informing them about RAIK's mission and asking them to provide information about antiquities and monuments in their area of jurisdiction.[107] In particular, the diplomats were requested to inform RAIK about the feasibility of research and information about local conditions, if antiquities were on sale or not, and if they were on sale, information about potential sellers and buyers. The letters produced positive results. Shortly afterwards Russian diplomats sent letters expressing their support and readiness to help RAIK.[108]

In his exchange with the Serbian and Bulgarian missions in the Ottoman Empire, Uspenskii referred to historical ties between these nations and Russia, the study of which was the reason why RAIK was established.[109] In addition, Serbian and Bulgarian diplomats were asked to be honorary members of the institute. RAIK not only established connections with the Balkan Slavs but also fostered connections with Athens. Already in 1900, RAIK secured a permanent building in the Greek capital. Rooms in the Petraki Monastery were offered to the Russian Embassy for the use of RAIK.[110]

In addition to its diplomatic contacts, RAIK established relations with the Orthodox Patriarchate of Constantinople, too. In 1896, a letter was sent to the Patriarch, asking information about ancient monuments, manuscripts or any other ancient objects worthy of interest. In exchange, Patriarch Anthimus VII (1895–6) asked clergymen in his jurisdiction about ancient religious buildings in their locality, any libraries or archives, or oral traditions that needed to be recorded.[111] Therefore, archaeology formed a basis for cooperation between RAIK, Russian diplomatic posts across the Ottoman Empire, the Orthodox Patriarchate and its local representatives.

RAIK also had scientific contacts with numerous prestigious universities and societies, and institutes in Britain, the United States, Denmark, Germany, Sweden, Austria, Greece, Romania, Switzerland and France. Its library was enriched through book exchange agreements with various academic institutions. The desire to catch up with European scholarship prompted Russian archaeologists to cooperate, if possible, with European scholars, and participate in international congresses and meetings. In its very first year, in 1895, Uspenskii and Pogodin visited Athens to familiarize themselves with archaeological methods used by foreign archaeologists in this city.[112] Another example of academic cooperation was R. K. Leper's participation in a German-led expedition in 1905 in the Aegean islands and the Aegean coast of Asia Minor, which was led by Professor Wilhelm Dörpfeld from the German Archaeological Institute in Athens.[113]

Archaeological cooperation was extended to other foreigners in the Ottoman Empire who had an interest in antiquities. For instance, Paul Gaudin, a Levantine engineer from İzmir, an ardent art and antiquities collector and amateur archaeologist, was one of the most frequent donors, and also an associate member of RAIK. Gaudin sent many ancient objects as gifts to the institute.[114] However, the closest relationship was established with the French Assumptionist Church in Kadıköy, Istanbul. This French Church also functioned as a research centre with a focus on the history of the Eastern Churches and the Byzantine Empire, and therefore had shared interests with RAIK. The Assumptionist Church published an academic periodical named *Les Echos d'Orient*.[115] While Uspenskii and other RAIK members frequently wrote articles for *Les Echos d'Orient*, the articles of clergy-scholars of the French Church appeared in the annual Bulletin of RAIK. The two institutions made an agreement and shared the study of Istanbul's history and archaeology. While the French Assumptionist Church was responsible for the expeditions and surveys on the Asian side of the city, RAIK was responsible for the study of the European side.[116]

In addition to Europeans, American scholars followed the establishment of RAIK with interest. In the first months of 1895, *The American Journal of Archaeology and of the History of the Fine Arts* reported the establishment of RAIK and described the bureaucratic structure and scientific objects of the institute.[117] In the coming years, this journal continued to regularly publicize the scientific activities of RAIK to its readers.

What emerges from this picture is the contrast between the explicitly stated political intentions of Russian bureaucrats, diplomats and scholars to justify archaeological studies and the international scientific collaboration that transcended political intentions. Scholars looking for financial support from governments usually find it convenient to make a political case for support. On the other side of the coin, governments are seldom interested in 'pure' research in the humanities. However, despite the obvious and openly stated political agenda, RAIK's activities prove that there was also academic cooperation between intellectual elites, a cooperation that went beyond imperial, national and religious boundaries. If archaeological discoveries were a distinctive sign of imperial prestige, scientific collaboration was a means of being integrated into the 'civilized' and cultured international community. National and imperial rivalries were expressed only within the confines of this code of behaviour. RAIK's relations with the Ottoman authorities and especially the Ottoman Museum will be examined more closely in Chapter 4, but suffice it to say that even with the Ottoman Museum, despite all the mutual suspicions, the relationship was formed on the basis of this code that governed the relations of cultured cosmopolitan intellectuals.

This brings us to the initial question that triggered this research – the complicity of scholars, in this case archaeologists, in political projects. Why certain questions are asked and why governments prefer to support one field of research over others shed light on the identity and the priorities that are promoted by the state. In the case of RAIK, the emphasis of a number of diplomats and Byzantinist scholars on shared identity with Balkan nations found support from government bodies and the Tsar himself. The importance given to shared ethnic and religious identity reflected the mindset of the imperial bureaucracy in the last decades of the Russian Empire. However, the conjunction of interests between scholarship and politics does not invalidate the academic value of RAIK's archaeological studies; neither does it mean that scholars who participated in these projects were mere tools in the hands of policymakers. It was not the scientists who set the political agenda, but existing political circumstances facilitated the emergence of certain modes of scholarship.

The Russian Empire's discovery of soft power was another theme that could be detected in the discussions that led to the creation of RAIK. Both diplomats and scholars frequently evoked the example of the French to point to the importance of cultural influence. Russian diplomats discovered that being a great power required more than mere military power, and realized the importance of cultural institutions. They were also aware of the fact that Russia was behind European powers in this respect. At this point, RAIK was designed as an institution that would facilitate academic and cultural contacts between Russia and the Balkan nations. If RAIK succeeded in this target, then it would reveal that Russian foreign policy was not solely based on military power and would hence contribute to Russia's prestige. However, as will be outlined in Chapter 4, political realities were not compatible with these hopes. Sharing Orthodox faith or Slavic background had little practical value in the late 19th century, considering the Macedonian dispute between the Greeks, Bulgarians and Serbians. Being ethnic or religious kinsmen (*edinovertsy i edinoplemmeniki*) did not keep the Balkan peoples together, therefore the image Russia tried to create, the protector of Slavs and the Orthodox, was gradually losing its meaning. Ideas emanating from Western Europe, like nationalism, liberal values, and parliamentary democracy were becoming more attractive to educated segments of Balkan societies, rather than Slavdom and Orthodoxy.

4

Expeditions of the Russian Archaeological Institute and contacts with Ottoman authorities

Russian archaeological activities in the Ottoman Empire started when the Ottoman Empire was already in the process of standardizing procedures to deal with foreign archaeologists. We know that there were unsystematic individual Russian expeditions in the late 1880s, conducted mainly by diplomats. The correspondence between Abdülhamid II's court and local military authorities reveal that these individual activities were perceived as suspicious and were immediately reported to the Sultan. For instance, in 1889 the Russian consul in Edirne made archaeological investigations in the countryside and local authorities immediately prepared a report stating that the consul was not accompanied by an Ottoman official.[1] On another occasion, Ambassador A. I. Nelidov's visit to ruins in Çanakkale was reported to Abdülhamid II.[2] In addition to such sporadic investigations by diplomats, the IPPO, established in 1882 upon the initiative of Grand Duke Sergei Aleksandrovich, carried out the first professional Russian archaeological expeditions in the Ottoman Empire. In addition to its theological work, the Palestine Society undertook archaeological excavations on an unsystematic basis. Documents reveal that the Ottoman government permitted investigations of a scientific nature as long as the excavation team obeyed Ottoman laws. In 1891, upon the Grand Duke's request to make archaeological investigations about Christian and Byzantine monuments in Syria, Palestine and the Sinai Mountain, the Ottoman government issued a permit on the condition that the excavation team acted in accordance with Ottoman laws and that the gendarmerie accompanied them.[3]

RAIK was not only the first Russian scientific community abroad, but also the first foreign archaeological institute in the Ottoman Empire. At first, Abdülhamid II and bureaucrats at the Sublime Porte displayed a reluctant attitude to RAIK's establishment, which bordered on outright suspicion. In 1894, Russian ambassador Nelidov communicated his desire to create a school of archaeology in Istanbul that was planned to be under the administration of the Russian Embassy. The Sublime Porte responded to this request with an official note trying to dissuade the Russian Embassy, but ambassador Nelidov insisted on his plan.[4] Eventually, RAIK opened its offices in the Ottoman capital in 1895. In April 1895, Osman Hamdi Bey, the director of the Ottoman Museum, sent a gift to RAIK, a photographical album of the antiquities collection of the Ottoman Museum as a gesture of support. In exchange, RAIK sent four fragments from bronze statues to the Ottoman Museum.[5] Finally in September 1897, two years after the opening of its offices, RAIK was officially authorized by the Ottoman government to make scientific investigations, surveys and excavations.[6]

Abdülhamid II's authorization of RAIK in September 1897 was communicated to the Russian Embassy by the Ottoman Minister of Foreign Affairs, Ahmed Tevfik Pasha.[7] According to the *irade* issued by the Sultan, members of RAIK could carry out archaeological studies in the Ottoman Empire, provided that they acted in accordance with existing Ottoman antiquities regulations. These rules included officially notifying local administrative authorities before expeditions and not undertaking research without proper permits.[8] Russian archaeologists were expected to give half of their findings to the Ottoman Imperial Museum. Officials from the Ottoman Ministry of Education were responsible for deciding which objects Russian and Ottoman sides would retain. At the same time, Russian archaeologists could enjoy some privileges; the books and pamphlets they brought from Russia were to be exempt from the customs tax and subject to only procedural examination at the custom.[9]

The note, sent by the Ottoman Ministry of Foreign Affairs, meant that both the Sultan and the Ministry recognized RAIK as an institution separate from the Russian Embassy. More importantly, the Ottoman government granted rights to RAIK that had never been granted to foreigners before. Since RAIK was the first and only permanent foreign archaeological institution in the Ottoman Empire, the 1897 *irade* that formed the basis for RAIK's activities in the Ottoman Empire did not have a precedent. Considering the initial Ottoman reluctance to accept RAIK's establishment, the rights granted in the *irade* looked very generous. It is possible that the Ottomans did not want to be regarded as uncooperative in the sphere of science and scholarship, as it would make the Ottoman government look 'uncultured' and therefore would be a blow to Ottoman prestige.

In 1897, a month after the authorization of RAIK by Abdülhamid II, Fyodor Uspenskii received an Imperial Order from the Sultan.[10] Next year, in 1898, Osman Hamdi Bey became an honorary member of RAIK. Therefore, a basis for scientific collaboration was established between Ottoman and Russian archaeologists in the highly politicized world of archaeology. Nevertheless, it is difficult to say that there was a genuine cooperation between Russian archaeologists and their Ottoman colleagues. On the contrary, Uspenskii frequently complained about Osman Hamdi Bey's lack of interest as regards RAIK's activities. Uspenskii recalled that although he tried to establish cordial relations with Osman Hamdi Bey, even visited his house twice, and offered to take Osman Hamdi's paintings to St Petersburg for an exhibition (his paintings were known to be Osman Hamdi's soft spot), Osman Hamdi's response to these gestures were cool, to say the least. Uspenskii noted, 'It is difficult to say if the director is our friend.'[11] The director of RAIK wrote to the Russian ambassador in 1906 that Osman Hamdi Bey ignored Russian archaeologists: he visited RAIK only once, and although he was the first person to whom Uspenskii always sent invitations for academic meetings and lectures held at RAIK, Osman Hamdi Bey never once visited any of the scholarly meetings. On top of that, the Sublime Porte was not totally free of suspicions vis-à-vis the Russians: Russian governmental emblems and signs with the name of RAIK could not be displayed on the institute building. What bothered Uspenskii the most, however, was the strict surveillance of their scientific activities by the Ottoman government.[12]

On their part, Russian archaeologists respected Osman Hamdi's life-long effort that manifested itself in the Ottoman Imperial Museum – Uspenskii stated that the Ottoman Museum was one of the most important museums in Europe in terms of the richness and importance of its collection.[13] However, he complained that besides the Ottoman Museum, there was not a serious interest in the scientific study of antiquities among the population of the Ottoman Empire.[14] Uspenskii argued that only some predominantly Greek educational societies and some Greek individuals had an interest in archaeology, but their studies lacked a scholarly methodology.

In order to familiarize themselves with the surviving historical monuments from the Byzantine era, RAIK undertook numerous expeditions between 1895 and 1914. The relations between Russian archaeologists and the Ottoman government was sometimes smooth, but sometimes there were disagreements as regards the scope of RAIK's archaeological research. Even though RAIK's charter encompassed the study of pre-Christian Hellenistic antiquities, Uspenskii and his colleagues directed their attention primarily to the study of Byzantine history, theology, art and ancient Slavic history. Their expeditions targeted regions which were under Byzantine political or cultural influence; primarily, Macedonia, Mount Athos, Bulgaria, Serbia, Asia Minor, Greece, Syria and Palestine. During these expeditions Russian archaeologists gathered manuscripts from monasteries and made sketches of monuments, photographed buildings, made excavations and collected valuable monuments and objects, some of which were brought to Russia after the closure of RAIK. Consequently, the institute acquired a rich material base for scientific study. Throughout its existence, RAIK spent considerable effort at researching and preserving valuable manuscripts and earned a well-deserved reputation in international scientific circles for that effort. Uspenskii participated in most expeditions undertaken by RAIK and was responsible for most of the scientific work. In nearly all volumes of the *Izvestiia*, Uspenskii had an article. Even as regards articles written by his colleagues, he either supervised them or helped with the materials needed for the study.[15]

Even before the official recognition of RAIK by the Sultan, Uspenskii was given permission in May 1895 by the Ottoman Ministry of the Interior to make excavations on the Black Sea littoral, around the cities of Trabzon, Sinop and Samsun.[16] While local officials were requested to provide the necessary help to Uspenskii and his colleagues, on the other hand they were asked to keep an eye on his behaviour.[17] A few months later, when Uspenskii wanted to make investigations in Istanbul, the same caution was repeated. Local officials were asked to offer Uspenskii any kind of help he needed, while keeping him under surveillance 'without making this evident to him'.[18]

These first excursions were not systematic, rather they were intended to familiarize Russian archaeologists with Byzantine antiquities in the Ottoman Empire, and they laid the ground for more systematic archaeological studies in future. Both the Black Sea coast and Istanbul would be RAIK's favourite spots for research in the coming years. During the first Trabzon expedition in 1895, Russian scholars collected objects of Christian art, including ancient manuscripts and icons with Slavic inscriptions, which were thought to be made by the medieval Rus', from the period when Byzantine rule extended over to the northern shores of the Black Sea.[19] They also conducted research in the monasteries of Sumela, Vazelon, Perister in Trabzon, where they would carry out more systematic studies in later years.

In 1897, Ivan Alekseevich Zinoviev (1839–1917), who was the former head of the Asiatic Department of the Ministry of Foreign Affairs and the leading expert of the Ministry on the Near East, replaced Nelidov as the ambassador in Istanbul. The same year Zinoviev was appointed, RAIK made its first important acquisition: the discovery of the *Codex Purpureus Petropolitanus*, also known as Codex N, Purple Codex or the Sarmısaklı Codex. The Codex was found in 1896 in the Sarmısaklı village near Kayseri, in the middle of Anatolia.[20] This ancient Bible, which dated back to the 6th century, was written in silver and gold letters. Before the Russians arrived at Sarmısaklı, the Americans and the British bargained with villagers for the acquisition of this ancient Bible. Russian archaeologist Ia. I. Smirnov coincidentally learned about this manuscript on his trip around Asia Minor and informed Uspenskii about it.[21] Uspenskii immediately asked the ambassador to find the means for the purchase of the Sarmısaklı Codex. Finally, the Codex was bought for 10,000 roubles through the personal donation of Tsar Nicholas II (r. 1894–1917), who presented it to the Imperial Public Library in St Petersburg.[22] The Emperor's personal donation is proof of his personal interest in RAIK's activities in the Ottoman Empire.

Encouraged by the Tsar's donation, Uspenskii made a request for monetary support in a letter to the Ministry of Public Education in August 1898. He reminded the Ministry that despite its very modest means, RAIK had achieved a lot in a short period of time: an impressive library, a valuable manuscript collection, a numismatics collection, numerous expeditions and a significant number of members in different parts of the Ottoman Empire. Uspenskii stated that RAIK's primary responsibility was to study Christian antiquities and prevent them from being smuggled abroad, 'and hence fulfil its scientific and political role in the East'.[23] However, given financial constraints, this duty was very hard to accomplish. Uspenskii stated that if RAIK did not acquire the Sarmısaklı Codex, it would end up abroad, too. In fact, being transported from Asia Minor to Russia, the Codex was indeed sent abroad. Obviously, what Uspenskii meant with 'abroad' was either Europe or the United States. The acquisition of a Christian antiquity, when there were rival Western collectors, was considered a success for RAIK and for Russia in the international competition over antiquities, and Russia's primary responsibility was defined as successfully competing with other foreigners in this race. Eventually, Uspenskii's repeated requests became successful. In 1898, RAIK's budget was raised by 7,500 roubles, upon the Emperor's approval.[24]

When Archbishop Arsenii Volokolamskii visited RAIK on his return trip from Palestine to Russia in the summer of 1900, he praised the efforts and dedication of Professor Uspenskii which resulted in the creation of a valuable research centre. Uspenskii and his secretary Farmakovskii showed Archbishop Arsenii the institute library and museum, where he also met three young researchers from Russian universities. The sight of a Russian scientific community in the Ottoman capital more than satisfied the archbishop.[25]

After a series of preliminary expeditions and investigations, Russian archaeologists asked for an excavation permit from the Ottoman authorities for the first time in 1898, during an expedition to Ottoman Macedonia. Although it was easier to obtain permissions for research trips, when trips involved excavations, the Ottoman government applied stricter regulations. In the summer and fall of 1898, there were two excursions to Ottoman Macedonia, to the Pateli village near the town of Sorovich[26] between Selânik (Thessaloniki) and Manastır (Bitola). Along the Selânik–Manastır railway, near Pateli, a necropolis from the late Bronze Age was discovered during the construction of the railway. Engineers working on the site informed RAIK about the discovery. One of the members of RAIK, Z. E. Ashkenazi donated 3,000 francs for the trial excavation.

This was the first instance when the relations between RAIK and the Ottoman Museum cooled. The major problem, according to Russian archaeologists, was that the privileges of the two institutions were doomed to come into conflict with each other.[27] On the one hand, the Ottoman Museum was the major governmental institution concerning antiquities and had a monopoly over archaeological activities in the Ottoman Empire since the 1884 antiquities regulation. On the other hand, RAIK demanded full and uninterrupted right to make excavations and research in Ottoman territories based on the *irade* issued by the Sultan in 1897. In practice, RAIK wanted to bypass the authority of the Ottoman Museum by relying on the privileges granted by Abdülhamid II.

In the summer of 1898, Uspenskii addressed the Governor of Manastır, Abdülkerim Pasha, through the Russian consul in the city, A. A. Rostkovskii. The Governor stated that he had to submit the question both to Istanbul and to the Administrative Council of the Manastır *Vilayet* (*Vilayet Meclis-i İdaresi*) for further discussion.[28] The Council, uninformed about the Sultan's *irade*, submitted an inquiry to the Porte about the legality of Russian archaeological activities in Pateli. Abdülkerim Pasha promised that as soon as he received an official note from the Porte, the question would be discussed at the Administrative Council and the response would be immediately communicated to the Russians. Abdülkerim Pasha also confidentially told Uspenskii that the Administrative Council was unlikely to risk giving a permit for excavation without formal approval from Istanbul because the village Pateli and the area lying around it was considered *emlâk,* that is, private land belonging to the Sultan. Finally in September 1898 Russian archaeologists received permission from the Ottoman Ministry of the Interior to start diggings in the area, but their excavation was strictly overseen by local representatives of the Ottoman government.[29] When Uspenskii and his colleagues initiated investigations in Pateli, the authorities gave a permit on the condition that their findings were to be exhibited at the Imperial Ottoman Museum in Istanbul.[30]

In Pateli, an interesting coincidence crossed RAIK's path with the famous liberal politician Pavel N. Miliukov (1859–1943). Before engaging in politics, Miliukov was a historian, who served as assistant professor at the Department of History and Philology at Moscow University from 1886 to 1895. Miliukov was fired from Moscow University in 1895 for the political messages of his public lectures.[31] He was first exiled to Ryazan, where he engaged in archaeological studies. While in exile, he received an invitation from the University of Sofia to take the chair of History.[32] He spent the period between 1897 and 1899 abroad, travelling around the Balkans and lecturing at Bulgarian institutions. In Sofia, he briefly gave lectures on Roman, medieval and Slavic history, as well as philosophy of history. However, Miliukov had to leave the University of Sofia in a few months. One reason for this hasty leave might be his acquaintance with several Bulgarian opposition figures. In addition, the Bulgarian government could not withstand the pressure from the Russian diplomatic representative in Sofia to dismiss him from the university. It was then he decided to spend time in Macedonia, partially to have first-hand information about this turbulent region. Until 1899, Miliukov mostly spent his time travelling around Macedonia and dedicated himself to archaeological studies. In later years, Miliukov left his mark on Russian politics as the founder of the Constitutional Democratic (Kadet) Party, as a member of the Duma from 1907 to 1912, and as the Minister of Foreign Affairs for the Provisional Government after the February Revolution in 1917.

When RAIK undertook the expedition to Macedonia, Miliukov was already dismissed from his position at the University of Sofia, and he was travelling in the Balkans. In 1897, he made a brief visit to Istanbul and was acquainted with Uspenskii. The excavation in Pateli, the very first excavation of RAIK, was initiated by Miliukov in the autumn of 1898. The RAIK secretary Farmakovskii took over the excavation from 14 October to 14 November 1898. The excavation team discovered numerous ceramic, bronze and iron objects from the late Bronze Age, as well as bones and skulls.[33] However, they had to stop excavations in mid-November 1898 due to the start of the cold and rainy season. After the expedition, Miliukov spent months in Istanbul to organize materials shipped off from Macedonia.[34] In the meantime, Uspenskii transmitted his desire to continue more systematic excavations next autumn in 1899 to the governor of Manastır, Abdülkerim Pasha.[35]

A few months later, in March 1899, the Ottoman Ministry of Foreign Affairs warned RAIK through the Russian Embassy that it was not legal to undertake excavations without receiving necessary permits beforehand from the Ottoman Ministry of Education, the ministry with which the Ottoman Museum was affiliated.[36] This warning meant that Abdülhamid II's *irade* was not sufficient on its own for RAIK to freely start archaeological activities, but the Russians should also consult the Ottoman Museum. The note also stated that the Ottoman Museum had not yet received any objects from the Pateli expedition, even though it was reported that sixteen chests of objects were brought to the Russian Embassy in Istanbul.[37] The Ottoman Ministry of Foreign Affairs required RAIK to comply with the previous agreement and send the findings to the Ottoman Museum for partitioning.

Secretary Farmakovskii and Director Uspenskii responded to this note by citing the rights accorded to them by the Sultan.[38] The Russian archaeologists stated that the Sultan's *irade* gave them the right to carry out research anywhere in the Ottoman Empire. On top of that special permit from the Sultan, Russian archaeologists also noted that in October 1898 they had informed local authorities, including the Governor of Manastır, Abdülkerim Pasha, about their expedition. Apparently, Uspenskii assumed that he could bypass the Ottoman Museum by referring to the *irade,* and that RAIK could engage in dialogue with local administrative authorities on its own, without the interference of the Russian Embassy.

In his defence against the Ottoman government, Uspenskii stated that RAIK operated totally openly and legally, using all sorts of assistance from central and local authorities: the Minister of the Interior communicated with the Governors in Selânik and Manastır about providing excavation permits to the Russian Institute. The Governor of Manastır Abdülkerim Pasha commanded a police officer to help the director, dispatched an official to oversee the excavation and to keep an inventory of found items. Uspenskii claimed that this official had never told them to send half of the items to the Ottoman Museum, either during the excavation or during the shipment of the items to Istanbul.[39] In view of the fact that the items found did not have a special monetary value, Uspenskii concluded that the Ottoman government was not interested and did not want to keep half of them. Besides, having a permit for excavation from the Sultan, he did not consider it a legal obligation to ask for a permit again from the Ottoman Ministry of Education, especially because excavations were carried out on the Sultan's private land. Uspenskii complained that he could not even understand how he could be seen to have violated existing regulations.[40] The director of RAIK presumed that the Ottoman Ministry of Education had been notified through administrative channels about RAIK's permission to undertake excavations in Pateli. The presence of a police officer detached to the excavation area, who closely followed the excavation, supported Uspenskii's view that this officer was a representative of the Ottoman Ministry of Education, while in fact he was commissioned by the local governor.[41] The misunderstanding stemmed from the fact that despite the Ottoman Museum's claim to full monopoly over archaeological activities in the Ottoman Empire, Russian archaeologists only notified the Ottoman Ministry of the Interior, not the Ottoman Museum and hence violated the bureaucratic chain.

With regard to the Ottoman Museum's demand to receive half of the findings from the expedition, Uspenskii claimed that out of the sixteen boxes sent to the Russian Embassy in Istanbul, only three had antiquities found during the excavations, of which two boxes contained pottery and only one box contained bronze and iron materials. The remaining boxes had not yet been opened and they only contained bones and skulls from the necropolis. He invited Osman Hamdi Bey, who was also an honorary member of RAIK, to personally visit and inspect the contents of the boxes whenever he wanted. Uspenskii stated that the excavations in Pateli were not carried out for commercial ends, but only for the sake of archaeological and 'pure scientific objectives'. This scientific concern was obvious, considering that the findings did not have any material value. Uspenskii asked to keep the objects until they were thoroughly investigated in their entirety. He stated, 'I dare to hope that the enlightened Ottoman government would consider it beneath their dignity to insist on the surrender of half of the materials, before they were researched and published by the Institute.'[42]

Next year, in August 1899, Uspenskii requested permission to continue the excavation in the same area through Ambassador Zinoviev. The director asked for all possible precautions to avoid any sign of suspicion on the part of the Ottoman government after the last year's crisis, and especially requested Zinoviev to consult the Ottoman Museum to prevent any misunderstanding.[43] During this second expedition, RAIK confirmed that they would send the objects after completing their investigation.[44] In spite of this assurance, the Porte sent Tevhid Bey, an official from the Ministry of Foreign Affairs and specialist in antiquities, to Manastır to oversee the excavation, in addition to sending a note to the Russian Embassy to specify the share of the Ottoman Imperial Museum.[45] On top of that, the Ministry of the Interior warned local officials in Manastır to ensure that Russian archaeologists acted within the confines of Ottoman laws.[46] Finally, the question was brought to a resolution thanks to the direct communication between Uspenskii and the director of the Ottoman Museum, Osman Hamdi Bey. Boxes full of objects discovered at the Pateli expedition were opened at the Ottoman Museum and the contents were equally divided.[47] Nevertheless, RAIK had to submit the materials to the staff of the Ottoman Museum before they were extensively studied at the Institute.[48]

The Macedonia expedition of 1898–9 showed the sensitivity of the Ottoman government about exercising its authority vis-à-vis Russian archaeologists within its boundaries. The Ottoman government, through its various ministries and state institutions, was reminding foreign archaeologists of its sovereign rights. The sensitivity of the Ottoman government, especially of the Ottoman Museum is worthy of attention, given the insignificance of the findings at the Pateli excavation – remnants from the Bronze Age without any contemporary political or religious connotation. This incident showed that the Ottoman government was not concerned with ownership rights over antiquities only because of the symbolic meaning attached to them, but that the very act of monitoring foreign archaeologists and compelling them to obey Ottoman laws was a political message in itself. In this context, even the politically insignificant Bronze Age materials could turn into a sign of sovereignty.

In fact, the site at Pateli was only a coincidental discovery in the Macedonian expedition of 1898–9. The major intention of this expedition was the study of Christian antiquities – especially Slavic monuments of Ottoman Macedonia.[49] During the expedition, Uspenskii was accompanied by A. A. Rostkovskii, the Russian consul in Manastır, Miliukov, and M. I. Rostovtsev. Like Miliukov, Rostovtsev was a world-famous historian, specialized in the history of southern Russia.[50] From a historical perspective this expedition was especially important to understand the history of medieval Bulgarian–Byzantine relations. Throughout the expedition, Russian historians gathered important information about the history of Ottoman Macedonia.[51] The most important discovery of the expedition was an inscription from the late 10th century, from the period of Tsar Samuil of medieval Bulgaria, which was the oldest-known example of Slavic letters. Another important achievement was the discovery of an inscription delineating the Bulgarian–Byzantine border in the early 10th century.[52]

More interesting than archaeological discoveries, however, were the observations of archaeologists about the contemporary political situation in Macedonia reflected in the institute report for 1898. The report was written by the archaeologists who participated in the Macedonia expedition, including Miliukov. Russian scholars stated that the most important part of Macedonia for Slavic history was the region around Selânik, Ohrid Lake, and Prespa, a region which was the setting for inter-communal fighting at the turn of the century.[53] Until then, little archaeological study was conducted in this area because of political instability.

Referring to the conflict between the Bulgarians and Serbs, Russian archaeologists deemed it necessary to make a correction with regard to a misunderstanding in Russian public opinion.[54] The Russian public, the report remarked, falsely blamed Greeks for destroying ancient Bulgarian and Serbian monuments that gave evidence to historical rights of the Slavs in Macedonia. 'Our observation in Macedonia did not confirm these complaints,' Russian archaeologists claimed. Ancient Slavic inscriptions were not smeared, scraped and replaced with Greek inscriptions. Likewise, there was no evidence proving the intentional destruction of frescoes and icons in Bulgarian churches by the Greeks. On the contrary, the report described mutual treatment of Bulgarians and Serbs as 'barbarian' (*v varvarskom obrashchenii*) and claimed that the current war between Serbs and Bulgarians threatened Slavic antiquities more than Turkish intolerance (*neterpimost'*) or

Greek phyletism.[55] Russian archaeologists noted that many times they had witnessed Bulgarians destroy Greek or Serbian monuments, and scrape or seriously damage frescoes with the images of Serbian tsars. The report argued that the only motivation for such behaviour could be political. There was serious danger for Slavic monuments if Bulgarian ecclesiastical authorities did not curb the intolerance of their representatives in Macedonia. Some examples of such intentional destruction were Treskavets Monastery near Pirlepe (Prilep) and Markov Monastery near Üsküp (Skopje). Given the Bulgarian-Russian political rapproachement at the time and considering that one of the writers of the report was Miliukov, who had strong pro-Bulgarian sentiments, the report was interesting for pointing to inter-communal struggles between Bulgarians and Serbs and for blaming the Bulgarians for the destruction of antiquities.

In fact, these observations indicated why Russia's self-inflicted role as the protector of Ottoman Christians, or more specifically, Balkan Slavs was a dead end. The primordial ties between Russia and the Balkan nations, which were frequently evoked to legitimize RAIK's establishment, did not have a practical meaning in an age when nationalism challenged supra-national, imperial identities in the Balkans.[56] As the expedition report documented, Orthodoxy or common Slavic heritage was far from being a uniting factor in the Balkans at the turn of the century. Exploring the past of Balkan nations to foster stronger ties with them in future – RAIK's primary goal – was easier said than done. The report hints at the fact that ancient monuments were regarded as solid evidence for territorial claims over Macedonia – therefore, were targeted and destroyed by rival groups.

RAIK's studies in Macedonia were not the only ones of its kind; archaeological and historical studies were conducted by scholars from different ethnic backgrounds, as the struggle over Macedonia reflected itself in the scientific realm. Especially after the Congress of Berlin in 1878, anthropologists, linguists and other scholars came up with theories and scientific studies to claim Macedonia for their respective ethnic groups. Bulgarian linguists indicated linguistic proximity with the Macedonian Slavs, as did the Serbs. On the other hand, Greek scholars emphasized the importance of the religious authority of the Orthodox Patriarchate of Constaninople in the formation of national identity.[57]

A very interesting aspect of RAIK's Macedonia expedition was the involvement of Pavel Miliukov, who published an atlas of Macedonian ethnography in 1900 as a result of this expedition.[58] For Miliukov, an intellectual with great interest in Balkan affairs, archaeological expedition was a scholarly enterprise as well as a useful excuse to travel around Macedonia without arising suspicion on the part of Ottoman or Russian authorities. At first sight, it may be surprising to see a staunch opponent of Russian autocracy, who was even jailed for his political views, as part of a government-sponsored archaeological project about Orthodox churches in Macedonia. Essentially, RAIK's collaboration with a well-known government critic further confirms that academic concerns of RAIK staff went beyond political considerations. Academic cooperation with such world-famous scholars like Miliukov and Rostovtsev indicated that RAIK was not merely a voiceless institution subordinate to the government's whims, but it was a platform in which scholars with different agendas could pursue individual goals and carve up their personal space independent of the government. Even though it was a very short-lived collaboration and Miliukov did not openly engage in political activities when he joined the RAIK team, it is still noteworthy that RAIK accommodated Miliukov at a time when University of Sofia had to fire him upon pressure from Russian diplomats in Sofia.

In his memoirs, Miliukov noted that his experience in Macedonia shaped his opinions on the Balkan question, hence he became a vocal supporter of the Bulgarian cause in the Third Duma during the Balkan crisis of 1908.[59] It should be noted that Miliukov was no less a supporter of active Russian involvement in the Balkan affairs than his right-wing opponents in the Duma, and he was not very much in contradiction with the official policy in this respect. Actually, his interventionist policy approach and firm belief in Russia's responsibility to protect Balkan Christians and especially Bulgarians only grew after his voyages in Macedonia. However, different from his political adversaries, Miliukov was inspired by the democratic movements in the Balkan Peninsula and advised his fellow Russians to follow the same path.[60]

One should be cautious when reaching a conclusion about the relationship between the state and intelligentsia in late imperial Russia only by looking at Miliukov's statements, but the fact that RAIK's archaeological projects received support from Nicholas II on the one hand and Miliukov on the other, people at the opposite ends of the political spectrum in domestic affairs, deserves attention. It is possible to argue that despite their different attitudes in domestic issues, there was a certain degree of consensus between intellectuals with different political inclinations as regards Russia's position and identity in international politics. If the political programme of conservative politicians and intellectuals as regards the Balkan question was characterized by Pan-Orthodoxy or Pan-Slavism, Miliukov was attracted by the democratic tendencies of young Balkan nationalists. Consistent in his democratic priorities, Miliukov was at first hopeful about reformist capacity of the Young Turks.[61] Despite these very different starting points, eventually, Russian intellectuals from different walks of life shared the belief that Russia should be actively involved in the affairs of its ethnic and religious brethren. Especially during the First World War, Miliukov came closer to the right wing, and supported Russian seizure of the Straits.[62]

The 1898 Macedonia expedition was an example of RAIK's interest in Slavic antiquities, and it was not the only one. The second excavation of RAIK was conducted in autonomous Bulgaria, near Shumen. The excavations in Aboba,[63] the ancient Bulgarian capital in the 7th–9th centuries, in 1899–1900 was the outcome of Russian–Bulgarian archaeological collaboration. During this excavation Uspenskii worked with Karel Škorpil, lecturer at Varna Gymnasium, M. IU. Popruzhenko from the Imperial Novorossiya University and V. N. Zlatarskii from Sofia High School.[64]

After the first preliminary expedition to Bulgaria in 1896, Director Uspenskii wrote a letter to the Princess of Bulgaria, Marie Louise:

> Your Royal Highness so deeply and correctly evaluates the meaning of archaeological science for national identity and for the development of respect for antiquities. Having before us the experience of European states, I have the firm conviction that only with the initiative of enlightened governments, can archaeological scholarship have a solid scientific basis ... I would be grateful if you had the opportunity to take archaeological study in Bulgaria under the protection of Your Royal Highness.[65]

In this letter, archaeological scholarship was seen both as an indicator of being enlightened and civilized, and as an indispensable part of national consciousness. Just like it was for the Ottoman elites, Europe was taken as an example that should be followed. It is particularly interesting that the director of a Russian national project such as RAIK should stress the role of Europe, not Russia, as a role model for Bulgarian scholarship. As a matter of fact, Europe was an example for Russian archaeologists as well, and increasing level of involvement in archaeological activities was an assertion of Russian equality with Europe in cultural terms. Taking the lead in an area closest to Russian history and identity – the history of Orthodoxy and Slavdom – would affirm that Russia had succeeded in catching up with its European role model in science.

In his letter to the Princess of Bulgaria, Uspenskii emphasized the importance of ancient history for the development of national consciousness with these words: 'Love for [their] antiquities characterises all cultured nations. [This love] stimulates a sense of national identity, which develops with the learning of national history and literature.'[66] Uspenskii stated that individual efforts to study ancient history were insufficient and measures for the preservation and collection of antiquities should be undertaken by the Bulgarian government.[67] He drew a road map for Bulgarian archaeology: he proposed the establishment of central organizations to study antiquities, the preservation and publication of manuscripts, and systematic excavations in ancient sites.[68]

Throughout 1898 Uspenskii tried to establish contact with the Bulgarian Ministry of Education to undertake expeditions in Bulgaria. Not receiving any response, he wrote directly to Prince Ferdinand I of Bulgaria for permission to undertake expeditions and excavations.[69] Upon receiving this letter, Ferdinand I, who was also an honorary member of RAIK,[70] sent a response assuring Uspenskii that he would inquire of the Bulgarian Ministry of Education. Finally, RAIK received permission for archaeological research with the following conditions:

1. RAIK would receive half of the discovered materials.
2. A commission formed by the Bulgarian Ministry of Education would assess the value of monuments.
3. RAIK should clearly delineate its area of excavation.
4. The excavation permit was given only for two years.
5. The Bulgarian Ministry of Education would employ officials from the National Museum in Sofia to help RAIK.
6. If the discovered objects were distinctive in terms of their aesthetic value and historical importance, RAIK had to turn them over to the National Museum in Sofia after the completion of studies. The commission from the Bulgarian Ministry of Education was responsible for determining the value of discovered objects.[71]

Obviously, it was not only the Ottoman government that was sensitive about ownership rights over antiquities, but the autonomous Bulgarian government also expressed its sovereign rights to Russian archaeologists in clear terms. This was after all a logical corollary to Uspenskii's own letter to the princess saying that archaeology was essential to Bulgarian national identity.

The RAIK report from the 1899 expedition to Aboba and Preslav recalled that Bulgarian nationalists blamed the Russians for smuggling Bulgarian antiquities to Russia following the 1878 Russian occupation.[72] The report found this thesis difficult to prove and claimed that Preslav was looted long ago, in addition to being destroyed by the Turks recently in the 19th century. In any case, the disagreement between Russian archaeologists and Bulgarian nationalists showed that the 'liberation' of Bulgaria by the Russian army in 1878 was remembered with mixed feelings by the Bulgarians.

The question of Bulgarian antiquities went back to the Russian occupation of Bulgaria during the 1877–8 Russo-Turkish War. After the retreat of the Russian armies at the end of the war, a large number of senior Russian officers and administrative personnel were left behind to ease the transition of the recently established state, but essentially with an intention to keep the Principality as a Russian dependency.[73] The Russian imperial attitude caused discontent among nationalist Bulgarian leaders, and the bitterness in Russian-Bulgarian relations continued in the next decades. Although by 1898 the relationship was ameliorating, it was still fragile. Whether the Bulgarian antiquities were really smuggled to Russia or not, in any case, the presence of a rumour against Russia among Bulgarian nationalists implied that despite the Russian Empire's self-perception as the saviour of Slavdom and Orthodoxy, the practical reality on the ground was different. Actually, as Uspenskii recalled in his letter to Princess Marie Louise, the love for antiquities indeed stimulated a sense of national identity for Bulgarian patriots. This national identity, however, was specifically marked by 'Bulgarianness', and could turn against Russia too, as the Bulgarian identity was not necessarily expressed within the framework of a broader Slavic and Orthodox identity.

After the preliminary studies in 1896 and 1899[74] and after the securing of permits from the Bulgarian government, excavations in Aboba started in 1900. The excavation team identified the oldest Bulgarian churches and revealed that the first capital of the first Bulgarian Kingdom was Aboba, not Preslav as it had previously been assumed.[75] Among the findings in Aboba was the palace from the early 9th century attributed to the medieval Bulgarian Khan Omurtag, which had an alley of columns with the names of cities Omurtag conquered in Thrace.[76] Part of these columns were brought to the National Museum in Sofia before Russians started excavations. The materials discovered in this expedition were important not only for Bulgarian history but also for the overall history of the Balkan Peninsula.

Among their excursions to the centres of Byzantine-Slavic heritage, RAIK's expedition to Syria in 1900 stood apart in terms of the geographical focus of interest. However, the Syria expedition reflected the same feeling of competition with European archaeologists. In this excursion that took place between April and June 1900, the painter Nikolai Karlovich Kluge (1869–1947) and the dragoman of the Russian consulate in Jerusalem, I. Huri accompanied Uspenskii. Financial support for the expedition came from the IPPO, which donated 5,000 roubles to RAIK for the expedition to ancient Palmyra in Syria.[77] This was a brave undertaking, considering that Syria was also at the centre of European scholarly attention and Russian archaeology was still behind European scholars in methodological and material terms. In fact, the acknowledgement of this shortcoming prompted Russian scholars to focus on Slavic and Byzantine archaeology, fields which were relatively less studied by Europeans, and fields in which Russia had comparative advantage.

The Palmyra expedition was originally motivated by the discovery of the Palmyra Customs Tariff in 1882 by the Russian archaeologist Prince Semyon Semyonovich Abamelek-Lazarev (1857–1916). This important monument, dated from 137 BC, outlined an ancient tax law. It was particularly important from a linguistic perspective, as the text was written in both Aramaic and Greek. In 1884, Abamelek-Lazarev published an article entitled 'Palmyra' about the importance of this monument. After this publication, an idea was born among Russian specialists to acquire the monument for a Russian museum.[78] On 4 May 1899, at a meeting of the Imperial Russian Archaeological Society, P. K. Kokovtsev, a professor from the Department of Hebrew and Assyrian Languages at the Imperial St Petersburg University, strongly supported this opinion. Shortly afterwards, the chairman of the Imperial Academy of Sciences, Grand Duke Konstantin Konstantinovich, wrote a letter to the Russian ambassador in Istanbul, Ivan Zinoviev, inquiring about the possible means for the acquisition of the Palmyra Tariff. Zinoviev showed great interest in this cause, and personally entered into dialogue with Abdülhamid II to acquire the Tariff.

RAIK assumed responsibility for the practical questions surrounding the transfer of the monument. After Uspenskii's preliminary analysis in Palmyra in May 1900, Zinoviev fulfilled the necessary procedures and on 13 October 1900, Abdülhamid II announced that he gave the Palmyra Tariff – seven chests of 'stone' as it was described in the original document – to Grand Duke Sergei Aleksandrovich, who was known to be interested in archaeology.[79] In 1901, Uspenskii visited Syria again to arrange the export of the monument, together with the dragoman, Huri. The stone plates were sent from Palmyra to Damascus, then to Beirut by railway, from Beirut to Odessa, and finally to the Imperial Hermitage in St Petersburg.[80]

While Uspenskii, Kluge, and Huri were busy with the transfer of the monument from Palmyra, they heard rumours circulating in St Petersburg.[81] In the imperial capital, there were concerns among scholars that the dragoman Huri, an incompetent person, was in charge of the transfer. They also feared that Arabs or the Turkish authorities could fool Huri and sell the original Palmyra Tariff to Europeans. Although this fear proved to be ungrounded, the anxiety was caused by the possibility of losing an archaeological trophy to European competitors.

Apparently, European competition was one of the motivations for the Palmyra expedition. Professor Kokovtsev, who worked on the tombstones acquired from Palmyra in 1901, proudly expressed the important achievement by Russian archaeologists in a field where Europeans took the lead.[82] The painter Kluge, who extended his trip to Palestine and Transjordan and made studies in Madeba (in modern Jordan), made a comparison with Catholic missionaries, and remarked that Catholics were very good at publishing and publicizing their studies. Russia, he claimed, could use its links with the Orthodox Arab population to make archaeological discoveries, as well.[83] Archaeological success was identified with imperial prestige and Russian civilizational status. Consequently, the ability to compete with European scholars had a particular importance for Russian archaeologists.

Acquisition of the Palmyra Tariff was definitely one of the most important achievements in RAIK's history, and a sign of increasing self-confidence vis-à-vis their European rivals. On the other hand, by offering the monument as a gift to the Russians, Abdülhamid II actually disregarded the antiquities law of 1884 that the Ottoman Imperial Museum was so sensitive about, since the law very clearly outlawed the transfer of antiquities abroad. Although the transfer of the Palmyra Tariff to Russia contradicted existing regulations, Abdülhamid II's authorization made the deal legal.

Nevertheless, it seems that in addition to such legal acquisitions, RAIK might have acquired antiquities through illegal means as well, although not on a large scale. Russian archaeologists were definitely not the only foreigners who attempted to smuggle antiquities outside Ottoman territories. In fact, with their very limited financial resources, they were less capable of doing so than their European and American competitors. The Russians also started archaeological studies in the Ottoman Empire at a time when the Ottomans had already grown sensitive about cultural property, another factor restricting the possibility of antiquities smuggling.

The exchange between Russian diplomatic representatives in Samsun, an important city on the Black Sea coast, and Uspenskii hint at the possibility of their involvement in a small-scale illegal antiquities trade. In November 1902, the Russian vice consul in Samsun, Viktor Fedorovich Kal', sent epitaphs to RAIK from the ancient city of Amisos near modern Samsun and asked Uspenskii to determine a price for these ancient objects.[84] The conversation about the prices of antiquities implied that Kal' probably received antiquities from a local dealer and acted as intermediary between RAIK and the dealer. In fact, a similar letter from Kal' to Uspenskii written a month later clarified this network a little more. In December 1902, Kal' sent artefacts, which he personally bought from a local resident, as gifts to RAIK. These artefacts included silver and bronze objects, necklaces, earrings, rings and pieces from an Apollo statue. However, he stated, these were not all the objects. In this letter Kal' explained that a certain Uzun Mihal, whom he described as the only person interested in archaeology in Samsun, conducted secret excavations around Amisos, especially in the ancient necropolis from the

Roman period.[85] According to Mihal's testimony, professional excavations in the nearby theatre and temple could produce promising results.

Kal' continued to send ancient objects to RAIK throughout 1903. In February 1903, he sent three bronze Byzantine crosses, found near Vona, Ordu on the Black Sea coast.[86] Kal' wrote that he bought these objects very cheap, and asked for the amount from Uspenskii. It is understood from the letter that Uspenskii specifically wanted these pieces. Kal' also promised that he would let Uspenskii know if there would be secret excavations around Samsun. In June 1903, he further sent two packages full of antiquities, including bronze plaques to RAIK. Some of these artefacts were Kal's gifts but for some he asked Uspenskii to pay an amount he deemed sufficient.[87]

Upon the information provided by Kal', it appeared that Samsun was a promising location for archaeological research. In 1904, Uspenskii sent RAIK member Leper to Samsun for preliminary research. On this trip, Leper did not encounter any obstacles from the Ottoman authorities. In addition to Samsun, Leper visited Sinop, Giresun, Inebolu and Ordu on the Turkish Black Sea coast. He investigated the cultural links between Amisos near Samsun and Panticapaeum near Kerch, and the overall connection between the Turkish Black Sea coast and southern Russia, which were linked by the common Pontic heritage.[88]

In June 1904, Uspenskii asked Ambassador Zinoviev to help him secure a permit to make excavations in Samsun in the autumn of 1904, explaining that there were already illegal excavations in the region and proper excavations would save antiquities from being plundered.[89] After Pateli, this was the second time RAIK asked to undertake excavations in the jurisdiction area of the Ottoman Imperial Museum. This time, the excavation request failed from the start and the Ottoman government did not allow the Russians to undertake excavations in Samsun. Nearly a year later, in May 1905, Zinoviev notified Uspenskii that the Ottoman government was in the process of promulgating a new antiquities law and would not allow excavations until its finalization.[90] In his letter to Zinoviev from May 1905, Uspenskii complained that the promulgation of the new law did not prevent the Ottoman government from granting excavation permits to the Berlin Museum in Didyma; even the German ambassador was present at the excavation site.[91] Uspenskii stressed that RAIK was different from such individual projects – RAIK had a permanent status and a permanently valid permit received from the Sultan in 1897. He stated that the privileges granted by the Sultan could not be abrogated by another institution, even in case of the promulgation of a new antiquities law. Only the Sultan himself, Uspenskii noted, could change the legal basis on which RAIK operated in the Ottoman Empire.

Uspenskii asked Zinoviev to bring the issue to the attention of the Porte again. After examining Uspenskii's objection, the Ottoman Ministry of the Interior stated that the right to make excavations on Ottoman territories belonged only to the Ottoman Imperial Museum, hence foreign scientific societies and foreign researchers could excavate only exceptionally and with a special permission from the Ottoman Imperial Museum. In case of a second appeal by the Russians, the Ministry of the Interior suggested to the Ottoman Ministry of Foreign Affairs to notify the Russian Embassy about this situation in an appropriate manner.[92] In the end, Uspenskii could not get permission for the planned excavation in Samsun.

The general discontent about Ottoman antiquities regulations prompted foreign scholars to solve the issue through diplomatic and political channels. In 1906, the director of the Royal Museum in Berlin, Theodor Wiegand (1864–1936) visited RAIK, where he discussed the issue of Ottoman surveillance with Uspenskii.[93] Uspenskii adamantly argued that the question regarding the new Ottoman antiquities regulation of 1906 should be brought before the embassies, since the rights of foreigners in the Ottoman Empire were at stake. Wiegand, in response, assured Uspenskii that he would inform relevant German institutions and the German government would join every step taken by the Russian Embassy in the desired direction.

Nevertheless, to the dismay of Uspenskii and other foreign archaeologists, the new antiquities regulation had a clause restricting the possibility of an appeal through diplomatic action in cases of conflict with the existing law. Article no. 33 of the new regulation had a clear clause about that matter: 'Conflicts with the existing law are within the responsibility of civil courts.'[94] Uspenskii particularly expressed his disappointment about this article.[95]

Criticizing the response of the Ottoman government, Uspenskii referred to the 1897 *irade* of the Sultan, which provided a legal basis for the studies of Russian archaeologists.[96] He concluded that it was clearly expressed in the text of the *irade* that RAIK was recognized as a special foreign institution operating in the Ottoman Empire. Although the *irade* contained a provision about the necessity of compliance with Ottoman regulations, like asking for permission from the Ottoman Ministry of Education and notifying them about the exact time and location of research, the privileges bestowed upon RAIK were granted permanently. Nelidov viewed this *irade* as a special kindness on the part of the Sultan and thought that it would permit RAIK to engage in archaeological activities without obstacle. The recognition of RAIK as a scholarly institution receiving special privileges should not only liberate it from the proposed regulations concerning archaeological excavations, but should also create a special legal basis for its activities.

Uspenskii complained that the Ottoman government unilaterally changed the laws regarding antiquities, and with the promulgation of this new law RAIK's interests were disregarded. In fact, it was only natural for the Ottoman government to issue the mentioned law without consulting foreigners, because the antiquities question was undoubtedly a domestic matter. However, since the name of RAIK was not openly mentioned in the law, Uspenskii felt that RAIK was being ignored. He stated, 'Not having the opportunity to negotiate, [RAIK] was put face to face with the already approved and issued law.' The 1906 law included an article that practically abolished the privileges granted by the Sultan to RAIK: 'provisions regarding antiquities that are contrary to this law will be repealed.'⁹⁷ In fact, as previous excavation in Pateli proved, RAIK's privileges were largely non-functional and it is difficult to say that Russian archaeologists enjoyed any real advantages derived from the Sultan's earlier decree.

Despite Uspenskii's complaints about Ottoman double standards against Russians, not only Russians but all foreign archaeologists were compelled to obey Ottoman antiquities regulations. By mid-1905, even Germans, Abdülhamid II's allies, were at an all-time low in their relations with Osman Hamdi Bey. The reluctance of some German archaeologists to comply with Ottoman regulations brought excavations at Babylon, Assur and Pergamon to a halt, while the future of digs at Baalbek, Miletus and Didyma was uncertain. The German archaeologist Robert Koldewey (1855–1925) expressed his dissatisfaction about the strict order from the German Embassy in Istanbul asking German archaeologists to obey Ottoman regulations. Koldewey complained, 'If I take the communications from Istanbul seriously, we would do well here, when his Excellence Hamdi Bey slaps us on the left cheek, not only to offer him the right cheek, but to thank him most politely.'⁹⁸ The letters of the Russian consul in Baghdad to Uspenskii from 1911 recounted that the failure to comply with regulations brought German archaeologists into conflict with Ottoman authorities and that the Ottomans were very unlikely to give ancient objects to the Germans.⁹⁹

Particularly after 1906 the Ottoman government monitored foreign archaeologists more seriously. Suspicion of Russian archaeologists was especially evident, if the expeditions were made in strategic locations. For instance, when local authorities noticed that one of the members of RAIK and his interpreter were drawing maps around the Sakarya River, which ran from the east of Istanbul before reaching the Black Sea, it was seen as a highly dubious act and the Ministry of the Interior warned local authorities not to allow map-drawing in this region.¹⁰⁰

Uspenskii and his colleagues received permission to make scientific investigations from 1908 to 1914, mostly examining Byzantine monuments around Istanbul, but there is no document from this period complaining either about suspicious activities on the part of Russian archaeologists or about the failure to enforce Ottoman regulations.[101] After 1906, there are significantly fewer documents about Russian archaeological activities in the Ottoman archives. Right after the new regulation was promulgated, the Russian Embassy requested an official permit for the continuation of archaeological investigations by RAIK.[102] Uspenskii received permission to make some investigations, take photographs and make drawings of ancient monuments in the Edirne province and around Istanbul.[103]

Unable to receive permission for excavations and seriously restricted in their scientific studies both by Ottoman regulations and financial constraints, Russian archaeologists turned their attention to areas they could more easily handle. Receiving permits for surveys was easier to obtain than excavations in Ottoman territories. Therefore, after 1906 RAIK devoted its energy to make surveys of Byzantine monuments, mostly in regions within close proximity to Istanbul. One of the most successful examples of such a survey was their study in the Kasımiye Mosque in Selânik.

In late 1907 and early 1908 the Turks started to restore the Kasımiye Mosque in Selânik. This monument was originally a Byzantine church from the 5th century, the Church of Hagios Demetrios, before being converted into a mosque by the Ottomans in the late 15th century. In January 1908, N. V. Kokhmanskii, the Russian consul general in Selânik, sent a letter to Uspenskii to inform him about the repairs.[104] The Russian consulate general engaged in dialogue with the governor of Selânik, Mehmed Şerif Rauf Pasha, to facilitate studies in the church-converted-mosque. Kokhmanskii said that the governor of Selânik was especially amiable and concerned with the 'benefits of science', which should be used as an advantage.[105] The Governor Mehmed Şerif Rauf Pasha inquired if an album would be published about the mosaics after the scientific work was completed.

As a result of the restoration, the plaster covering the frescoes and mosaics was removed from the walls and magnificent works of art were revealed. Hearing this, Uspenskii went to Selânik in the winter of 1908, but when he arrived at the city the refurbishment of the mosque was nearly done. Most parts of the walls were again covered with plaster and workers started drawing Muslim signs on the walls. Because the apse was totally covered with Muslim signs and it was not possible to touch them after they were made, Uspenskii restricted his analysis to other parts of the church.[106] The painter Kluge copied the mosaics and frescoes that were not yet covered. The mosaics of the church-mosque were mostly about the life and miracles of St Demetrius, the patron saint of Thessaloniki, and were important for the history of Orthodox Christianity and Byzantine iconography.[107]

4.1 Studies in Istanbul

Of course, as the former capital of the Byzantine Empire and cradle of Orthodoxy, Istanbul was the focus of RAIK's scholarly attention from the start, and deserves to be analysed under a separate heading. In the course of the twenty years of its existence, RAIK made numerous studies around Istanbul and regularly published them in the *Izvestiia*. As soon as RAIK's office was opened in 1895, the archaeologists undertook a preliminary expedition to familiarize themselves with the monuments of the city. The capital of the Byzantine emperors received the lion's share in terms of the numbers of articles and lectures RAIK produced. The archaeological interest in Istanbul echoed the political sensitivities of significant numbers of influential Russian intellectuals, who dreamed that one day Istanbul would be 'liberated' from the Turkish rule, and might indeed be governed by Russia.[108]

The first remarkable study of RAIK in Istanbul was carried out in Kariye Mosque, or the Chora Church before its transformation into a mosque by the Ottomans. Built as part of a monastic complex in the 5th century, Chora Church was transformed into a mosque by the Ottomans in the early 16th century. The mosaics and frescoes in the interior were examples of the Palaeologian Renaissance of the 14th century. In March 1899, Uspenskii asked permission through Ambassador Zinoviev to make architectural plans, take photographs and make sketches of mosaics and frescoes inside Kariye.[109] He pointed to the danger posed for the monument, whose art treasures were threatened by neglect. Uspenskii was already in communication with the president of the Imperial Academy of Arts, Count I. I. Tolstoy, to commission a painter and photographer to help prepare the reproductions of mosaics. The Imperial Academy entrusted N. K. Kluge with this task.[110] Shortly after Uspenskii's request, the Ministry of Religious Foundations granted a permit for the study of the monument.[111] The Minister notified the Russian ambassador that he would provide any necessary help in case need arose.[112] The work in Kariye was completed in 1904 and results of the study were published as an album. Tsar Nicholas II made a personal donation of 10,000 roubles for the publication of Kariye mosaics.[113] This donation was another instance showing the Tsar's sympathy for the RAIK enterprise.

RAIK started the systematic study of the topography of Istanbul in 1902. Even though the investigations of Russian archaeologists in this period were closely followed by Ottoman officials, the Russians were allowed to take photographs, draw sketches of monuments and were provided with assistance when necessary.[114] In 1903, after much difficulty, Uspenskii managed to receive a permit to do research in the library of the Topkapı Palace, which he continued with intermittently until 1914. In addition to a large collection of Islamic manuscripts, this library also contained books and manuscripts that the Ottomans inherited from the Byzantine emperors.[115] Here Uspenskii discovered the famous Topkapı Octateuch Bible from the 12th century, also known as the Seraglio Octateuch.[116] Important both for its artwork and for its content, the Topkapı Octateuch was an important literary monument from the Comnenos dynasty. The foreword of the Topkapı Octateuch was written by Isaak Comnenos, son of Alexios I Comnenos.[117] In 1903, RAIK received an additional permit to take photographs of the miniatures in the manuscript. The Imperial Russian Archaeological Society gave Uspenskii an award for his work on the Topkapı Octateuch.[118] Uspenskii recalled that he could not see all parts of the Topkapı library due to the suspicious attitudes of the Ottomans, who monitored him closely during his study at the Palace.[119]

RAIK undertook important studies at the İmrahor Mosque, or the Monastery of Stoudios in the years 1906–9, under the guidance of B. A. Panchenko. Historically, the Monastery of Stoudios was the most important Byzantine monastery in Istanbul. The only remaining part of the original monastic complex in the 19th–20th century was the remnants of a 5th-century basilica, which was converted into a mosque by the Ottomans in the late 15th century. Until 1906, RAIK could not receive a permit to make studies in the interior of İmrahor, as it was closed after the 1894 earthquake. After two years of struggle, the Russians finally secured a permit in late 1906 from the Ministry of Religious Foundations to make a survey, at a time when there was a restoration going on at the building. However, this permit was short-lived and Russian archaeologists were not allowed to continue their studies in 1907.[120] Uspenskii recalled that in 1907 the Ottoman government created obstacles to foreigners who wanted to visit mosques converted from churches, even Hagia Sophia.[121]

In 1909, thanks to repeated requests of the Russian ambassador to the Grand Vizier Hüseyin Hilmi Pasha and the Minister of Religious Foundations Halil Hamdi Hamada Pasha, RAIK finally received permit to remove the plaster on the walls and to make excavation in the interior of the half-ruined mosque.[122] Until then there had been a number of Europeans who made topographic and architectural studies in Istanbul, but receiving excavation permits in the Ottoman capital was nearly impossible. The only exception was the British archaeologist Charles Newton's excavation in the Hippodrome in 1855, when Britain and the Ottoman Empire were allies during the Crimean War.[123] The Russian excavation in İmrahor was important in the sense that it was the first excavation linked to Istanbul's Christian past. The excavations continued from September to December 1909.[124] Although it was inferior to Kariye in artistic terms, historically, the Monastery of Stoudios had a particular importance for Russian religious history. The monastic charter of the Kiev-Pechersk Lavra was based on the example of the Monastery of Stoudios.[125]

At the end of July 1912 a great fire in Istanbul destroyed the Turkish quarters of the city from the east of Hagia Sophia and Hippodrome nearly up to the sea. The Great Palace of the Byzantine emperors, constructed in the 4th century during the reign of Constantine the Great, was believed to be in this area. After the fire, among the burnt stones of Turkish houses, the terraces, foundation and even the lower floors of the imperial palace were revealed. Before the reconstruction of the burnt quarters started, it would be very convenient to study the topography of the imperial palace. RAIK secured permission from the Ottoman government to make plans, drawings and take photographs, and topographical studies started in spring 1913 under the guidance of RAIK's co-secretary B. A. Panchenko.[126] Before 1914, Russian archaeologists were in preparation of a large-scale excavation in this part of the city, but the outbreak of the First World War interfered in this first systematic study of Istanbul's Byzantine past.

Conclusion

The Balkans and Istanbul received by far the lion's share in RAIK's expeditions and excavations. RAIK not only contributed to the study of Byzantine and Slavic history and archaeology but also to the study of Orthodox theology, as was exemplified by the close collaboration between RAIK and the Holy Synod. Sometimes by its own staff and sometimes in collaboration with fellows from the Holy Synod, RAIK made extensive research in the churches, monasteries and monastic libraries in Bulgaria, Ottoman Macedonia, Mount Athos, Mount Sinai, as well as in the archives of the Orthodox Patriarchate of Constantinople.[127] These clergy-scholars delved into the history of the Orthodox Church, as well as examining theological, liturgical and canonical questions. The confluence of religion and archaeology hints at the motivation behind Russian archaeological activities and imperial Russian policy in the Ottoman Empire.

In addition to scholars from theological academies, RAIK cooperated with world-wide famous historians such as Mikhail Rostovtsev, Pavel Miliukov, A. A. Vasiliev and Pavel Kokovtsev. Foreign scholars such as Josef Strzygowski, Theodor Wiegand, Karel Škorpil and Konstantin Jireček also made contributions to RAIK's studies. Notwithstanding the obvious political motivations of diplomats and bureaucrats for supporting archaeological studies in the Ottoman Empire, the existence of an academic network that divided across ideological, national and imperial lines indicated a genuine scientific concern on the part of scholars.

What does this scientific network tell the modern reader about the independence of researchers from the state? In fact, the relationship between state and researchers was too complex to fit into the dependent–independent dichotomy. Two secretaries of RAIK, Pogodin and Shmit, had familial relations with two notable bureaucrats, Tertii Filippov and Aleksandr Nelidov, respectively, but these personal relationships did not necessarily compromise RAIK's status as a scholarly institution. After all, it was not bureaucrats but scholars, Uspenskii, Kondakov and Kirpichnikov who drafted the institute's charter, and once RAIK was established, it was Uspenskii who determined the direction of expeditions. Uspenskii, as the mastermind and the principal decision-maker for RAIK, tried to achieve his vision of reclaiming Byzantine antiquities by using the government's resources. Yet, his financial dependency on the government did not mean that he received orders from the Russian Embassy in Istanbul. The director's accommodation of Pavel Miliukov, a well-known political dissident, in Istanbul was a case in point. Uspenskii was not subordinate to the Embassy, but he also did not contradict the diplomats' political vision with his scientific activities. Therefore, he independently pursued his scientific goals without posing a political alternative to Russian diplomatic representatives.

Just like Osman Hamdi Bey was identified with the Ottoman Imperial Museum, Uspenskii was identified with RAIK, and rightfully so, as RAIK was mostly Uspenskii's personal project. Other scholars, even secretaries, witnessed certain periods of RAIK's history, yet Uspenskii was the only person who shaped the institute's path from its establishment to its demise. This is why this study was mostly mute about the perspectives of other scholars affiliated with RAIK.

Compared to the Ottoman Empire, Russia had a longer history of university education, and even though the autonomy of universities in the autocratic Russian Empire was very much open to speculation, at least scholars could push their limits to create an independent scholarly space. The same cannot be said for the Ottoman Empire, which lacked the institutional basis for the development of archaeology in an academic setting.

One similarity between the two empires, though, was that both Ottomans and Russians learnt archaeological methodology from European scholars and they took Europe both as an example and as a rival at the same time. In the expedition reports, in private correspondence, and in other documents, Russian archaeologists and diplomats explained the necessity of establishing an archaeological institute with reference to rivalry with European powers, but they also expressed themselves in the context of values and objectives defined by Europe. Acquisition of ancient monuments in Ottoman territories, when European collectors were competing for the same antiquities, was seen as a victory, as was exemplified by the acquisition of the Palmyra Tariff and the Sarmısaklı Codex. If archaeological glories reflected imperial prestige and if the Louvre, the British Museum, and later the Pergamon Museum competed with each other to visualize the grandeur of their respective empires, then the Imperial Hermitage had to be a part of this competition, too.

In the discourse of Russian archaeologists and diplomats, being a great power was identified with investment in the academic study of history. Certainly, linking historical studies to imperial status was not limited to Russian scholars, as European governments were also supporting historical studies with similar motivations and European scholars were also competing with each other in academic terms. Actually, Russian scholars' allegiance to an initially Western concept of academic excellence and value showed the internalization of these values by Russian elites. In their legitimization of RAIK's activities, Russian diplomats and scholars regarded historical consciousness and interest in antiquities as a sign of being enlightened. Therefore, falling behind Europe would be detrimental to the international prestige of the Russian Empire. The establishment of an archaeological institute in Istanbul was partly an attempt to prove Russia's imperial standing. Archaeological studies, the very act of bringing a monument to Russia was regarded as a sign of imperial glory.

A very often and explicitly repeated reason for supporting RAIK's activities was extending influence over the Near East through science and cultural institutions. Both Russian diplomats and scholars cited examples from European powers, most notably France, to point to the importance of cultural influence. 'Soft power', in modern parlance, was Russia's weak side and Russian diplomats who came up with the RAIK project were aware of this shortfall. Nevertheless, they tried to infiltrate Ottoman territories and the Balkans through an archaic identity and used slogans from another century, like Orthodoxy and Slavdom. Although in the late 19th century some intellectuals in the imperial centres propagated pan-nationalist programmes, the intellectuals of the newly emerging nation-states prioritized local identities over pan-national identities. In the age of rising micro-nationalism in the Balkans, ancient monuments were not defined as 'Slavic' or 'Orthodox', but as the remnants of particular nations. Strict Bulgarian surveillance of Russian archaeologists proved that the 'Orthodox and Slavic' brethren of Russia were not any less likely to monitor foreign archaeological activities than the Ottomans.

The Ottoman government, on the other hand, was on the defensive in its relationship with Russian archaeologists, as the provider of antiquities. Russian archaeologists arrived in the Ottoman Empire relatively late, compared to the French, the British or Germans. As long as their activities remained scientific and they acted within the confines of Ottoman laws, members of RAIK received permission for archaeological expeditions. Nevertheless, even in this case, their activities were closely supervised by the authorities both in the provinces and in the centre, and Russian archaeologists were frequently reminded of the procedures they should follow. Actually, RAIK's relationship with the Ottoman government was characterized by a combination of cooperation and conflict. On the one hand, Ottomans were suspicious of Russian archaeological activities, and very strictly monitored Russian archaeologists. The openly stated political agenda of RAIK shows that this suspicion was not totally baseless. Also, the Russians were frequently seeking study permits in politically instable regions that were at the forefront of international interest, such as Macedonia, which further increased Ottoman suspicions. On the other hand, Ottoman sensitivity about ownership rights over antiquities was part of a broader Ottoman policy, and was not exercised peculiarly vis-à-vis the Russians.

In addition to suspicions, however, there was also a certain degree of cooperation between the Ottoman government and RAIK. Although the director of the Ottoman Museum Osman Hamdi Bey was described as very distant by Russians, in the end, the Ottoman legal framework made RAIK's studies possible. RAIK even found the opportunity to make excavations in Istanbul, a very rare opportunity for foreign scholars. Despite their reservations, the Ottoman government provided necessary conditions for archaeological research. In this context, being supportive of science was a sign of being part of the 'enlightened' and 'civilized' world, and the Ottoman Empire could not risk being perceived as backward and unsupportive of scientific activities by foreigners. Ottoman sensitivity made sense in the context of the highly fluid international political atmosphere of the late 19th–early 20th century and of the dominant values of the era. In an attempt to survive as a viable political entity and reinforce its vulnerable sovereignty, the Ottoman Empire launched its project of modernity, and archaeology was a symbolic manifestation of this endeavour.

There was a radical transformation in both countries after the First World War and the patterns of relationship fundamentally changed. The contrast between the periods before and after the First World War further proved the political nature of RAIK's activities. The radical political change and the new identity promoted by the Bolsheviks indicated why Byzantine studies lost their appeal for the Soviet regime.

5

On the eve of the Balkan Wars: Archaeology in the midst of political unrest

As repeatedly noted in this book, the Balkans, along with Istanbul and the Black Sea littoral were the key regions that attracted RAIK's scholarly interest. However, amidst the growing political tensions in the first decade of the 20th century, it became more and more difficult for RAIK to undertake expeditions in the Balkan region, especially in Macedonia. The story of RAIK's expeditions in the Balkans illustrated why the ideological background that characterised the establishment of RAIK, was not a viable political project. Since the Russian Empire based its foreign policy to a certain extent on religious and ethnic principles like Orthodoxy and Slavdom the rise of micro-nationalism caused Russian foreign policy many problems. When the Orthodox believers and Slavs fought with each other, Russia found itself in a delicate position. Therefore, the primary motivation behind RAIK, extending influence over the Balkan Peninsula through studying the history of Orthodoxy and Slavdom was problematic, because ancient monuments were no longer defined broadly as remnants of Orthodox or Slavic civilization. Instead, they were seen as symbols of particular national histories. The causes of conflict in the Balkans were so complicated and multifaceted that it would be a crude simplification to assume that the only obstacles on Russia's path were other European powers and the Ottoman Empire. In fact, shortly before the Balkan Wars, ethnic tensions in the Balkans reached a level beyond the control of any imperial entity, including Russia.

The political background of RAIK's expeditions in the Balkans testified to the complications Russia faced in the region at the turn of the century. One example was RAIK member Fyodor Ivanovich Shmit's (1877–1956) visit to Selânik in 1903 for a brief observation of Byzantine monuments of the city.[1] The year 1903 was a very tense one for Russian-Ottoman relations, especially in Macedonia. After the failed Ilinden Uprising precipitated by the Internal Macedonian Revolutionary Organization (IMRO), Austria-Hungary and Russia compelled the Ottoman Empire to follow the Mürzsteg reform program to consolidate order in the region. Very unwillingly, the Sultan accepted the Austro-Russian terms; however, this made things only worse: an article in the program called for the redrawing of districts according to ethnic lines once order was restored, which brought more nationalistic propaganda and violence as rival Balkan states and nationalist bands struggled to create 'facts on the ground' in Macedonia.[2]

On an international scale, Russian rapprochement with Austria after the Mürzsteg talks secured the status quo on the Balkan front, as Russia turned its face towards Asia in the very first years of the 20th century. After the Russian defeat at the Russo-Japanese War of 1904, Russia redirected its attention back to the Balkans, which automatically brought Austria and Russia against each other. In fact, Mürzsteg happened to be the last instance of cooperation between Russia and Austria-Hungary in Balkan affairs.[3] The events that followed the last decade before the First World War antagonized Russia's relations with Austria and Germany, while bringing the former closer first to France, and then to Britain.[4]

During Shmit's Selânik expedition, interethnic violence in Macedonia resulted in the murder of a Russian diplomat. In a letter to Uspenskii, Shmit expressed his sadness about the recent murder of the Russian consul in Manastır (Bitola), Aleksandr Arkadievich Rostkovskii, who had always been a supporter of RAIK's activities in Ottoman Macedonia.[5] On 8 August 1903, Rostkovskii was shot dead by an Ottoman soldier of Albanian origin.[6] The Russian government responded strongly: although Abdülhamid II and ministers of the Ottoman government sent condolences, Russia sent part of its Black Sea fleet to Ottoman territorial waters and demanded a reform program for Macedonia. Abdülhamid II accepted Russia's terms and a more serious diplomatic crisis was avoided. In fact, this was not the first time a Russian diplomat was murdered in Ottoman Macedonia. Earlier in 1903, the Russian consul in Mitrovitsa, G. Shcherbin was also murdered by an Albanian, who protested against the opening of a Russian consulate in the city.[7]

Shmit reported that as was the case of the previously murdered Russian consul, Shcherbin, the murderer of Rostkovskii was sentenced to paying 10,000 roubles to the family of the victim.[8] Although the Sultan gave condolences to Zinoviev, Shmit criticized the decision of the Turkish government to take the murder to a civil court instead of a military court, and commented that the murderers had no reason to fear, when they knew they would be pardoned.

From 1904 to 1908, the breakdown of the Ottoman authority increased lawlessness in Macedonia. Not only Macedonian Christians but also Muslims were uneasy about great power intervention, and the murder of Russian consuls were only two instances reflecting the resentment of the

Muslim population at the interference of European powers. The violent conflicts between Greek, Bulgarian and Serbian bands in Macedonia forced local populations to identify themselves with one of these national groups, thereby legitimizing the nationalists' territorial claims for Macedonia's future 'liberation.' As Mark Mazower commented, 'Ethnicity was as much the consequence as the cause of this unrest; revolutionary violence produced national affiliations as well as being produced by them.'[9]

For a short time, it seemed that at least the Bulgarian and Serbian governments could come to an agreement. After the failed Ilinden Uprising, Serbian and Bulgarian nationalists realized that the support of European powers, including Russia, was inconsistent, unreliable and depended on power politics. The disillusionment with imperial powers brought Serbian and Bulgarian nationalists together against foreign intervention, although the Serbo-Bulgarian cooperation did not last long.[10] The two Balkan governments signed two treaties – a treaty of friendship and a treaty of political alliance in 1904. Despite this brief rapprochement, the Macedonian question continued to be a bone of contention between the two Balkan countries. In fact, the 1904 agreement between Serbia and Bulgaria proved to be short-lived and fell short of sorting out differences between the two governments.

The Macedonian Crisis reached a climax in 1908, when a number of factors combined to create a crisis at both international and domestic levels. The 1908 crisis also paved the way for future alliances and antagonisms that eventually led to the Balkan Wars and the First World War. The 1908 Young Turk Revolution originated in the crisis-ridden Macedonia. The Young Turks gave utmost importance to preserving the integrity of the Ottoman Empire through centralizing the administration. They were uncomfortable both about European breach of Ottoman sovereignty and the expansion of young nation-states in their vicinity. The Young Turks were more heterogeneous in their political outlook than is generally argued and the overall orientation of their foreign policy fluctuated over time.[11] Until the outbreak of the First World War, different political figures from the Young Turk government sought alliances with Britain, France, Germany and Austria. Although they generally maintained a suspicious attitude towards the Russians for their involvement in Balkan affairs, it would be incorrect to say that the Young Turks had a consistently anti-Russian policy line. The eventual alliance with the Germans, who had significant economic interests in the Ottoman Empire, was a contextual outcome, rather than the result of a systematic policy.

The year 1908 was stage to other important developments of international scale, as immediately after the Young Turk Revolution, Austria-Hungary annexed Bosnia, Greece annexed Crete and Bulgaria declared independence. In the meantime, the balance of power in European diplomacy changed from the late 19th century to the first decade of the 20th century. After the Austrian annexation of Bosnia, Russia actively worked to create a Serbian-Bulgarian alliance to contain Austro-Hungarian influence in the Balkans, although in time it was revealed that Serbia, Bulgaria and Russia had contradicting motivations for entering into this alliance.[12] Not surprisingly, Austria-Hungary was also worried about the expansion of Russian influence in the Balkans and the spread of nationalist propaganda within its borders.

In this political atmosphere, Russia came closer to France and Britain, its former rivals over the Near East. Although the traditional British anxiety about Russian control of the Straits did not calm down, the nature of Russian-British relations changed in the first decade of the 20th century. For one reason, Russia's agreement with the French meant that any conflict with Russia would automatically bring Britain into a conflict with France, which was a deterrent factor for the British.[13] Moreover, Britain's strengthened position in Egypt, and sophisticated naval methods made the Royal Navy less concerned about Russia's position in the Straits than it was in the past.[14] At the same time, Russian diplomats were aware that protecting the balance of power was crucial until Russia was strong enough to capture the Straits. After a series of talks between Russian and British diplomats from 1904 to 1907, the two countries ironed out their differences and signed the Anglo-Russian Convention in August 1907, which brought Russia closer to fulfilling its desires over the Straits question.[15] Eventually, by 1908, Austria-Hungary and Germany grouped on one side, while Russia, Britain and France grouped on the other side.

Although the Austro-Russian reform programme of 1903 was intended to reduce violence in Macedonia, in fact the tension never decreased in the province between then and the outbreak of the Balkan Wars in 1912. To the already existing conflicts between Greeks, Bulgarians, Serbs and the Ottoman government, Albanian discontent was added as a new element in the early 20th century, a development that would impact the future of Macedonia. Originally, Albanian elites were not interested in total independence from Ottoman rule, they rather sought moderate reform. Many educated Albanians, either Christian or Muslim, sided with the Young Turk Revolution because they saw a promise of liberty in the Young Turk regime.[16] However, the relations between Albanians and the Young Turks soon got sourer as the new regime pursued a policy of centralization and Turkish nationalism.

The agitation among Muslim Albanians caused anxiety on the part of the Slav population of Macedonia, who feared an independent Albania might be detrimental to their interests. On the other hand, the Ottoman government was also uneasy about Albanian demands, because increasing political instability meant weakening of effective Ottoman rule.[17] Albanian demands for autonomy coincided both with the overall Macedonian crisis and with a reaction against the Young Turk regime.[18] The lands demanded by the Albanians were contested both by Greeks and Serbians, and the situation only resulted in the further escalation of violence.

RAIK's expedition to Old Serbia in 1908 was carried out under the shadow of the Albanian crisis and the above-mentioned political background. The aim of the expedition was to investigate the Decani Monastery near the town İpek (Pecs), which was built in the 14th century by the Serbian King Stefan Uroš III. The Decani Monastery had a significant place in Serbian nationalist imagination, as it was the patriarchal seat of the medieval Serbian Kingdom. In the early 20th century, the monastery was also the setting for an interethnic conflict between Albanians and Serbians. Threatened by Albanian raids and irresponsible administration on the part of Serbian monks, the monastery was on the brink of collapse. In order to attract Russian financial and political support, Nikephor, the Metropolitan of Rashka and Prizren, decided to invite Russian monks from Mount Athos to Decani in 1902.[19]

Uspenskii recalled that in the midst of anarchy, he managed to collect valuable ancient materials in Decani that were until then unknown in the scientific world. In the expedition report, in addition to making scientific analyses about ancient monasteries in Old Serbia, Uspenskii gave information about the sociopolitical conditions in the region and the relations between the Albanians, Bulgarians and Serbs. He made remarks about the level of welfare of the region's inhabitants and the inappropriate conditions in which he made the expedition.

The inspector general of the Three Macedonian *Vilayets*, Hüseyin Hilmi Pasha, offered help to Uspenskii on his expedition to Decani, provided the Russian archaeologists with a military escort and suggested the least dangerous routes.[20] In the expedition report, Uspenskii explained that 'limitless arbitrariness' ruled over Old Serbia and Macedonia: there was intense animosity between Muslims and Christians, Albanians and Slavs, and even among different Albanian tribes. The Serbian Patriarchate and monasteries were threatened by armed Albanian bands. In Decani, the monastery was protected by the Turkish garrison stationed inside the monastery but as soon as the Ottoman forces left, the monastery faced destruction.[21] Ottoman authority was practically non-existent in the region. In their correspondence, the Russian consul in Skopje, Arkadii Aleksandrovich Orlov explained to Uspenskii that the major reason behind the conflict was economic, but in the absence of an authority to resolve economic problems, the question evolved into an ethnic conflict.[22]

There was also a minor disagreement between Serbian authorities and Uspenskii following the 1908 Decani expedition. Already irritated by the presence of Russian monks in their premises, Serbian monks complained that Russians took out valuable manuscripts from the monastery. The issue was raised by the Serbian Royal Academy and finally by Serbian Ministry of Foreign Affairs. In May 1908, Uspenskii assured the Serbian diplomats in Istanbul that the manuscripts were safe in his hands and pledged to return them to the monastery once his research was over.[23]

In the aftermath of the Balkan Wars, shortly before the closure of RAIK, Uspenskii made a plea for financial support from the Russian government to undertake a second expedition to Old Serbia.[24] He pointed out that in the changing political climate after the war, the most historically important regions passed into Serbian possession, which therefore opened up new scientific opportunities for RAIK. Since the systematic study of Serbian antiquities exceeded the financial means of Serbian archaeologists, the burden, Uspenskii claimed, fell on Russia's shoulders. However, the outbreak of the First World War in 1914 made this plan impossible.

5.1 The establishment of the Slavic Department within RAIK

No other project reflected the ideological motivation of RAIK as clearly as the efforts at creating a Slavic Department within the institute in 1911. Despite being a failed project, the circumstances in which it failed indicates the complexities and limits of Russian foreign policy in the Balkans at the turn of the century. In fact, the failure to create a Slavic Department in RAIK shows the discrepancy between the political realities of the Balkans and the ambiguous Pan-Slav sympathies of Russian diplomats and scholars. Russia's religious and ethnic brethren – *edinovertsy i edinoplemenniki* – did not necessarily define themselves on the grounds of being Slav or Orthodox. The umbrella identity of which Russia saw itself as the protector, was already crumbling on the eve of the Balkan Wars.

Russian foreign policy in the Macedonian crisis – creating Pan-Slavic solidarity with mixed messages about Slavdom and Orthodoxy – accorded with RAIK's academic interests. In the practical world of politics, the Russian government viewed itself as the 'big brother' of the Orthodox Slavs of the Balkan Peninsula. In this regard, the focus of RAIK's studies suited the government's direction: Russian archaeologists studied the history of Byzantium, but emphasized the influence of Slavs on Byzantine institutions, and collaborated with Serbian and Bulgarian, rather than Greek scholars. It was explained in Chapter 2 that Russian Byzantine studies was very much linked to Slavic studies and many Russian Byzantinists studied the relations between the Byzantine Empire and the Slavic world. Ideologically, academic interest in Slavic studies was shared by both liberal and conservative intellectuals, as was exemplified by the works of Miliukov on the one, and Lamanskii on the other end of the political spectrum.

From early on, RAIK served as a meeting place for young archaeologists from Balkan countries, meaning Bulgaria and Serbia. Russian archaeologists tried to establish close contacts with Serbian and Bulgarian archaeologists and museums. Article 13 of the RAIK Charter gave the opportunity to foreign scholars to become members and conduct research within RAIK facilities. In the course of RAIK's existence the Serbian government sent three students: I. Radonich and S. Stanoevich were commissioned in 1898–9 and M. Vukchevich in 1902. In 1899–1900 the Bulgarian government sent G. Balaschev to Istanbul to continue his studies under the guidance of Uspenskii.[25] These students completed their studies under the supervision of Uspenskii and returned to their countries as experts in their fields. All of them worked on the history of relations between South Slavs and the Byzantine Empire. Even after they left, the cooperation between RAIK and these scholars continued.

RAIK also financed and jointly directed archaeological field trips with Bulgarian colleagues. One example was the excavation at Aboba in Bulgaria in 1899–1900, which was conducted by Uspenskii and Karel Škorpil.[26] As another sign of scientific collaboration, the bulletin of RAIK was published in Sofia from 1898 to 1912, the remaining issues being published in Odessa.

In early 1910, Uspenskii submitted a note to the Ministry of Public Education and to the Russian ambassador in Istanbul outlining the importance of Balkan history for Russia, as well as pointing to important archaeological discoveries made by RAIK in this region.[27] Uspenskii recalled the discovery of the Tsar Samuil inscription, the excavations in Aboba, extensive research in Macedonia and Old Serbia. Comparing them to RAIK's activities in Asia Minor, Syria and Palestine, Uspenskii concluded that the strength of RAIK, especially considering its material capabilities and the competence of its staff, lay in the Balkans. However, Article 3 of the Charter left the Balkans out of RAIK's geographical scope and did not provide a basis for scientific studies in this region. Considering the successful studies carried out in the Balkans, Uspenskii proposed the enlargement of RAIK's programme. He stated that there were also demands from Bulgarian and Serbian scholars in this direction. He cited a Serbian archaeological journal, *Starinar*, from 1907, which had an article by Dr M. Vasich, the director of the National Museum in Belgrade, arguing that RAIK should enlarge its scope and incorporate prehistorical archaeology to reveal ethnographical and cultural questions. Dr Vasich proposed to divide RAIK into specialized units with secretariats in Serbia, Bulgaria and southern Russia with its centre being in Istanbul.

In November 1909, Vasich and Uspenskii discussed the possible enlargement of RAIK. Vasich reminded Uspenskii of Russia's cultural mission among the Slavs and the 'threatening danger' posed by the West.[28] It appears that Uspenskii was in contact with the representatives of Balkans Slavs in the Ottoman capital, because in the December of the same year, he paid a visit to Bulgarian Exarchate in Istanbul.[29] In order to combine the demands of Balkan scholars with RAIK's activities, Uspenskii proposed the following measures:[30]

1. A department would be established within RAIK for the study of the prehistorical archaeology of the Balkans.
2. A body with representatives from Serbia and Bulgaria would be responsible for the administration of the Slavic Department. A committee of six scholars would be selected; two from Bulgaria, two from Serbia and two from Russia, and the committee would be chaired by the director of RAIK.
3. The committee would be responsible for planning and organizing the activities of the Slavic Department, for securing financial resources, and establishing contacts with relevant institutions to carry out projects, especially with regard to prehistorical study.
4. In order to guarantee that the Slavic Department would not be a financial burden on the RAIK budget, the costs would be split between Bulgaria, Serbia and Russia; that is, each government would allocate 5,000 francs for the Slavic Department.
5. The publication organ of the Slavic Department would be RAIK's *Izvestiia*. Articles would be chosen by the above-mentioned committee and would be published either in Slavic languages or in their Russian translation. Excerpts from specialized research articles from local journals might also appear in *Izvestiia*.
6. Bulgarian, Serbian and Russian scholars should undertake collaborative research in Turkish Thrace and Macedonia. In order to eliminate any pretext for suspicion on the part of the Ottoman administration – Uspenskii noted that the Ottomans had many reasons to have suspicions about their closest neighbours, Russia – it would be helpful to integrate the Ottoman Ministry of Education into the Slavic Department. Uspenskii thought that the presence of a Turkish member in the committee might facilitate excursion and research permits for politically unstable regions of the Ottoman Empire. The Turkish member

would not make a financial contribution to the budget of the Slavic Department.

7. In order to guarantee that the Slavic Department would not go against the RAIK Charter, it would be sufficient to enlarge the first article, which explained the founding principles of RAIK, and to provide it with the features of an international scholarly institution. The Slavic Department would be subordinate to RAIK in its activities.

Ambassador N. V. Charykov, totally sharing the opinions outlined in the above note, recognized the timeliness and desirability of the project proposed by Uspenskii. Upon the ambassador's approval, the note was sent to the Bulgarian, Serbian and Russian Ministries of Education, with a request of annual 5,000 francs allowance from the Bulgarian and Serbian Ministries and 3,000 roubles for two years from the Russian Ministry.[31] To develop the project and put it into practice, Uspenskii visited Belgrade and Sofia in the summer of 1910, and exchanged opinions with local scholars on the subject. On 11 March 1910, Nicholas II approved the allocation of 3,000 roubles from the treasury from the 1910 budget to cover the expenses of collaborative archaeological research by Russian and South Slavic scholars in the Balkan Peninsula. The Serbian Ministry of Education and Church Affairs and the Royal Serbian Academy of Sciences also approved the project. The Serbian government allocated 5,000 dinars from the 1911 budget for this end.

It is no coincidence that the efforts to create a Slavic Department within RAIK occurred at a time when Russia was working hard to create a Serbo-Bulgarian military and diplomatic alliance, that is, the later Balkan League. In other words, Russia's 'soft power' symbolized by RAIK reflected the political agenda set by the Russian 'hard power'. Russia's role in forging alliances between Bulgarians and Serbs was an expression of Pan-Slavic sympathies of certain segments of the Russian Foreign Service. In addition, with the 1905 Revolution in Russia, the Balkan question became a public concern the Russian government could not neglect.[32] No doubt that the Russian government used Balkan Christians as foreign-policy instruments various times throughout the 19th century, but on the other side of the coin, independent Balkan states also used Russian military power to their advantage. The Balkan alliance of 1911 was articulated by the Balkan nations more than by Russian diplomats.

In February 1911, Uspenskii invited the representatives of Serbia, Bulgaria and Russia to a meeting to discuss the details of the Slavic Department. The Serbian government sent academician A. Stefanovich and the director of the Belgrade National Museum, Dr M. Vasich. The Bulgarian government sent G. Katsarov, a professor at Sofia University, the director of National

Museum in Sofia, B. Filov, and a former researcher at RAIK and a teacher at Varna Gymnasium, K. Škorpil. From Russia, the director of the Kiev Museum of Art and Antiquities, V. V. Hvoyko participated in the meeting, in addition to Uspenskii and RAIK secretary F. Shmit. The meeting protocol for the discussion of a prehistorical archaeology department was signed on 21 February 1911 by the Russian and Serbian delegates.[33] In this meeting, the status of the Slavic Department within RAIK was discussed and a work plan for 1911 was laid down. The Bulgarian delegates did not agree with the resolutions and left the meeting because of a difference of opinion with the Serbian delegates. In other words, the Slavic Department came to life as incomplete from the start.

Unfortunately, RAIK's report from 1911 and the reports sent to the Ministry of Public Education did not reveal the nature of the quarrel between Bulgarian and Serbian delegates, but it is interesting that the two governments could not cooperate in a seemingly less political matter when they could enter into a military alliance, although the military alliance was also not free of friction. Actually, the territoriality of archaeological scholarship added a political element to it, and it is this territorial aspect that can explain the sensitivity of Bulgarian and Serbian government representatives, especially on the eve of a war that changed the boundaries of the states in question. Ancient monuments demarcated the boundaries of the nation, and therefore archaeological record could be read as testimony to the continuous existence of distinctly demarcated cultures and ethnic groups across a landscape.[34] Whether the landscape and the monuments on it belonged to Serbian or Bulgarian nation was difficult, if not impossible, to decide.

As a result of the meeting, the Russian and Serbian delegates agreed upon conducting prehistorical research together, especially in the Vardar and Maritsa Valleys. Necessary permits from the Ottoman government would be requested through the director of RAIK. Planned expeditions for 1911 were determined as follows: an expedition would be carried out in Strandzha, Sakar-Planina and Eastern Rhodopes under the guidance of K. Škorpil; and in Eastern Serbia under the guidance of Dr Vasich.[35] Despite the possible obstacles the Bulgarian government could create, the Russian and Serbian members of the Slavic Department decided to proceed with the studies planned in the protocol.

On 2 March 1911, the charter of the Slavic Department was authorized by the Serbian and Russian delegates.[36] The charter laid out the following points:

1. A department dedicated primarily to the study of the prehistory of the Balkan Peninsula would be established with the intention to create a

common academic platform for Slavic scholars, its chairman being the
director of RAIK.

2. The Slavic Department would be composed of the director and
   secretaries of RAIK and representatives from Slav countries.
3. Scholars from Balkan nations with an interest in archaeology would
   first be appointed as members of RAIK before becoming members of
   the Slavic Department.
4. The director of RAIK would choose two representatives for each
   country from the members mentioned above.
5. One member from each country would serve as secretary. The secretary
   would be appointed by the relevant government upon preliminary
   agreement with the director of RAIK.
6. The responsibilities of the secretary would be the organization of
   scientific capabilities in his country and channelling them in a fashion
   that would enable the Slavic Department to achieve its goals.
7. Upon the invitation of the director of RAIK, the Slavic Department
   would meet once every year with the intention of
   a. discussing work already undertaken the previous year.
   b. preparing plans for the next year.
   c. appointing staff for these projects.
8. The Slavic Department could recommend new members to RAIK.
9. The Slavic Department would have financial resources at its disposal
   allocated by the Russian government and the governments of other
   representatives, the latter contributing evenly to the budget.
10. The Slavic Department would submit annual budget reports to each
    government, signed by the chairman and secretaries in charge.
11. The results of the studies and annual reports would be published as an
    addendum to *Izvestiia*.
12. The Slavic Department would publish its studies primarily in Russian,
    but publications in Bulgarian and Serbian were also allowed.
13. As for excavations, the Slavic Department was bound by the legal
    regulations of the country where the studies were to be conducted.
14. In case of need, the Slavic Department could make additions to these
    provisions.
15. This charter would come into force after its approval by the relevant
    governments.

The Serbian government immediately approved these provisions and
appointed Dr Vasich, the director of the National Museum in Belgrade, to
the Slavic Department upon the recommendation of Uspenskii. The work
plan for 1911 presented by Vasich was approved by Uspenskii. In the summer

of 1910, from 21 July to 17 September, Vasich undertook excavation in Vinci in Serbia, on the coast of Danube.[37] The excavations in this region continued until the First World War.

Because of the interruption of the Balkan Wars and the First World War, the Slavic Department could not succeed in leading extensive fieldwork. Yet, the establishment of such a department suggests the ideological orientation of RAIK. The reluctance of the Bulgarian delegates to undertake archaeological studies in collaboration with the Serbs hinted at the difficulty of the Russian desire to create a Pan-Slav solidarity.

Eventually, Russian effort at creating a Balkan alliance not only failed in the sphere of archaeology. In fact, Russia's role in fostering the Balkan League ended up being paradoxical in itself. The Russian government encouraged the Balkan alliance as a bulwark against Austria-Hungary in the Balkans, not as a step towards anti-Ottoman mobilization, because the dissolution of the Ottoman Empire would bring complications Russia did not want to cope with at that point. However, Russian support gave Balkan nations, especially Bulgaria, sufficient self-confidence to drive the Ottomans out of the European continent.[38] At the end of the Balkan Wars, the Ottoman presence in the Balkans nearly came to an end. Arguments over the division of the spoils as a result of the First Balkan War triggered Greece and Serbia to turn against Bulgaria, which initiated the Second Balkan War. Romania and the Ottoman Empire also took advantage of the conflict between Serbs, Greeks and Bulgarians, and seized lands acquired by Bulgaria in the first war. As a result of the Second Balkan War Bulgaria had to cede most of the territories it gained in the first war.

Expansionist Bulgarian dreams also contradicted Russian military, economic and political interests in the Balkans. Although Russia was instrumental in the Bulgarian independence and had been a supporter of the Serbo-Bulgarian alliance of 1912, the economic, military and political confrontation over the issue of the Straits brought Bulgaria and Russia against each other. In 1912, Russian minister of foreign affairs Sergei D. Sazonov warned the Bulgarian government that Russia would not tolerate any Bulgarian pretensions over Istanbul.[39] Bulgarian government on its part turned against Russia because they believed that the Russian government backed Serbia in the Second Balkan War. This was yet another instance where Pan-Slavic and Pan-Orthodox ideas came into conflict with pragmatic foreign-policy principles. Until the ultimate capture of Istanbul by the Russian armies, Russian Foreign Service preferred to see the imperial city at the hands of the Turks and were not likely to make concessions even to Bulgarians, their Slavic and Orthodox brethren, in this regard. If Byzantium

had to be re-enacted, it would be Russia who should take the lead, not
Bulgaria or any other Balkan nation.

On the eve of the First World War, staunch monarchists and liberals like
Miliukov shared similar concerns about extending Russian influence in the
Balkans and the Near East, although their motivations were different.[40] At
the same time, there were a number of factors that complicated Russian
foreign-policy options in the Near East. On the one hand, there was a desire
to counter European propaganda and influence in the Balkans and Near East.
On the other hand, this desire contradicted with the existing alliances with
France and Britain.

Conclusion

The archaeological study of Byzantine monuments in the Balkans offered
a perfect example of the intersection of ancient history with contemporary
Russian imperial identity and political interests. Between 1895 and 1914,
and especially right before the Balkan Wars, the areas that attracted
RAIK's scholarly interests were ridden with a violent interethnic conflict.
In addition to Russian archaeologists, scholars from Balkan nations also
tried to legitimize the territorial claims of their nations with archaeological
evidence. Therefore, archaeological research was more divisive than unifying
among the Orthodox nations of the Balkans. The establishment of the Slavic
Department coincided with the last time the Russian Empire sponsored an
alliance between Bulgarians and Serbians, but eventually both the Slavic
Department and the Balkan Alliance failed, although for different reasons.
Despite its failure, the Slavic Department was the ultimate showcase of RAIK's
raison d'être: fostering ties between Russia and the Balkan Slavs, exactly what
ambassador Nelidov and other advocates of RAIK's establishment had in
mind in the early 1890s.

Although in a general sense Russian foreign policy was driven by issues
of security and national interest, Russian policymakers often had illusions
about Orthodox and Slavic solidarity. In fact, the basis of Russian imperial
identity, Orthodoxy and Slavdom, was out of touch with the political realities
of the day. By the time RAIK was established in 1894, neither Orthodoxy nor
Slavdom were viable political appeals in the Balkans, as the inter-communal
conflict in Macedonia exemplified. The failed project to create a Slavic
Department and the Bulgarian reluctance to join it was a reflected the limits
of Russian foreign policy.

6

The doom of empires: The fate of the Russian Archaeological Institute after 1914

With the outbreak of the First World War, the Russian diplomatic corps in Istanbul left the city on 16 October 1914. On the same day RAIK staff joined diplomats and closed down their office, leaving the library, antiquities collection and museum behind, as well as the personal property of the director, Fyodor Uspenskii. In a report sent to the Ministry of Foreign Affairs and Ministry of Public Education, Uspenskii blamed Ambassador Mikhail Nikolaevich Girs for the situation.[1] Recalling the institute charter which placed RAIK under the protection of the Russian Embassy, Uspenskii claimed that before the outbreak of hostilities he was in constant communication with Ambassador Girs. Although the general atmosphere in the Russian Embassy 'left no doubt that [we] were on the eve of great events', Girs recommended Uspenskii not to give reason to the Turks to suspect that the Russians were preparing to evacuate the city. As a result, the ambassador did not recommend taking precautions for the preservation of RAIK's property. Until October 1914 RAIK functioned as usual, continuing its lectures and studies. After the hostilities started, Uspenskii and his wife left Istanbul with the Russian diplomats in a hurry, leaving their personal belongings behind, taking only the most important things. Uspenskii noted that none of the Russian institutions had taken any precautions regarding the protection of their property in Istanbul.

At first the war gave Uspenskii and other monarchist scholars the hope that Russia might indeed capture the capital of the Byzantine emperors. Some Byzantinist scholars, including I. I. Sokolov, dreamt that now the Byzantine Empire could be resurrected under the rule of the Russian Tsar, accompanied by the unification of Russian Church with the Orthodox Patriarchate of Constantinople.[2] Uspenskii was more modest in his expectations. In a memorandum from December 1914 entitled 'On the Arrangements Connected to the Expected Occupation of Constantinople by Russia', Uspenskii wrote that the possible occupation of Istanbul would bestow responsibilities upon Russia.[3] He repeated the argument that Russian military power should be accompanied by moral and cultural influence over Orthodox people. Uspenskii deemed Orthodoxy as a very efficient tool to strengthen Russia's cultural influence; therefore, he pointed to the appeal of a Russian patriarch for Orthodox Slavs once Istanbul was captured. Uspenskii stated that in terms of the wealth of its antiquities and its historical importance, Istanbul, the 'last Rome', was one of the most important historical cities in the world. Even though ancient Byzantine monuments were not directly related to Russian national history, Uspenskii claimed that religious and historical ties between Russia and the Byzantine Empire gave a historic mission to Russia. In anticipation of a Russian victory at the end of the war, Uspenskii called for the establishment of a commission to oversee the systematic investigation and preservation of Byzantine monuments in Istanbul to fulfil this mission. He particularly suggested the conversion of the Hagia Sophia back into a church after the expected Russian victory. Uspenskii hoped that the first service in the historic cathedral after the Russian conquest of Istanbul would be held in Russian language.

In fact, a committee was established during the war to survey, record and preserve archaeological monuments in Istanbul and its environs, although it never functioned.[4] The mission of the committee was described as studying the monuments in Istanbul from a scholarly perspective, taking necessary precautions for their preservation, and collecting ancient materials and manuscripts. After the monuments and archaeological artefacts were categorized, the committee would undertake excavations. The Russian Ministry of Foreign Affairs was supposed to provide financial support. The chairman of the committee was the president of the Imperial Academy of Sciences, Grand Duke Konstantin Konstantinovich. Other members included Count S. D. Sheremetyev, Count Aleksey Aleksandrovich Bobrinskii, Prince A. A. Shirinskii-Shihmatov, Countess P. S. Uvarova, F. I. Uspenskii, N. N. Pokrovskii (last foreign minister of the Russian Empire) and two unnamed representatives from the Holy Synod and the Ministry of Foreign Affairs.

Russian preparations for ruling Istanbul after the war were actually grounded on a reasonable expectation. The secret Straits Agreement of March 1915 between Britain, France and Russia granted Istanbul and the Straits to Russia as a war prize.[5] Had it not been for the Russian Revolutions of 1917, it was possible that Istanbul and the Straits would have been given to Russia at the end of the war.[6] Therefore, Russian plans for reshaping the urban landscape of Istanbul through archaeological preservation after the expected victory accorded with the political context.

Not only the Ottoman capital but Syria and Palestine were also on the agenda of Russian scholars on the eve of the Great War. In 1914, Petrograd University professors and members of the Academy of Sciences organized a meeting in Petrograd, as St Petersburg was then called, to discuss Russian scientific interests in the Near East.[7] Scholars agreed upon the creation of a Russian archaeological institute in Jerusalem based on the example of RAIK once the war was over. Next year in 1915, the Academy of Sciences even elected a commission to oversee the establishment of the planned institute. The commission included Nikodim Kondakov, Fyodor Uspenskii and Nikolai Marr, among others.[8]

However, these hopes were dashed soon when it became obvious that Russia was going through a turbulent and revolutionary period, let alone not capturing Istanbul. After the Revolution, Uspenskii decided to devote his attention to the repatriation of the RAIK property that remained in Istanbul. Shortly after leaving Istanbul, he wrote a letter to the Ministry of Public Education about the need to reclaim RAIK property, to which the Ministry responded positively.[9]

By the time RAIK ceased to operate in 1914, it possessed a rich museum and library collection, especially noteworthy for the wealth of manuscripts it held. Both the library and the antiquities collection were acquired mostly through donations, but also through the funds allocated to RAIK by the Russian government. In total, the materials in the library had a value of 134,000 roubles by Uspenskii's estimate, with 22,622 books under 8,909 titles, including books, journals, maps and brochures. The museum collection was partly moved to the Russian Embassy and partly brought to Russia during evacuation. The museum collection included pieces of Byzantine, Greco-Roman and Slavic art; a large numismatics collection; documents and manuscripts in Greek and Slavic languages; church paraphernalia and other ancient objects. In total, the value of RAIK property was estimated to be nearly 200,000 roubles.[10] In addition to RAIK property, Uspenskii estimated that the value of his personal property that remained in Istanbul was about 20,000 roubles.[11] The status of RAIK property was determined by war conditions and changing governments in both countries, and was solved only by agreement between Republican Turkey and the Soviet Union in 1929.

Already in 1901, part of the collection was moved to the Russian Embassy, for preservation and because there was not enough space at the RAIK building.[12] After the Russians evacuated Istanbul on 16 October 1914, the Italian Embassy took over the property of the Russian Embassy. Uspenskii entered into direct communication with the Italian ambassador, who agreed to take necessary measures for the protection of RAIK's property left at the Embassy building.[13] During the war, one of the members of RAIK, B. A. Panchenko delivered certain objects of Christian art, coins, seals and mostly golden materials from the RAIK building to the Russian consulate general in

Istanbul in early 1915.[14] In addition, part of the RAIK archives and materials were brought to Odessa after the evacuation.[15]

According to the information received by the Russian Ministry of Foreign Affairs from the Italian Embassy in Istanbul in December 1914, the Turkish government sequestered RAIK's library that remained at the institute building, and sent the contents to the Imperial Ottoman Museum.[16] Furthermore, two plots of land purchased for the construction of a Russian commercial high school were taken over by the Turks and the RAIK building was transformed into a military hospital. In later years, RAIK's remaining property in the Ottoman Museum would constitute a diplomatic problem in the relations between the Turkish and Soviet governments.

The Sèvres Peace Treaty, signed in 1920 between the Ottoman Empire and the Allies, stipulated that the Turkish authorities were responsible for the protection of RAIK's property and must return it to the Allied powers, when requested.[17] Halil Ethem Bey (1861–1938), who became the director of the Ottoman Museum after Osman Hamdi Bey died in 1910, claimed that with the outbreak of the First World War, the Russians brought the most valuable manuscripts, coin collections and other ancient objects to Russia. In a book that was published in 1937, Halil Ethem claimed that the library of RAIK, which remained in Istanbul, was on the point of being distributed, when the Ottoman Museum intervened and took care of the books and the few remaining artefacts with an intention to preserve them.[18]

The final expedition of RAIK was made to Trabzon, a city on the south-eastern coast of the Black Sea in 1916–17, when the region was occupied by the Russian forces.[19] In fact, during and after the First World War, local groups as well as occupying British, French and Russian forces resorted to archaeology to claim land in occupied Ottoman territories in Anatolia as well as in Mesopotamia, where borders were fluid and contested.[20] RAIK's Trabzon expedition was only one of the many archaeological and ethnographical studies conducted in the Russian-occupied regions in Eastern Turkey during the First World War. Russian scholars undertook a number of expeditions, especially around the cities of Van, Erzurum, Trabzon and neighbouring towns. Among them, Nikolai Marr's expedition to Van and his studies on Armenian antiquities is quite well-known.[21] There was also a unit responsible for archaeological preservation within the Russian military administration of Trabzon.[22] Russia's wartime scientific activities fall outside the scope of this project but suffice it to say that the Russian occupation of the Ottoman Empire was much more than a military invasion: Russian armies were accompanied by ethnographers, geographers, archaeologists and architects who devised projects to reconstruct the landscape of the occupied regions. In this context, Russian archaeologists projected themselves as the saviours of antiquities. As Austin Jersild pointed out, Russian archaeologists constructed a contrast between the sacred antiquity of the Orient and its contemporary deplorable condition. The 'original', 'authentic', 'glorious' Orient had to be made known by the scholars so that the Russian Empire could legitimize its role as the restorer of this once-glorious past.[23]

The decree issued by Nikolai Yudenich, the commander-in-chief of the Caucasian Armies in March 1916 testified to the saviour mission the Russian Empire embraced. Yudenich stated, 'While our forces enter deep into Turkey, a rich variety of monuments from the earliest times of human culture are coming into our hands, the necessity of whose preservation has been brought to my attention several times by leading people.'[24] The commander regretfully acknowledged that he received information about Russian citizens, some of them from the ranks of the army, who thoughtlessly caused the destruction of the monuments and even secretly engaged in antiquities trade. Yudenich declared that this was totally unacceptable and stated that ancient monuments, without exception, were under state protection. Churches, monasteries, mosques, both secular and religious buildings, archives, libraries, museums, ancient manuscripts, books in any languages, inscriptions were all counted in this list. Yudenich commanded that destruction, plundering, sale, purchase, unauthorized collection of ancient books, manuscripts and other ancient objects were strictly forbidden in the areas occupied by the Russian army. People who held old manuscripts and books, inscriptions and religious-historical materials were ordered to hand them to military superiors in their districts. These objects would be exhibited in the Caucasian Museum in Tbilisi. Excavations were allowed only for people with appropriate certificates from district headquarters. Archaeological research and excavations were strictly forbidden for people who failed to produce necessary documents, even if they had legitimate scientific grounds.

Trabzon had a particular historical significance for Byzantinists. The Empire of Trebizond, its centre being modern-day Trabzon, was one of the three successor states to the Byzantine throne along with the Nicaean Empire and the Despotate of Epirus after the fall of Constantinople to the Latins following the Fourth Crusade in 1202–4.[25] The Trebizond Empire was founded by Alexios I Comnenos (r. 1204–14) with the help of the Georgian Kingdom in the early 13th century. Culturally, the Trebizond Empire brought together various elements – Georgian, Armenian, Greek, Caucasian and Seljukid. It was the longest-surviving Byzantine successor-state; Trabzon was captured by the Turks only in 1461, eight years after Constantinople.

RAIK undertook two expeditions to Trabzon during the war, in the summer of 1916 and in the summer of 1917.[26] The major aim of the Trabzon expedition was making a detailed architectural and archaeological study of

Christian monuments, taking necessary precautions for their preservation, as well as the protection of Muslim monuments from plundering and destruction. Valuable objects in mosques would be brought from the war zone to safer locations, and Greek antiquities would be placed under the protection of the Trabzon Metropolitan.[27] The report particularly laid emphasis on the preservation of mosques built by the Turks, thereby supporting Russia's self-ascribed role as the saviour of antiquities from different cultures.[28]

F. I. Shmit and N. K. Kluge accompanied Uspenskii on the Trabzon expedition. Russian archaeologists especially devoted their attention to the monasteries around Trabzon and focused not only on their archaeological study but also their preservation. Upon Uspenskii's petition, the Ministry of Foreign Affairs made generous donations for the benefit of monasteries in the city of Trabzon in 1917.[29] In line with Uspenskii's demand, the Ministry sent 6,000 roubles; 2,000 roubles was donated to each of the metropolitan seats of Trabzon and Rodopolis (today known as Maçka), and 2,000 roubles was divided between the monasteries of Sumela, Peristera and Vazelon.[30] Upon the withdrawal of Russian forces from the region in 1917, Uspenskii made copies of manuscripts he found in these monasteries. He published these findings in 1927 with V. N. Beneshevich under the title *Vazelonskie Akty*.[31] Uspenskii's *Ocherki iz Istorii Trapezuntskoy Imperii* (Essays from the History of Trabzon Empire) was also based on his research in Trabzon during the war. In addition to Trabzon, Uspenskii made studies in the Batum oblast' as well.[32] With the defeat of the Turks in parts of Eastern Turkey, there were plans to organize a new expedition to the south of Trabzon in autumn 1917, but this plan was not realized given wartime conditions and domestic turmoil in Russia.[33]

In Trabzon city centre, the most important archaeological studies were made in the churches of Hagia Sophia, Panagia Chrysocephalos Church (Ortahisar Mosque) and St Eugene Church (Yeni Cuma Mosque). All three monuments were Byzantine churches which were converted into mosques after the Ottoman conquest. In early 1916, the Commission for the Preservation and Registration of Ancient Monuments, affiliated with the Russian military administration, issued a resolution about these monuments. The resolution ordered that these mosques, all of which were converted from churches, would not hold Muslim services any longer. The fate of the monuments would be decided after a comprehensive archaeological study and removal of plasters on their walls.[34] A decree by the Russian military administration, issued on 30 June 1916, extended the scope of archaeological research about converted Byzantine churches in the Trabzon area. According to this decree, all churches that were converted into mosques by the Ottomans would be first examined by archaeologists and, later, Muslim service would be prohibited in these churches. The report counted seven such churches in Trabzon. In addition, the decree concluded that all mosques constructed by the Turks should continue Muslim services as usual.[35]

An interesting conjunction of archaeology, religious practices and daily life was staged with the discovery of the burial ground of the Emperor of Trebizond, Alexios III Comnenos (r. 1349–90). After the discovery, the Russian military administration of Trabzon organized a church service in the Emperor's honour.[36] In this example, the Russian administration in Trabzon not only acted as the saviour of antiquities but also linked ancient history to daily religious practice. This tribute, paid to a medieval Byzantine emperor, projected Russia as the representative of Byzantine emperors in the modern world.

During the wartime expeditions to Trabzon and environs, Uspenskii collected over four hundred manuscripts from churches, mosques and private residences. Among them, there were several Quran copies and Turkish-Arabic manuscripts. In a report, Uspenskii acknowledged that he found these books in houses and mosques abandoned by residents during the Russian occupation.[37] Particularly valuable Islamic manuscripts were found in the Panagia Chrysocephalos Church, or the Ortahisar Mosque. Uspenskii, in consultation with the Transcaucasian Committee Interim Administration, decided to send these valuable manuscripts to Batum.[38] While some manuscripts were kept in Batum, others were sent to Petrograd before the end of the war. One reason Uspenskii collected the Islamic manuscripts was because he wanted to use these objects as leverage against the Turks. He hoped that 'in future negotiations with the Turks [the books] could be used in exchange for the transfer of the Institute's books and manuscripts'.[39]

Not only Turkish-Islamic manuscripts but also Greek antiquities were brought to Russia during the occupation. Konstantin Papoulidis brought to light a local Greek view about Russian archaeological activities in Trabzon. In June 1917, a Greek journalist from Trabzon, N. A. Leontidis, accused Russian scholars of smuggling four trunks of objects with religious and artistic value to Russia.[40] The discontent of local Greeks about the smuggling of antiquities by Russian archaeologists echoed some previous examples, such as the Bulgarian nationalists who blamed Russians for smuggling Bulgarian antiquities after the 1877–8 Russo-Ottoman War. In an age of nationalism, Russian appropriation of either Orthodox or Slavic symbols was met with local resistance from other groups that shared the same cultural heritage.

The First World War was followed by dramatic regime changes in both the Russian and the Ottoman Empires. After the Bolshevik Revolution Byzantine studies lost the ideological justification and popularity it enjoyed under the Tsarist regime. At the same time, the nature of relations between

Russia and Turkey was very different from the prewar years. In May 1920, the communist regime officially abolished RAIK and established a bureau within the Academy of Material Culture that was responsible for overseeing RAIK's affairs and negotiating with the young Republican regime in Turkey for the repatriation of RAIK's property. Although at first the Academy of Material Culture appointed someone else as the chairman of the bureau, in 1924 Uspenskii was appointed as the chairman, upon his repeated requests.[41] Uspenskii's appointment to the bureau, although it took a few years, suggested that his political views were not regarded as seriously threatening by the Soviet regime.

In the first years after the Revolution, Fyodor Uspenskii did not give up his hope that RAIK would resume its activities after the war. He even submitted a petition to the Soviet government in 1918 for the enlargement of RAIK. This petition was the exact copy of a proposal that had been submitted to the Ministry of Public Education before the outbreak of the war. Despite the radical ideological change in the country, Uspenskii used the same arguments as he had used vis-à-vis the Imperial government. He argued that a country which 'claim[s] to have an important role in history should not refrain from taking part in a noble competition in the scientific sphere'.[42] He requested financial support and an increase in the number of staff, and proposed to create subdivisions for Balkan, Asia Minor, Western European, prehistorical, Roman-Byzantine, Slavic and Oriental studies within RAIK. Not surprisingly in 1918, this proposal did not receive a positive response.

In the tumultuous years of the Russian Civil War (1918–22) discussion about an archaeological institute was too much of a luxury and questions about RAIK were shelved for a few years. Nevertheless, Uspenskii never gave up his hope that RAIK might be re-established once the political situation consolidated. In 1918, the Imperial Archaeological Commission was transformed into the Academy for the History of Material Culture, which was dedicated to the study of art, archaeology and ethnography of ancient cultures. Within this Academy the section of Early Christian and Byzantine Archaeology continued research and publication about Byzantine history, art and archaeology, albeit at a slower pace compared to the Imperial period.[43] In August 1924, the Board of the Russian Academy of the History of Material Culture convened to discuss Uspenskii's request to reopen RAIK.[44] The meeting was chaired by Nikolai Marr, and attended by Vasilii V. Bartold, S. A. Yasebelev and the former RAIK secretary, B. V. Farmakovskii, among others. Discussions continued for more than a year. In a report to the USSR Academy of Sciences on 21 December 1925, Uspenskii, as the chair of the newly established Russian-Byzantine Commission, outlined the principles that would shape the regenerated institute:[45]

1. The report argued that a research-based institution was necessary for a scientific and in-depth study of the Near East and especially the neighbouring Turkey, particularly in order to cultivate strong cultural relations with the Turkish government. Uspenskii's report especially emphasized the political nature of the proposed institute, stating that the institute would serve a 'scientifically and politically important task' with its studies.[46] The proposed institution would have two branches, one being humanities-oriented and the other with a focus on natural sciences, their centres being in İstanbul and Ankara, respectively. The humanities branch would be the successor of RAIK and would specialize in the literature, history, linguistics, ethnography and archaeology of Turkey. The institution would carry out expeditions, excavations and research with the permission of Turkish authorities. Both departments were planned to be under the same administrative structure.

2. Considering that RAIK had a library and antiquities collection, which were seized by the Turkish government in November 1914 and kept in the Ottoman Museum until the time of the report, the return of this property would be requested from the Turkish government. Together with the property of RAIK, Uspenskii's personal property should also be demanded. On his part, Uspenskii reminded that he seized Islamic manuscripts during the occupation of Trabzon in 1914–17 from the Ortahisar Mosque, which were kept in Batum and Leningrad. Uspenskii proposed their return to Turkish authorities in exchange for RAIK's property.

3. If the negotiations between the USSR and Turkey resulted positively, the legal basis for the proposed Scientific Research Institute would be laid down.

Apparently, the re-establishment of RAIK, or rather the establishment of a new scientific institute with a new scientific policy looked like a close possibility, as information to this effect appeared even in Soviet newspapers. An unidentified newspaper from 17 July 1927 announced that the USSR Academy of Sciences would establish a scholarly institute in İstanbul.[47] The newspaper article stated that upon the proposal of the Ankara government, the Academy was also planning to create an institute in Ankara to study natural resources around the new capital city of Turkey, for which the Soviet Academy of Sciences would provide the necessary scientific support. In August 1927, the draft principles of the Research Institute were elaborated once again by Uspenskii. The former RAIK director stressed that the establishment of a research-based institution required a detailed discussion of technical requirements but also careful choice of words 'so as not to cause foreigners to reach wrong conclusions'.[48]

However, Uspenskii's ardent attempts at the recreation of RAIK or a substitute institution in the end failed. In April 1928, the Department of Scientific Institutions within the Council of Peoples Commissars (Sovnarkom) notified the permanent secretary of the USSR Academy of Sciences that the Department had decided to postpone the establishment of the planned Research Institute in Turkey until the resolution of the property question. Nevertheless, the basic principles of the institute were laid down, in case a future opportunity arose for its creation:[49]

1. The institute would be a Turkish-Soviet institution; its staff would be made up equally of Turkish and Soviet scholars.
2. The focus of the institute would be the study of Turkey from a variety of academic perspectives.
3. The institute would only function within the borders of Turkey.

In response to Sovnarkom's above-mentioned proposal, the Byzantine Commission, including Uspenskii and V. Bartold, wrote a report to the Academy of Sciences.[50] Contrary to Sovnarkom's opinion, the Commission raised doubts about the first article of the memorandum. Uspenskii and Bartold claimed that even though there were some Turkish scholars who produced valuable studies, like the member of the USSR Academy of Sciences Köprülüzade Mehmed Fuad, overall, they believed that the level of science in Turkey was far from meeting European standards. Therefore, the Byzantine Commission advised the establishment of an institute staffed by Soviet scholars, rather than a collaborative Turco-Soviet enterprise.

In the meantime, the question over RAIK property was still being discussed between the two governments. A secret resolution from the Main Scientific Directorate (Glavnauk) to the USSR Academy of Sciences, written on 14 July 1927, stated that agreement had been reached with the Ankara government about bartering RAIK property for Islamic manuscripts from Trabzon.[51] Apparently, it was the Ankara government that pursued Islamic manuscripts because Glavnauk did not know of the Trabzon manuscripts, let alone their whereabouts, and was asking the opinion of the USSR Academy of Sciences on the subject. The Academy of Sciences informed Glavnauk that the manuscripts were partly in the Batumi Gymnasium and partly in the Asiatic Section of the Academy of Sciences Library in Leningrad. After consulting Uspenskii, the Academy of Sciences agreed to give them back to the Turkish government.[52]

Finally on 17 August 1928, the USSR Academy of Sciences formally announced that agreement had been reached with the Turkish government over the years-long property dispute.[53] However, there was no mention of Islamic manuscripts in the memorandum sent to Uspenskii. In 1929, the Soviet government officially demanded RAIK's property from the Turkish government through the Soviet Embassy in Turkey. That year Turkey returned the remaining property and library of RAIK to the Soviet Union. In addition to the materials at the İstanbul Archaeological Museum, – the previous Ottoman Imperial Museum – antiquities were found in the attic of the old Russian Embassy building.[54] Although the first exchange of letters between the two governments implied that the RAIK's property would be exchanged with Islamic manuscripts Uspenskii brought from Trabzon, the final agreement did not have a clause about this barter. On his part, the director of the Istanbul Archaeological Museum Halil Ethem Bey displayed a stubborn attitude, and insisted that the library of RAIK could be returned only on the condition that the historical treasures taken by Uspenskii from Turkey were returned, too.[55] However, in the end, on 16 July 1929, the library of RAIK, consisting of 26,703 books and manuscripts, was handed by the Turkish authorities to their Soviet colleagues with an inventory of the objects submitted.[56]

The objects and books delivered by the Turkish authorities were shared between the Hermitage, the USSR Academy of Sciences, and the Academy of Material Culture, after their preliminary analysis by the Academy of Sciences. While manuscripts and books were sent to the Academy of Sciences Library in Leningrad, the museum collection was sent to the Hermitage in 1930.[57] Following the Revolution, in the early 1920s, smaller museums, palace museums and private collections were dismembered and museums were centralized. In this process the Hermitage was given the lion's share.[58]

However, most of the materials that were previously delivered to Russian diplomatic posts for preservation were either damaged or lost. Briefly after 1917 the building of the former Russian Embassy in Istanbul served as an émigré diplomatic mission. According to the 1921 Moscow Agreement between the USSR and Turkey both parties agreed not to tolerate each other's political opponents. In line with this, the Turkish authorities displayed an uncooperative attitude towards anti-Bolshevik representatives.[59] After 1921, émigré groups had to move from the Embassy building, which was taken over by the Americans.[60] Most of the materials that remained from RAIK were lost in the process.

The Bolshevik Revolution brought destruction to Russian Byzantinology. The publication of scholarly journals and books significantly decreased and many proposed multivolume books produced only their first volumes. Uspenskii's *Istorii Vizantiiskoi Imperii* (History of the Byzantine Empire) shared the same fate.[61] Bolsheviks viewed the field of Byzantine studies as an ideological vestige of the old regime, a field promoted by the Tsarist regime for political reasons.[62]

Uspenskii's letters to the USSR Academy of Sciences indicated that he was in a difficult position under the new regime. For instance, he was not allowed to travel to Istanbul to settle the property question with the Turkish government, even though he was the most competent person to deal with this issue.[63] In a letter from August 1928, Uspenskii complained to the permanent secretary of the Academy of Sciences that in addition to the government's reluctance to send him to Istanbul, he was not allowed to participate in the international congress of Byzantinists in Belgrade in 1927. Uspenskii was concerned that European scholars would assume he was out of favour with the Soviet government.[64]

After the Revolution, RAIK members scattered to different places, and only Uspenskii and Farmakovskii continued their academic career as archaeologists in the Soviet Union.[65] The painter N. K. Kluge left for Istanbul in 1920, and lived there until the end of his life. B. A. Panchenko died from typhus in 1920 somewhere in Ukraine, even the exact place of his death was unknown. R. H. Leper died in Petrograd in 1918. F. I. Shmit, Uspenskii's former colleague and member of RAIK, converted to Marxism and identified 'institutionalized' Byzantinism of the Tsarist period as the extension of an aggressive foreign policy vis-à-vis the Ottoman Empire.[66] Nevertheless, Shmit fell into conflict with the Soviet regime after the 1930s. He was arrested in 1933 and was executed in 1937.

Many prominent archaeologists and Byzantinists who collaborated with RAIK preferred to leave Russia after the Bolshevik Revolution. Among them, M. I. Rostovtsev left for Oxford in 1920, and finally ended up in Yale. From abroad, Rostovtsev wrote articles against the new Bolshevik regime. N. P. Kondakov left first for Bulgaria and then for Prague, where he continued to give lectures on Byzantine art.[67] A. A. Vasiliev, one of the most prolific names among émigré Byzantinist scholars, left Russia in 1925 for the University of Wisconsin, and finally accepted a position at the Dumbarton Oaks Byzantine Institute of Harvard University. Therefore, Russian Byzantinism was seriously damaged within the USSR, but the academic tradition born in the Russian Empire continued to thrive elsewhere in Europe and the United States, although at a slower pace.

Uspenskii's death in 1928 was followed by the interruption of Byzantine studies in the USSR. A relative revival began in the 1940s. *Vizantiiskii Vremennik* reappeared in 1947 after years of suspension, a department was re-established within the Academy of Sciences dedicated to Byzantine studies and a number of scholarly works on Byzantine history were published.[68] Like their predecessors, the Soviet Byzantinists focused on socio-economic history of the Byzantine Empire and Byzantine-Russian relations, but of course within the confines of a Marxist framework.

On the Turkish side, foreign archaeological activities, conducted mainly by the French, British, German and American archaeologists, resumed in the first years of the Republic. In Republican Turkey, archaeological policies were determined by the legal framework laid out by Osman Hamdi Bey in the 19th century. As in the Ottoman period, the main policy was to maintain scholarly cooperation with Western institutions, while strictly regulating and overseeing their activities. Antiquities smuggling was seen as a breach of sovereignty more than ever. In the Republican period, Turkish scholars demanded to be seen on an equal footing with their Western counterparts, and this demand was much more pronounced than it had been in the Ottoman Empire. As part of Republican reforms, academic archaeology was institutionalized in Turkey especially after the 1930s. The Turkish Historical Society was established in 1930, a Turkish Archaeology Institute was established at Istanbul University in 1934 and the first Department of Archaeology was opened at Ankara University in 1936.[69] Different from archaeologists in the Ottoman period, archaeologists of the Republican Turkey made studies on Anatolian civilizations, especially on the Hittites, in an attempt to promote Anatolia as the historical Turkish *patria*.

In his memoirs, the Italian Ambassador in Ankara, Giulio Cesare Montagna (1874–1953), referred to French attempts at creating an institute of Byzantine Studies in İstanbul in the first years of the Republic. The project was not realized, according to Montagna, because 'in the face of Turkish hostility towards everything concerning research and study which recalls the charm of Byzantium, the French government had to change tack'.[70] Consequently, the French government decided to transform the project into a Turkish Oriental Institute. Montagna suggested the establishment of an Italian Research Institute in Turkey considering the political role of foreign scientific institutes and the rivalry between European powers in the scientific field.[71]

Referring to discussions between the Turkish and Russian authorities about the fate of the RAIK library, the Italian ambassador argued that Soviet academic activities in Turkey were linked to their desire to create a sphere of influence over the young Republican regime. Montagna argued, 'It is known that in Moscow studies of the Orient, particularly its economics and politics, have for some time experienced a lively revival – as another weapon serving the renewed and transformed but still present Russian activity in these regions.'[72] Especially from 1929 until 1935, Soviet-Turkish relations were characterized by strong political, economic and cultural cooperation. The first Turkish Five-Year Plan was realized thanks to financial support from the Soviet Union, and the two countries shared a common antagonism to the Western political order.[73] Close economic relations had repercussions in other spheres, most notably in culture. Although eventually Soviet plans to establish a research institute in Turkey failed due to economic reasons, the proposal to create an institute should be seen in the context of Turco-Soviet rapprochement.

The final discussion about RAIK in Soviet academia took place in April 1945, when the Department of History and Philosophy within the USSR Academy of Sciences organized a meeting dedicated to the memory of Uspenskii, for the 100th anniversary of his birthday.[74] As a result of the meeting, the Department reached a decision about the re-establishment of RAIK, but like other previous re-establishment efforts, this project also ended without a result.

Conclusion

The outbreak of the First World War and the Revolution in its aftermath was an unexpected blow to RAIK. In fact, briefly with the occupation of Trabzon, RAIK found the opportunity to apply its academic studies to the practical realm. The symbolic funeral service for Emperor Alexios Comnenos III illustrated the image the Russian imperial administration evoked with the help of archaeological studies. Moreover, reconversion of Byzantine churches, which had been converted by the Ottomans into mosques was a step towards reshaping the landscape of the city. In this sense, the occupation of Trabzon was a showcase of what RAIK stood for: linking ancient past to present, and the Byzantine Empire to Russia.

The transformation in the nature of relations between Russia and Turkey in the aftermath of the First World War and the internal transformation of both countries created a contrast with the imperial period. The fall of Byzantine studies from favour in the Soviet era makes it clearer that RAIK was a political project, and reflected Russian imperial identity. There were discussions about the re-establishment of RAIK in the Soviet period, but the institute the USSR Academy of Sciences had in mind was quite different than RAIK. It was planned as a two-branched institute with a focus on natural sciences, in addition to humanities. Even within the humanities branch, Byzantine studies were regarded as a minor subfield. With the disintegration of the Russian Empire, the conditions that brought RAIK to life disappeared, as therefore did its reason for existence.

Conclusion

Broadly, this research was motivated by a curiosity about the relationship between academic scholarship and politics in the late 19th century and the early 20th century, right before the First World War. Among other academic fields, archaeology was especially useful in linking past to present, and legitimizing contemporary political projects with historical references. On the one hand, European empires projected themselves as the spiritual inheritors of classical civilizations and competed with each other for this role. Imperial rivalries were echoed in the museum halls and excavation fields. On the other hand, local nationalists contested this imperial vision by claiming ancient heritage for themselves. Each actor used archaeology to found their competing visions on a supposedly 'objective' and scientific basis.

The political use of ancient objects and monuments proves that cultural heritage does not have a fixed meaning, rather, 'heritage should be understood as a process, related to human action and agency, and as an instrument of cultural power in whatever period of time one chooses to examine.'[1] The meaning of cultural heritage is dynamic; constructed and reconstructed by individuals, groups or states. New and sometimes contradictory meanings may be attributed to the same monument by different groups across time and space. The way cultural heritage is interpreted reflects the social, cultural and political context in which it is created. In the words of Cornelius Holtorf, 'Cultural memory is hence not about giving testimony *of* past events, accurately or truthful, but about making meaningful statements *about* the past in a given present. Ancient monuments represent the past in the landscape and cultural memory gives them meaning and cultural significance.'[2]

In terms of their appreciation of ancient monuments, especially Byzantine monuments, the Russian and Ottoman empires embraced competing identities. On the one hand, Russian archaeologists emphasized Russia's cultural and historical links with the Byzantine Empire, and deemed themselves responsible for unearthing Byzantine history. Through their archaeological studies, Russian scholars created an imaginary link between the Byzantine Empire and Russia. They viewed Russia as the protector of Orthodoxy and thus the rightful heir to the Byzantine legacy. On the other hand, Ottoman archaeologists did not make such historical claims, neither did they embrace ancient Byzantine or Greco-Roman monuments as part of their national identity. Apart from a handful of intellectuals in the last years of the Empire, most Ottoman intellectuals did not integrate Byzantine history into the overall narrative of Ottoman history. Different from European empires, the Ottoman Empire failed to present a clear ideological basis to legitimize its claim over antiquities. The Islamic identity of the Ottomans as interpreted at the time made it hard to mobilize a Hellenistic-Roman past as part of its own and claim a European identity.

Ottoman interest in antiquities and cultural property rights was more linked to contemporary concerns than historical sensitivities. The Ottoman Empire was on the defensive in its relations with foreign archaeologists not because Ottomans were protecting monuments they saw as linking them to their ancestors, but because they were sensitive about protecting territories on which these monuments were found. Ottoman intellectuals adopted archaeological methods from Europe only in their external form, as a practice of collecting valuable ancient objects, but could not create a coherent discourse for integrating ancient monuments into their national identity. While Greek, Italian, Iranian and Egyptian archaeologists – legitimately or not – established historical links with their modern nations and ancient heritage on their 'historic' lands, Ottomans did not even attempt to do so, except for a few intellectuals. Only a handful of Ottoman intellectuals claimed an Ottoman identity on the basis of the Roman-Byzantine heritage. Clearly, the Byzantine Empire was destroyed by the Ottomans themselves; therefore the Ottoman Empire had a complicated relationship with the history of territories under its jurisdiction. Under these conditions, Ottoman claims over Byzantine and Greco-Roman antiquities remained only territorial – Ottomans claimed ownership rights over Byzantine antiquities only because these objects were found within the borders of the Ottoman Empire. There was definitely a political dimension behind Ottoman archaeological activities, but it was not a nationalist one. In a sense, what characterized Ottoman archaeology was a disconnect with ancient past.

Ottoman archaeology developed primarily as a reaction to foreign scholarly activities. Ottoman attitudes to foreign archaeologists was shaped by a mixture of mistrust and toleration within legal limits. Actually, Ottomans laid claims over antiquities only because Europeans also did so. For Osman Hamdi Bey and the first generation of Ottoman archaeologists, archaeology was a means of proving that the Ottoman Empire was on the same cultural level with European powers. If making archaeological discoveries was a sign of being enlightened, then the Ottoman Empire should also be a part of this cultural activity. Archaeological activities and the exhibition of findings in the Ottoman Imperial Museum displayed the European face of the Ottoman Empire – European because of the Sultan's and the Sublime Porte's official support for archaeology, not because of descent from ancient Greek or Roman civilization. Compelling foreign archaeologists to abide by a set of laws implied that the Ottoman Empire was capable of inducing foreigners to respect its sovereign rights within its borders. In a sense, Ottoman elites tried to protect the sovereignty of the Empire by becoming a part of the European world. To achieve this, it was necessary to compel foreigners to obey Ottoman laws, instead of being subject to extraterritorial rights.

When RAIK was established, the Ottoman Empire had already developed standard methods to monitor and regulate foreign archaeological activities. The 1884 antiquities regulation laid the groundwork for archaeological policies of the Ottoman Empire for the years to come. Similar to other foreign archaeologists, the Ottomans approached RAIK members with caution. Scholarly activities were permitted within legal limits, but were also strictly regulated. Considering the political background and RAIK's openly stated mission to extend Russian influence among Russia's ethnic and religious kinsmen, this suspicion was not completely baseless.

Although at first Ottoman government was reluctant to authorize RAIK and raised difficulties for their studies from time to time, it would be wrong to say that Ottoman attitudes towards Russian archaeologists were totally obstructive. On the contrary, RAIK received permits that no other foreign archaeologists had received until then. For instance, Russian excavations in the interior of the Imrahor Mosque was the first archaeological excavation in a functioning mosque in Istanbul. When Russian scholars justified their archaeological studies with scientific premises, the Ottoman government provided support, on the condition that Russian archaeologists respected Ottoman laws. For the Ottoman government, archaeology was a means of projecting its image as a modern empire, and scholarly cooperation with foreigners was a display of modernity. Therefore, the Ottomans did not demonstrate a totally uncooperative attitude. At the same time, enforcing Ottoman laws was a message about complete Ottoman sovereignty within its borders.

RAIK was established at a time when there was increasing political tension in Europe with regard to the fate of Ottoman territories. Especially, the Balkans were the boiling cauldron of international politics. It does not come as a surprise that the idea to create a scholarly institute in Istanbul was born in Russian diplomatic circles. In this political context, Russian diplomats saw RAIK as a means of furthering political influence in the

Ottoman Empire, especially in the Balkans. Archaeological research was regarded as an opportunity to facilitate closer academic and cultural contact between Russian and Balkan scholars. This mission was stated very openly and frequently in official ceremonies, letters and RAIK reports. Establishment of a scientific institute was regarded as a supplement to political influence. Russian diplomats and scholars realized that being a great power required more than military power, and emphasized the importance of cultural institutions. They made comparisons with European powers, especially with the French, and concluded that Russia lagged behind European governments as regards extending influence through cultural institutions.

In fact, Russian scholars and bureaucrats had similar concerns to their Ottoman counterparts. Both Russia and the Ottoman Empire adopted museum-building practices and archaeological scholarship from Europe, and for both empires archaeology was a means of asserting their place in an all-European competition for status and respectability. For Russian archaeologists, bringing historical monuments to Russian museums was a victory vis-à-vis Europeans, whereas for the Ottomans, keeping monuments at home was a success. The archaeological rivalry between empires started first between the British Museum and the Louvre. The Hermitage and the Ottoman Imperial Museum made a late, but ambitious start. In this competitive atmosphere, falling behind Europe was considered negative for the imperial prestige of both Russia and the Ottoman Empire. Sharing similar concerns with the Ottomans, Russians did not want to be left outside the scramble for ancient glories. Russian scholars often expressed the necessity to catch up with Europe in terms of the quality of scholarship, if Russia sought to be respected as a great power.

RAIK's scholarly activities centred mostly in the Balkans, Istanbul and the Black Sea coast. Partly as a result of the expertise of RAIK staff and partly because of the political mission of the institute, the major focus of RAIK's archaeological projects was Slavic and Orthodox monuments. On a side note, RAIK did not undertake any systematic study of Armenian antiquities, although there were a number of imperial Russian scholars producing valuable studies in this field, most notably Nikolai Marr, whose academic career stretched from the imperial to the Soviet period.

RAIK made detailed research in the monastic libraries around the Ottoman Empire, Greece and the Balkans, and made significant contributions to the study of Orthodox theology, liturgy and history. While undertaking studies on the history of the Orthodox Church, RAIK collaborated with IPPO and the Holy Synod. Russian archaeologists also concentrated on the study of Slavic history and made excavations in cooperation with Bulgarian and Serbian archaeologists. These collaborative studies resulted in the establishment of a Slavic Department in 1911 to enhance cultural and academic cooperation between South Slavs and Russia, although the Slavic Department failed to produce important studies because of the outbreak of the Balkan Wars and the First World War. The convergence of religion, ethnicity and archaeology reflected the motivation behind Russian archaeological activities in the Ottoman Empire.

The fact that the leading Russian scholars collaborated with RAIK, an institute supported by the Russian government with political motivations, indicated that the relationship between the state and intellectuals was not always conflictual in Tsarist Russia, but there were different possibilities of cooperation. RAIK first and foremost symbolized Russia's Pan-Orthodox orientation with its emphasis on the shared Byzantine-Orthodox tradition, but RAIK's activities opened up different possible avenues for Russian involvement in the Balkans and Ottoman territories as well. In addition to Byzantine studies, RAIK also served as a centre for Slavic studies. Miliukov's cooperation proved that liberal intellectuals, who were not quite likely enchanted with the Byzantine civilization, could be attracted to RAIK for different reasons. The Miliukov case further proved that there was a combination of cooperation and conflict between the state and intellectuals. Despite different attitudes as regards not only domestic policy but also Russia's Balkan policy, a certain degree of cooperation was more likely outside of Russia's borders.

Since RAIK prioritized the study of Byzantine antiquities, RAIK's activities shed light into Russian appropriation of the Byzantine legacy and how this legacy was moulded according to contemporary political concerns. The image of Byzantium had a very complicated meaning for Russian statesmen, clergy and intellectuals, ranging from admiration and critical reception to total repudiation. However, from Miliukov to Nicholas II, there was a shared belief that Russia should be politically active in Balkan politics and in other regions that were once Byzantine strongholds, although the sources of their inspiration and the conclusions they derived as regards the Balkan and Near East affairs were different. RAIK's activities suggested that both the regime's and the intellectuals' perceptions of the so-called Eastern Question was very much influenced by religious and cultural concerns, in addition to economic and strategic considerations.

Although the establishment of RAIK was first proposed by a handful of diplomats at the Russian Embassy in Istanbul, the idea received support from the Ministry of Foreign Affairs, the Ministry of Public Education, the Holy Synod and Imperial Academy of Sciences. Nicholas II showed personal interest in RAIK and made generous donations for the acquisition of valuable antiquities. The motivations of Russian diplomats, bureaucrats at the Ministry of Public Education, the Holy Synod and the Tsar for supporting RAIK's studies give insight about political priorities of the Russian government.

However, the governmental support did not undermine the value of RAIK's academic studies. Despite the often-stated political motivations, scholars affiliated with RAIK followed universal academic principles, which made their studies noteworthy outside the political context. As a result of its studies, RAIK maintained a respectable reputation in international academic circles, engaged in a scholarly dialogue and cooperation with prominent universities, institutions and societies in Europe and the United States. Russian archaeologists also established links with other foreign scholars in the Ottoman Empire.

Looking at the political rivalry between European empires on the one side of the coin and international scholarly cooperation on the other, there seems to be two opposing dynamics with regard to archaeologists' academic independence from politics. On the one hand, Russian diplomats, bureaucrats and scholars vocally expressed political motivations for the establishment of RAIK. On the other hand, even in this highly sensitive political atmosphere, and despite national and imperial rivalries, there were also scholarly contacts that transcended imperial and national boundaries. Common scientific concerns shared by scholars from different ideological and national backgrounds made scholarly collaboration possible. Therefore, what I intended to question throughout the book was not whether RAIK's studies were distorted by political considerations or not, but why the Russian government preferred to support an archaeological institute with a proclaimed intention to study Byzantine antiquities.

Director Uspenskii, consecutive Russian ambassadors in Istanbul and bureaucrats who supported the creation of RAIK all hoped that studies on Orthodox and Slavic antiquities would facilitate the infiltration of Russian cultural influence in the Balkans. Russian imperial identity as expressed in relations with the Ottoman Empire rested on shared faith and history with Balkan nations. RAIK reflected both Slavic and Orthodox images of Russia, melting them in the same pot. However, by the late 19th century, this supranational identity was contested by rising nationalism in the Balkans and was therefore far from being a unifying factor. On the one hand, the late 19th–early 20th century was an era of dreams about supranational ethno-civilizational blocs, such as Pan-Germanism, Pan-Slavism and Pan-Turkism. On the other hand, these supranational identities were contested by micro-nationalism. For the Russian Empire, reaching the Balkan nations with messages about Orthodoxy and Slavdom in the midst of the Macedonian crisis was not a very strong weapon. In an age of violent micro-nationalism, for the Balkan nations' ancient monuments did not signify the 'historic' lands of Orthodox and Slavic peoples, but were manipulated by particular ethnic groups – either Bulgarians, Serbs or Greeks – to delineate the territories each perceived to be its own legitimate historic land.

In the first months of the First World War, there were dreams about conquering Istanbul and regenerating Byzantine monuments in the city. These hopes were not unrealistic at all; on the contrary, Russian designs over Istanbul were grounded on the secret alliances concluded with the Allies during the First World War. According to the agreement between the Allies, Istanbul was promised to the Russians in case of an Allied victory. Although Russian armies fell short of capturing Istanbul, they briefly occupied eastern coasts of the Black Sea. Russian archaeological activities in Trabzon give insight about possible practical applications of RAIK's scholarly activities. Immediately after military occupation, Russian archaeologists started investigations in the most important Byzantine churches in the city, most of which were converted into mosques by the Ottomans. The interim Russian military administration of the city issued decrees to reconvert these monuments back into churches after archaeological surveys were completed. In a sense, Russian archaeologists' perceived role as the saviours of Byzantine heritage was taken to a practical level. With its archaeological studies and rehabilitation of churches to their original purpose, RAIK linked the Byzantine past to the Russian present.

In his study on monuments and collective memory, Pierre Nora argued that the physical transformation of places of memory (*lieux de mémoire*) during critical junctures of history reflects the struggle among different political groups for the symbolic capital represented by these sites.[3] Therefore, the meanings attributed to such objects of memory may change and fluctuate. For the Ottomans in the 15th century, transforming the largest cathedral of a conquered city into a mosque signified the triumph of Islam over Christianity, and marked a break with the Byzantine past.[4] On the contrary, for Russians during the First World War, reconversion of these churches meant the triumph of Orthodoxy, and heralded that Russia would repair the severed links with the Byzantine Empire.

Both Russia and the Ottoman Empire went through radical transformations following the First World War. In the aftermath of the Bolshevik Revolution, Byzantine studies no longer reflected the identity of the new regime, and consequentially lost official support. Throughout the 1920s and later in the 1940s the Soviet government formulated several projects for the establishment of a scholarly institute in Turkey. Despite close economic and cultural collaboration between Turkey and the Soviet Union in the 1930s, this project was never realized. Besides, the institute Soviet government intended to create was very different from RAIK. It was designed as a research centre with a focus on the study of the natural resources of Turkey, reflecting the industrialization drive that characterized the economic policies of both countries. A humanities branch was also planned within this institute, but Byzantine studies was only regarded as a minor subfield among the many interests of this branch. The Bolshevik Revolution severed the mythical links between the Byzantine Empire and Russia. Consequently, RAIK remained anachronistic and a thing of the past after 1917.

Notes

Introduction: Regenerating distant past: Nationalist and Imperialist uses of ancient history in the 19th century

1 David Lowenthal, *The Past Is a Foreign Country* (New York: Cambridge University Press, 1985), p. 238.
2 The ancient city fell to ISIS militants once again in December 2016 and is still under ISIS rule by the time these sentences were written in January 2016.
3 'Russian Orchestra Holds Concert in Ruined City of Palmyra', last modified 5 May 2016, http://www.themoscowtimes.com/arts_n_ideas/news/article/ russian-orchestra-holds-concert-in-ruined-city-of-palmyra/568161.html. Accessed 20 March 2017; 'Praying for Palmyra: Russian Orchestra Performs Concert Honoring Victims of Syria War', last modified 5 May 2016, https://www.youtube.com/watch?v=9b0hFIf4Zaw&feature=youtu.be. 20 March 2017.
4 Antiquarian interest in ancient monuments and systematic collection of such objects can be traced back to much earlier periods, even as far as Renaissance, but archaeology became a scientific discipline only in the 19th century, during the heyday of nationalism and imperial competition in Europe. For the beginnings of scientific archaeology first in Scandinavia, then in Britain and France, see Bruce G. Trigger, *A History of Archaeological Thought* (Cambridge: Cambridge University Press, 1989), pp. 73–103.
5 There was also a significant interest in the ancient history of colonial possessions, as illustrated by British archaeological activities in British India. But the major focus of this book is classical archaeology, so colonial archaeology will be left outside the scope of discussion.
6 Magnus Bernhardsson, *Reclaiming a Plundered Past: Archaeology and Nation Building in Modern Iraq* (Austin: University of Texas Press, 2005), pp. 23–4.
7 Margarita Díaz-Andreu García, *A World History of Nineteenth-Century Archaeology: Nationalism, Colonialism, and the Past* (New York: Oxford University Press, 2007), p. 128; Stephen L. Dyson, *In Pursuit of Ancient Past: A History of Classical Archaeology in the Nineteenth and Twentieth Centuries* (New Haven, CT: Yale University Press, 2006), pp. 86–7.
8 Bernhardsson, *Reclaiming a Plundered Past*, p. 23.
9 Deborah Harlan, 'Travel, Pictures, and a Victorian Gentleman in Greece', *Hesperia: The Journal of the American School of Classical Studies at Athens*, Vol. 78, No. 3 (July–September 2009), pp. 421–6.

10 Neil Asher Silberman, 'Promised Lands and Chosen Peoples: The Politics and Poetics of Archaeological Narrative', *Nationalism, Politics, and the Practice of Archaeology*, ed. Philip L. Kohl and Clare Fawcett (Cambridge: Cambridge University Press, 1995), p. 255; Bruce G. Trigger, 'Alternative Archaeologies: Nationalist, Colonialist, Imperialist', *Man*, Vol. 19, No. 3 (1984): p. 365; Shawn Malley, 'Layard Enterprise: Victorian Archaeology and Informal Imperialism in Mesopotamia', *International Journal of Middle East Studies*, Vol. 40, No. 4 (November 2008), pp. 637–40.

11 Bernhardsson, *Reclaiming a Plundered Past*, pp. 23–4.

12 'Layard and the Discoveries at Nimroud', *The Illustrated Magazine of Art*, Vol. 1, No. 4, (1853), p. 206.

13 Díaz-Andreu García, *A World History of Nineteenth-Century Archaeology*, p. 127.

14 Silberman, 'Promised Lands and Chosen Peoples', p. 256.

15 Examples include the T. E. Lawrance, Gertrude Bell, Leonard Woolley, David Hogarth from Britain and Theodor Wiegand from Germany. Dyson, pp. 172–3; Bernhardsson, *Reclaiming a Plundered Past*, pp. 69–70, 59–65.

16 Tsargrad is the historic Slavic name for Istanbul, which had a meaning far beyond geographic connotations. The word implied the dignity and sacredness of the city.

17 Trigger, 'Alternative Archaeologies: Nationalist, Colonialist, Imperialist', p. 363.

18 Anderson limits his analyses to Southeast Asia. Benedict Anderson, *Imagined Communities* (New York: Verso, 1991), pp. 163–4.

19 Anderson, *Imagined Communities*, p. 185.

20 Nick Baron, 'New Spatial Histories of 20th-Century Russia and the Soviet Union: Exploring the Terrain', *Kritika: Explorations in Russian and Eurasian History*, Vol. 9, No. 2 (Spring, 2008): pp. 433–47.

21 Warwick Bray and Ian C. Glover, 'Scientific Investigation or Cultural Imperialism: British Archaeology in the Third World', *Institute of Archaeology Bulletin*, Vol. 24 (1987): p. 116.

22 Bruce G. Trigger, 'Romanticism, Nationalism, and Archaeology', in *Nationalism, Politics, and the Practice of Archaeology*, ed. Philip L. Kohl and Clare Fawcett (Cambridge: Cambridge University Press, 1995), p. 272.

23 Selim Deringil, ' "They Live in a State of Nomadism and Savagery": The Late Ottoman Empire and the Post-Colonial Debate', *Comparative Studies in Society and History*, Vol. 45, No. 2 (April 2003): p. 313.

24 Since the completion of this study, the organization of the Turkish state archives has been restructured. In July 2018, the institution of Prime Ministry was abolished, and the archives are since then affiliated to the Presidency. Hence, Ottoman archives are currently identified as Presidential Ottoman Archives. However, since this research was conducted before these organizational changes, I will cling to the former classification method for the sake of clarity.

25 For further information, please visit http://www.ranar.spb.ru/eng/. Accessesd 16 November 2016.
26 *Fond* is an archival record group in Russian archival system. *Fond* refers to an entire set of documents from a particular individual or institution. Under *fonds*, there is *opis*, and under *opis*, there is *delo.*
27 Trabzon is a large port city on the Eastern Black Sea. The city was also the seat of the Trebizond Empire, one of the successors of the Byzantine Empire, until its conquest by the Ottomans in the 15th century.
28 I. P. Medvedev, *Arkhivy Russkikh Vizantinistov v Sankt-Peterburge* (St Petersburg: Izd-vo Dmitry Bulanin, 1995), p. 62.

1 Double-headed eagle flying over Russia: Russian appreciation of the Byzantine heritage

1 From Gavriil Romanovich Derzhavin's (1743–1816) poem 'Ode on the Capture of Izmail'. G. R. Derzhavin, *Sochineniia* (Moskva: Pravda, 1985), p. 98.
2 M. G. Popruzhenko, *Sorokaletie Uchenoi Deiatel'nosti Akademika Feodora Ivanovicha Uspenskogo (rech', skazannaia v zasdanii Istoriko-Filologicheskogo Obshchestva pri Imperatorskom Novorossiiskom Universitet v den iubileia – 3 Noiabria 1911 g.)* (Odessa: Ekonomicheskaia Tipografiia, 1912), p. 16.
3 George Vernadsky, *Russian Historiography: A History* (Belmont, MA: Nordland, 1978), p. 208.
4 L. P. Lapteva, *Istoriia Slavianovedeniia v Rossii v XIX Veke* (Moskva: Indrik, 2005), p. 376.
5 Alexander A. Vasiliev, 'Byzantine Studies in Russia, Past and Present', *The American Historical Review*, Vol. 32, No. 3 (April 1927): p. 540.
6 Popruzhenko, *Sorokaletie*, pp. 1–3.
7 F. I. Uspenskii, *Vizantiiskii Pisatel' Nikita Akominat iz Khon*, 1874.
8 Popruzhenko, *Sorokaletie*, pp. 10–11.
9 A. A. Spasskii, 'Noveyshii Vizantinizm i Ego Znachenie', *Bogoslovskii Vestnik*, T. 2, No. 4 (1894): p. 49.
10 Popruzhenko, *Sorokaletie*, p. 6.
11 Ibid., p. 15.
12 F. I. Uspenskii, *Ocherki Po Istorii Vizantiiskoi Obrazovannosti: Istoriia Krestovykh Pokhodov* (Moskva: Mysl', 2001), p. 320.
13 Fyodor Ivanovich Uspenskii, 'Iz Istorii Vizantinovedeniia v Rossii', *Annaly* (Petrograd: RAN, 1922), pp. 111–12.
14 Ibid., p. 110.
15 PFA RAN, f. 127, op. 1, d. 1, l. 99–100 (Uspenskii to Ministry of Public Education, 1914).
16 A. A. Spasskii, 'Noveyshii Vizantinizm i Ego Znachenie', p. 50.
17 Uspenskii, 'Iz Istorii Vizantinovedeniia v Rossii', p. 119.

18 Igor L. Tikhonov, 'Archaeology at St. Petersburg University (From 1724 Until Today)', *Antiquity*, Vol. 81, No. 312 (2007): p. 446.

19 Lev S. Klejn, *Fenomen Sovetskii Arkheologii* (St Petersburg: FARN, 1993), p. 17.

20 Igor L. Tikhonov, 'Deiatel'nost' Akademika A. S. Lappo-Danilevskogo v Arkheologii', in *Ocherki Istorii Otechestvennoi Arkheologii, Vyp.* 2 (Moskva: Gosudarstvenny Istoricheskii Muzei Institut Arkheologii RAN, 1998), pp. 154–66.

21 Lev S. Klejn and Igor L. Tikhonov, 'The Beginnings of University Archaeology in Russia', in *The Beginnings of Academic Pre- and Protohistoric Archaeology [1890–1930] in a European Perspective* (International Meeting at Humboldt-University Berlin, 13–16 March, 2003.), ed. Callmer, Meyer et al. (Rahden: Marie Leidorf), p. 197; Anatole G. Mazour, *Modern Russian Historiography: A Revised Edition* (Westport, Conn.: Greenwood Press, 1975), pp. 35–36; Dimitri Obolensky, *Byzantium and the Slavs* (London: Variorum Reprints, 1971), p. 67.

22 Theophilus C. Prousis, *Russian Society and the Greek Revolution* (DeKalb: Northern Illinois University Press, 1994), p. 167.

23 A. A. Spasskii, 'Noveyshii Vizantinizm i Ego Znachenie', p. 47.

24 Klejn and Tikhonov, 'The Beginnings of University Archaeology', p. 197.

25 Ibid.

26 Igor Tikhonov, 'Russia', in *The History of Archaeology: An Introduction*, ed. Paul Bahn (New York: Routledge, 2014), p. 156.

27 A. D. Priakhin, *Istoriia Otechestvennoi Arkheologii* (Voronezh: Voronezhskii Gosudarstvenny Universitet, 2005), pp. 69–70.

28 Ibid., pp. 73–5.

29 Victor A. Shnirelman, 'The Faces of Nationalist Archaeology in Russia', in *Nationalism and Archaeology in Europe*, ed. by M. Díaz-Andreu García and T. C. Champion (Boulder, CO: Westview Press, 1996), p. 225.

30 Pavel M. Dolukhanov, 'Archaeology in Russia and Its Impact on Archaeological Theory', in *Theory in Archaeology: A World Perspective*, ed. Peter J. Ucko (London: Routledge, 1995), p. 327.

31 I. V. Tunkina, *Russkaia Nauka o Klassicheskikh Drevnostiakh Iuga Rossii (XVIII-seredina XIX v.)* (St Petersburg: Nauka, 2002), p. 608.

32 Austin Jersild, *Orientalism and Empire: North Caucasus Mountain Peoples and the Georgian Frontier, 1845–1917* (Montreal: McGill-Queen's University Press, 2002), p. 67.

33 N. B. Strizhova, 'Moskovskii Arkheologicheskii Institut po Materialam Otdela Pis'mennykh Istochnikov Gosudarstvennogo Istoricheskogo Muzeia', in *Ocherki Istorii Russkoi i Sovetskoi Arkheologii*, ed. A. A. Formozov (Moskva: Akademiia Nauk SSSR, 1991), p. 102.

34 I. I. Sokolov, 'Vizantologicheskaia Traditsiia v S.-Peterburgskoi Dukhovnoi Akademii', *Khristiyanskoe Chtenie*, No. 1 (1904): p. 143.

35 Priakhin, *Istoriia Otechestvennoi Arkheologii*, p. 93.

36 N. V. Pokrovskii, 'Zhelatel'naia Postanovka Tserkovnoi Arkheologii v Dukhovnykh Akademiiakh', *Khristiyanskoe Chtenie*, No. 3 (1906): p. 349.

37 N. V. Pokrovskii, 'O Merakh k Sokhraneniiu Pamiatnikov Tserkovnoi Stariny', *Khristiyanskoe Chtenie*, No. 4 (1906): pp. 471–4.

38 Klejn and Tikhonov, 'The Beginnings of University Archaeology', p. 199.

39 A. E. Musin, *Imperatorskaia Arkheologicheskaia Komissiia, 1859–1917: U Istokov Otechestvennoi Arkheologii i Okhrany Kul'turnogo Naslediia: K 150-letiiu so Dnia Osnovaniia* (St Petersburg: DB, 2009), p. 47.

40 Vasiliev, 'Byzantine Studies in Russia, Past and Present', pp. 539–45; Alexander Kazhdan, 'Russian Pre-Revolutionary Studies on Eleventh-Century Byzantium', in *Byzantine Studies: Essays on the Slavic World and the Eleventh Century*, Vol. 9, ed. Speros Vryonis, Jr. (New Rochelle, NY: Aristide D. Caratzas, 1992), p. 110.

41 Igor Pavlovich Medvedev, *Peterburgskoe Vizantinovedenie* (St Petersburg: Aleteiia, 2006), pp. 130–42.

42 For biographical information about the secretaries of RAIK, see Ye. Yu. Basargina, *Russkii Arkheologicheskii Institut v Konstantinopole* (St Petersburg: DB, 1999), pp. 87–120.

43 A. A. Spasskii, 'Noveyshii Vizantinizm i Ego Znachenie', pp. 47–8.

44 Kazhdan, 'Russian Pre-Revolutionary Studies on Eleventh-Century Byzantium', pp. 111–20.

45 Medvedev, *Peterburgskoe Vizantinovedenie*, p. 133.

46 Obolensky, *Byzantium and the Slavs*, p. 68.

47 Semavi Eyice, 'Türkiye'de Bizans Mimarisi Hakkındaki Yabancı Araştırmaların Kısa Tarihçesi', in *Sanat Tarihi Yıllığı VI, 1974–1975* (İstanbul: İstanbul Üniversitesi Edebiyat Fakültesi, 1976), pp. 453–69.

48 Şule Kılıç Yıldız, 'A Review of Byzantine Studies and Architectural Historiography in Turkey Today(1)', *METU Journal of the Faculty of Architecture*, Vol. 28, No. 2 (2011/12): p. 64.

49 Robert Ousterhout, 'The Rediscovery of Constantinople and the Beginning of Byzantine Archaeology: A Historiographical Survey', in *Scramble for the Past: A Story of Archaeology in the Ottoman Empire, 1753–1914*, ed. Zainab Bahrani, Zeynep Çelik and Edhem Eldem (İstanbul: SALT, 2011), pp. 181–2.

50 A. A. Spasskii, 'Noveyshii Vizantinizm i Ego Znachenie', pp. 34–7.

51 Lora A. Gerd, *Konstantinopolskii Patriarkhat i Rossiia: 1901–1914* (Moskva: Indrik, 2012), pp. 39–40.

52 Priakhin, *Istoriia Otechestvennoi Arkheologii*, p. 60.

53 Gocha R. Tsetskhladze, *North Pontic Archaeology: Recent Discoveries and Studies* (Leiden: Brill, 2001), p. XI.

54 Priakhin, *Istoriia Otechestvennoi Arkheologii*, p. 56.

55 Of course, the Kunstkammer in St. Petersburg was established long ago, in the first half of the 18th century, which made it the first museum in the Russian Empire. However, the Kunstkammer was not a conventional antiquities collection, it was rather an incoherent collection of rare objects,

mostly natural rarities. The Hermitage, on the other hand, evolved from a royal collection to a public museum only in 1852. Priakhin, *Istoriia Otechestvennoi Arkheologii*, p. 48; Aleksandr Mongait, *Archaeology in the USSR* (Moscow: Foreign Languages Publishing House, 1959), p. 49.

56 For a detailed discussion on how Crimea simultaneously belonged to different historical and cultural spaces and how its natural and built environment were imagined by Tsarist officials in the 18th century, see Kelly O'Neill, *Claiming Crimea: A History of Catherine the Great's Southern Empire* (New Haven, CT: Yale University Press, 2017), pp. 11–23.

57 Lori Khatchadourian, 'Making Nations from the Ground up: Traditions of Classical Archaeology in the South Caucasus', *American Journal of Archaeology*, Vol. 112, No. 2 (April 2008): pp. 254–5.

58 Jersild, *Orientalism and Empire*, pp. 45, 67–9.

59 For 'archaeology of the Chersonessos legend' and the relation between science and religion in Imperial Russia, see Mara Kozelsky, 'Ruins into Relics: The Monument to Saint Vladimir on the Excavations of Chersonessos, 1827–57', *Russian Review*, Vol. 63, No. 4 (October 2004): pp. 658–61.

60 Mara Kozelsky, *Christianizing Crimea: Shaping Sacred Space in the Russian Empire and Beyond* (DeKalb: Northern Illinois University Press, 2010), pp. 83–8.

61 I. V. Tunkina, *Russkaia Nauka o Klassicheskikh Drevnostiakh Iuga Rossii*, p. 608.

62 Kozelski, 'Ruins into Relics: The Monument to Saint Vladimir on the Excavations of Chersonessos, 1827–57', p. 662.

63 Kozelsky, *Christianizing Crimea*, p. 11.

64 Kozelski, 'Ruins into Relics: The Monument to Saint Vladimir on the Excavations of Chersonessos, 1827–57', pp. 663–70.

65 Innokentii, Archbishop of Kherson and Tauride, *Izbrannye Sochineniia* (St Petersburg: Russkaia Simfoniia, 2006), pp. 571–5.

66 Ibid., p. 572.

67 Ibid., p. 574.

68 Kozelsky, 'Ruins into Relics: The Monument to Saint Vladimir on the Excavations of Chersonessos, 1827–57', pp. 670–1.

69 Musin, *Imperatorskaia Arkheologicheskaia Komissiia*, p. 186.

70 Kozelsky, *Christianizing Crimea: Shaping Sacred Space in the Russian Empire and Beyond*, p. 10.

71 Philip L. Kohl, Introduction to *Selective Remembrances: Archaeology in the Construction, Commemoration, and Consecration of National Past*, ed. Philip L. Kohl, Mara Kozelsky, and Nachman Ben-Yehuda (Chicago: University of Chicago Press, 2007), p. 21.

72 Musin, *Imperatorskaia Arkheologicheskaia Komissiia*, pp. 183–4.

73 Klejn and Tikhonov, 'The Beginnings of University Archaeology', p. 199.

74 Nikolay Mikhailovich Karamzin, *Istoriia Gosudarstva Rossiiskogo, Tom:1* (Moskva: Olma-Press, 2004), pp. 132–3; George [Yuri] Ivask, 'North and

South: Some Reflections on Russian Culture', *Russian Review*, Vol. 24, No. 3 (July 1965): p. 238.

75 Alexander A. Vasiliev, 'Was Old Russia a Vassal State of Byzantium?', *Speculum*, Vol. 7, No. 3 (July 1932): pp. 350–60.

76 John Meyendorff, *Byzantium and the Rise of Russia: A Study of Byzantino-Russian Relations in the Fourteenth Century* (Crestwood, NY: St Vladimir's Seminary Press, 1989), p. 14.

77 Michael Cherniavsky, 'Khan on Basileus: An Aspect of Russian Mediaeval Political Theory', *Journal of the History of the Ideas*, Vol. 20, No. 4 (October–December 1959): p. 463.

78 Vasily V. Zenkovsky, 'The Spirit of Russian Orthodoxy', *Russian Review*, Vol. 22, No. 1 (January 1963): p. 39.

79 Peter Chaadaev, 'Letters on the Philosophy of History', in *Readings in Russian Civilization*, Vol. 2, ed. Thomas Riha (Chicago, IL: The University of Chicago Press, 1969), pp. 304–8; Obolensky, *Byzantium and the Slavs*, p. 63.

80 Prousis, *Russian Society and the Greek Revolution*, pp. 86–7; Stephen L. Baehr, 'From History to National Myth: Translatio Imperii in Eighteenth Century Russia', *Russian Review*, Vol. 37, No. 1 (January 1978): p. 3; Hugh Ragsdale, 'Evaluating the Tradition of Russian Aggression: Catherine II and the Greek Project', *Slavonic and East European Review*, No. 66 (1988): pp. 93–4; Andrey Zorin, *Kormya Dvuglavogo Orla: Literatura i Gosudarstvennaia Ideologiia v Rossii v Posledney Tretii XVIII – Pervoy Tretii XIX Veka* (Moskva: Novoe Literaturnoe Obozrenie, 2001), pp. 33–4.

81 Obolensky, *Byzantium and the Slavs*, p. 62.

82 Rostislav A. Fadieev, 'What Should Be the Policy of Russia?', in *Readings in Russian Foreign Policy*, ed. Robert A. Goldwin (New York: Oxford University Press, 1959), pp. 67–73; Petrovich, *The Emergence of Russian Panslavism* (Westport: Greenwood Press, 1985), pp. 66–77.

83 Fadieev, 'What Should Be the Policy of Russia', pp. 70–1; Petrovich, *The Emergence of Russian Panslavism*, pp. 278–81.

84 F. M. Dostoievsky, *The Diary of a Writer*, trans. Boris Brasol (Santa Barbara, CA: P. Smith, 1979), p. 905.

85 Ivask, 'North and South: Some Reflections on Russian Culture', p. 238.

86 Andrey Korenevskiy, 'Russia's Byzantine Heritage: The Anatomy of Myth', *Novoe Proshloe / The New Past*, No. 1 (2016): pp. 66–70.

87 Prousis, *Russian Society and the Greek Revolution*, p. 166.

88 A. A. Spasskii, 'Noveyshii Vizantinizm i Ego Znachenie', p. 53.

2 Archaeology in the Ottoman Empire: Cultural property as a symbol of sovereignty

1 In this book, the term modernization broadly refers to Ottoman reactions to growing political, cultural and economic influence of Europe in 19th

century. Politically and economically, this influence manifested itself as
a tacit agreement between major European powers to control Ottoman
markets and political stage but keeping it as a separate entity to prevent a
possible inter-European conflict. Ottoman bureaucrats, who were influenced
by prevalent ideologies in Europe, tried to counter European demands
by a reform program that focused primarily on increasing administrative
centralization, thus trying to transform Ottoman Empire from a traditional
land-based empire to a modern state. For further information, see Erik
Jan Zürcher, *Modernleşen Türkiye'nin Tarihi* (Turkey, A Modern History)
(İstanbul: İletişim, 2007), pp. 18–19.

2 Suzanne Marchand, *Down from Olympus: Archaeology and Philhellenism
in Germany, 1750–1970* (Princeton, NJ: Princeton University Press, 2003),
p. xx.

3 Díaz-Andreu García, *A World History of Nineteenth-Century Archaeology*
(New York: Oxford University Press, 2007), p. 103.

4 Lucia Patrizio Gunning, *The British Consular Service in the Aegean and
the Collection of Antiquities for the British Museum* (Farnham: Ashgate,
2009), p. 46.

5 Ibid., p. 47.

6 Díaz-Andreu García, *A World History*, pp. 99–100.

7 James Goode, *Negotiating for the Past: Archaeology, Nationalism and
Diplomacy in the Middle East, 1919–1941* (Austin: University of Texas
Press, 2007), p. 24. Wendy Shaw argues for the opposite. She claims that
even though there were not protective measures for the preservation of
monuments, Ottoman officials and the ruling class were aware of the
value of ancient objects. Foreigners at least needed official permission to
remove objects even in the 18th century. See Wendy M. K. Shaw, *Osmanlı
Müzeciliği: Müzeler, Arkeoloji ve Tarihin Görselleşmesi* (Possessors and
Possessed: Museums, Archaeology, and the Visualization of History in the
Late Ottoman Empire) (İstanbul: İletişim, 2004), pp. 79–80.

8 Caroline Winterer, *The Culture of Classicism: Ancient Greece and Rome
in American Intellectual Life, 1780–1910* (Baltimore, MD: Johns Hopkins
University Press, 2002), 165.

9 Stephen L. Dyson, *In Pursuit of Ancient Past: A History of Classical
Archaeology in the Nineteenth and Twentieth Centuries* (New Haven,
CT: Yale University Press, 2006), pp. 137–8.

10 Şükrü Hanioğlu, *A Brief History of the Late Ottoman Empire* (Princeton,
NJ: Princeton University Press, 2008), pp. 43–5.

11 Niyazi Berkes, *Türkiye'de çağdaşlaşma* (Modernisation in Turkey)
(İstanbul: Yapı Kredi Yayınları, 2003), pp. 171–8.

12 Hanioğlu, *A Brief History of the Late Ottoman Empire*, p. 73.

13 Şerif Mardin, *Türk Modernleşmesi: Makaleler IV* (Essays on Turkish
Modernisation) (İstanbul: İletişim, 1991), pp. 138–41.

14 İlber Ortaylı, *İmparatorluğun En Uzun Yüzyılı* (The Longest Century of the Empire) (İstanbul: Alkım Yayinevi, 2006), p. 105.

15 Zeynep Çelik, *The Remaking of İstanbul: Portrait of an Ottoman City in the Nineteenth Century* (Seattle, 1986), pp. xv–xviii.

16 İlber Ortaylı, 'Tanzimat'ta Vilayetlerde Eski Eser Taraması' (Antiquities Survey in Provinces During Tanzimat), in *Tanzimat'tan Cumhuriyet'e Türkiye Ansiklopedisi* 6 (Encyclopedia of Turkey from Tanzimat to the Republic), ed. by Feroz Ahmad (İstanbul: İletişim Yayınları, 1985): pp. 1599–603.

17 Ussama Makdisi, 'Ottoman Orientalism', *The American Historical Review*, Vol. 107, No. 3 (June 2002): p. 783.

18 Mehmet Özdoğan, 'Ideology and Archaeology in Turkey', in *Archaeology Under Fire: Nationalism, Politics and Heritage in the Eastern Mediterranean and Middle East*, ed. Lynn Meskell (London: Routledge, 2002), p. 112.

19 Ortaylı, *İmparatorluğun En Uzun Yüzyılı*, pp. 236–7.

20 İsmail Günay Paksoy, 'Bazı Belgeler Işığında Osmanlı Devleti'nin Kültür Mirası Üzerine Düşünceler', in *Osman Hamdi Bey ve Dönemi, 17–18 Aralık 1992*, ed. Zeynep Rona (İstanbul: Tarih Vakfı Yurt Yayınları, 1993), pp. 202–8.

21 Başbakanlık Osmanlı Arşivi (Prime Ministerial Ottoman Archives, İstanbul; hereafter BOA); İrade, Mesail-i Mühimme (İ. MSM.), 17/387, 18 Safer 1262 (15 February 1846). For previous antiquities collections in the Ottoman Empire, see Selin Adile Atlıman, 'Museological and Archaeological Studies in the Ottoman Empire During the Westernization Process in the 19th Century' (Unpublished master's thesis, Middle East Technical University, Ankara, 2008), pp. 16–19.

22 Mustafa Cezar, *Müzeci ve Ressam Osman Hamdi Bey* (İstanbul: Türk Kültürüne Hizmet Vakfı Sanat Yayınları, 1987), p. 13.

23 Théophile Gautier, *Constantinople* (Paris, 1856), pp. 287–8.

24 Semavi Eyice, 'Arkeoloji Müzesi ve Kuruluşu' (The Establishment of the Archaeology Museum), in *Tanzimat'tan Cumhuriyet'e Türkiye Ansiklopedisi* 6 (Encyclopedia of Turkey from Tanzimat to the Republic), ed. Feroz Ahmad (İstanbul: İletişim Yayınları, 1985): pp. 1596–9.

25 BOA, Sadaret Mektubî Kalemi (A. MKT.), 51/75, 17 Şevval 1262 (8 October 1846.)

26 Artun argues that Ottoman elites failed in projecting the Museum as an institution embodying the linear evolution of Ottoman society, and the Museum remained an elitist project to the end. Ali Artun, 'İmkansız Müze' (The Impossible Museum), http://www.aliartun.com/content/detail/1, accessed 21 November 2016.

27 Zeynep Çelik, *Asar-ı Atika: Osmanlı İmparatorluğu'nda Arkeoloji Siyaseti* (İstanbul: Koç University Press, 2016), pp. 112–14.

28 BOA, Hariciye Mektubi Kalemi (HR. MKT.), 287/24, 11 Şevval 1275 (14 May 1859); HR. MKT., 293/92, 24 Zilkade 1275 (25 June 1859); HR. MKT.,

198/64, 29 Zilkade 1273 (21 July 1857); HR. MKT., 300/90, 16 Muharrem
1276 (15 August 1859); HR. MKT., 301/48, 19 Muharrem 1276 (18 August
1859). Only in 1857–8, several Russian aristocrats paid visit to the Ottoman
Museum. See, HR. MKT., 190/98, 06 Şevval 1273 (30 May 1857); HR. MKT.,
238/35, 04 Şevval 1274 (18 May 1858); HR. MKT., 243/68, 17 Zilkade 1274
(29 June 1858); HR. MKT., 251/78, 09 Muharrem 1275 (19 August 1858).
29 Gautier, *Constantinople*, pp. 287–8.
30 BOA, Sadaret Mektubî Kalemi – Nezaret ve Devâir (A. MKT. NZD.),
223/73, 04 Şevval 1273 (28 May 1857).
31 Makdisi, 'Ottoman Orientalism', p. 783.
32 Ibid., pp. 784–5.
33 Artun, http://www.aliartun.com/content/detail/1, accessed 21 November
2016. Selim Deringil argues that for Ottoman elites, adopting European
colonial discourse with regard to the periphery of the Empire was a
survival tactic in an era when the Ottoman Empire itself was subject to
the imperialist policies of European powers. He calls Ottoman imperial
discourse in the late 19th century as 'borrowed imperialism'. Selim Deringil,
' "They Live in a State of Nomadism and Savagery": The Late Ottoman
Empire and the Post-Colonial Debate', *Comparative Studies in Society and
History*, Vol. 45, No. 2 (April 2003): p. 313.
34 BOA, İrade, Şura-yı Devlet (İ. ŞD.), 11/547, 04 Şevval 1285 (18 January
1869); Shaw, *Osmanlı Müzeciliği: Müzeler, Arkeoloji ve Tarihin Görselleşmesi*,
pp. 102–3.
35 Existing literature generally dates the first antiquities law to 1874. However,
Halil Çal has brought the law of 1869 to the attention of researchers. See,
Halil Çal, 'Osmanlı Devletinde Asar-ı Atika Nizamnameleri' (Antiquities
Regulations in the Ottoman Empire), *Vakıflar Dergisi*, No. XXVI, Ankara
(1997), pp. 391–400; Ferruh Gerçek, *Türk Müzeciliği* (Turkish Museology)
(Ankara: Kültür Bakanlığı, 1999), pp. 91.
36 Çal, 'Osmanlı Devletinde Asar-ı Atika Nizamnameleri', p. 395.
37 Mustafa Cezar, *Sanatta Batı'ya Açılış ve Osman Hamdi*, Vol. 1
(İstanbul: Türkiye İş Bankası Kültür Yayınları, 1971), p. 168.
38 Gerçek, *Türk Müzeciliği*, pp. 91–5.
39 Rezan Kocabas, 'Müzecilik Hareketi ve İlk Müze Okulunun Açılışı'
(Opening of the First School of Museology), *Belgelerle Türk Tarihi Dergisi*,
No. 21 (1969): pp. 76–7.
40 Shaw, *Osmanlı Müzeciliği: Müzeler, Arkeoloji ve Tarihin Görselleşmesi*,
pp. 114–17.
41 Mustafa Cezar, *Sanatta Batı'ya Açılış ve Osman Hamdi*, p. 177.
42 BOA, Maarif Mektubî Kalemi (MF. MKT.), 18/97, 23 Rebiülahir 1291 (9
June 1874).
43 BOA, MF. MKT., 18/147, 09 Cemaziyelahir 1291 (24 July 1874).
44 Díaz-Andreu García, *A World History*, p. 113.

45 Nurettin Can, *Eski Eserler ve Müzelerle İlgili Kanun, Nizamname ve Emirler* (Laws, Regulations, and Acts about Ancient Objects and Museums) (Ankara: Milli Eğitim Bakanlığı, 1948), pp. 1–5.

46 Gerçek, *Türk Müzeciliği*, pp. 91–3; Çal, 'Osmanlı Devletinde Asar-ı Atika Nizamnameleri', pp. 391–2, Cezar, *Sanatta Batı'ya Açılış ve Osman Hamdi*, p. 168.

47 Goode, *Negotiating for the Past*, pp. 12–13.

48 Zürcher, *Modernleşen Türkiye'nin Tarihi*, p. 119; Mardin, *Türk Modernleşmesi: Makaleler IV*, pp. 15–16.

49 For biographical information, see Shaw, *Osmanlı Müzeciliği: Müzeler, Arkeoloji ve Tarihin Görselleşmesi*, pp. 122–6; Ahmet Cemil Tan, 'Osman Hamdi Bey', *Ankara Sanat*, No. 10 (1 February 1967), pp. 8–9; Arif Müfid Mansel, *Osman Hamdi Bey* (Ankara: Ankara Üniversitesi, 1959), pp. 189–93; *Osman Hamdi Bey* (İstanbul: Devlet Güzel Sanatlar Akademisi, 1967); Cezar, *Müzeci ve Ressam Osman Hamdi Bey*; Edhem Eldem, 'An Ottoman Archaeologist Caught between Two Worlds: Osman Hamdi Bey (1842–1910)', in *Archaeology, Anthropology, and Heritage in the Balkans and Anatolia: The Life and Times of F. W. Hasluck, 1878–1920*, Vol. 1, ed. David Shankland (İstanbul: Isis Press, 2004), pp. 126–9.

50 Makdisi, 'Ottoman Orientalism', pp. 785–6. In a costume catalogue Osman Hamdi Bey prepared for the Vienna International Exhibition of 1873; he praised the quality and beauty of Turkish fabric as opposed to those produced in Europe. Osman Hamdi Bey and Marie de Launay, *1873 Yılında Türkiye'de Halk Giysileri: Elbise-i Osmaniyye* (The Popular Costumes of Turkey in 1873) (İstanbul: Sabancı Üniversitesi, 1999), p. 261; pp. 223–5.

51 Cezar, *Müzeci ve Ressam Osman Hamdi Bey*, p. 14.

52 Gerçek, *Türk Müzeciliği*, pp. 320–5.

53 Banu Ahibay, 'Theoretical Approaches in Turkish Archaeology' (Unpublished master's thesis, Bilkent University, Ankara, 2007), pp. 12–13.

54 Edhem Eldem, 'An Ottoman Archaeologist Caught between Two Worlds: Osman Hamdi Bey (1842–1910)', p. 129.

55 Cezar, *Müzeci ve Ressam Osman Hamdi Bey*, pp. 17–18.

56 BOA, İrade, Meclis-i Mahsus (İ. MMS.), 78/3401, 23 Rebiülahir 1301 (21 February 1884). With minor revisions, this act remained in effect until 1974.

57 Çal, 'Osmanlı Devletinde Asar-ı Atika Nizamnameleri', p. 393.

58 Quoted in Edhem Eldem, 'An Ottoman Archaeologist Caught between Two Worlds: Osman Hamdi Bey (1842–1910)', p. 132.

59 Ibid., pp. 134–5.

60 Zeynep Çelik, *Asar-ı Atika: Osmanlı İmparatorluğu'nda Arkeoloji Siyaseti*, p. 88.

61 Osman Hamdi Bey and Osgan Efendi, *Le Tumulus de Nemroud-Dagh* (The Tumulus of Mount Nemrud) (İstanbul: Archaeology and Art Publications, 1987), Osman Hamdi Bey and Osgan Efendi, *Le Voyage à Nemrud Dağı*

d'Osman Hamdi Bey et Osgan Efendi (1883): Récit de voyage et photographies (Paris: Institut français d'études anatoliennes-Georges Dumézil, 2010).

62 Mustafa Cezar, *Sanatta Batı'ya Açılış ve Osman Hamdi*, p. 273.

63 Ibid., p. 275.

64 Osman Hamdi Bey and Theodore Reinach, *Une Nécropole Royale à Sidon: Fouilles de Hamdy Bey* (A Royal Necropolis in Sidon: Excavations of Hamdi Bey) (Paris: Ernest Leroux, 1892).

65 BOA, İrade, Hususi (İ. HUS.), 1/1310-M-074, 10 Muharrem 1310 (4 August 1892).

66 BOA, Bab-ı Âli Evrak Odası (BEO.), 95/7104, 04 Rebiülahir 1310 (26 October 1892).

67 Gerçek, *Türk Müzeciliği*, p. 122.

68 Nezih Başgelen, *Ölümünün 100. Yılındu Osman Hamdi Bey: Yaptığı Kazılar – Bulduğu Eserler* (Osman Hamdi Bey on the 100th Anniversary of His Death: His Excavations and Findings) (İstanbul: Arkeoloji ve Sanat Yayınları, 2010), pp. 15–25.

69 Nur Akın, 'Osman Hamdi Bey, Asar-ı Atika Nizamnamesi ve Dönemin Koruma Anlayışı Üzerine' (Osman Hamdi Bey, Antiquities Regulations, and the Preservation of Antiquities in His Period), *Osman Hamdi Bey ve Dönemi, 17–18 Aralık 1992* (İstanbul: Tarih Vakfı Yurt Yayınları, 1993), pp. 237–8.

70 Mustafa Cezar, *Sanatta Batı'ya Açılış ve Osman Hamdi*, p. 274.

71 Refik Epikman, *Osman Hamdi* (İstanbul: Milli Eğitim Basımevi, 1967), pp. 5–6.

72 Mustafa Cezar, *Sanatta Batı'ya Açılış ve Osman Hamdi*, p. 211.

73 Ibid., pp. 276–83.

74 Makdisi, 'Ottoman Orientalism', p. 784.

75 BOA, DH. MKT., 555/16, 02 Cemaziyelevvel 1320 (7 August 1902).

76 For example, railroad concessions granted constructing countries the right of ownership of discoveries made along the right-of-way. Deutsche Orient-Gesellschaft was granted the right to make excavations in Mesopotamia in 1898, one year before the Germans initiated the Berlin–Baghdad railway project. For further information, see Goode, *Negotiating for the Past*, p. 24; Bernhardsson, *Reclaiming a Plundered Past*, pp. 52–6.

77 Goode, *Negotiating for the Past*, p. 25.

78 BOA, BEO., 1726/129384, 16 Cemaziyelahir 1319 (30 September 1901).

79 BOA, BEO., 1731/129825, 27 Cemaziyelahir 1319 (11 October 1901).

80 Wendy M. K. Shaw, 'Islamic Arts in the Ottoman Imperial Museum, 1889–1923' *Ars Orientalis*, Vol. 30, Exhibiting the Middle East: Collections and Perceptions of Islamic Art (2000), p. 57.

81 Özdoğan, 'Ideology and Archaeology in Turkey', p. 115.

82 Çal, 'Osmanlı Devletinde Asar-ı Atika Nizamnameleri', p. 393.

83 Shaw, 'Islamic Arts in the Ottoman Imperial Museum, 1889–1923', p. 60.

84 Can, *Eski Eserler ve Müzelerle İlgili Kanun*, pp. 67–77; Çal, 'Osmanlı Devletinde Asar-ı Atika Nizamnameleri', p. 393.
85 Bernhardsson, *Reclaiming a Plundered Past*, pp. 73–4.
86 Marchand, *Down from Olympus*, pp. 212–15.
87 Şükrü Hanioğlu, *The Young Turks in Opposition* (New York: Oxford University Press, 1995), pp. 17–18.
88 Mardin, *Türk Modernleşmesi: Makaleler IV*, pp. 97–101.
89 Feroz Ahmad, *The Making of Modern Turkey* (New York: Routledge, 1993), p. 46.
90 Marchand, *Down from Olympus*, p. 216.
91 BOA, Dahiliye, Hukuk Müşavirliği (DH. HMŞ.), 9/8, 16 Recep 1329 (13 July 1911).
92 BOA, Dahiliye Nezareti Muhaberât ve Tensîkât Müdüriyeti Belgeleri (DH. EUM. MTK.), 13/12, 22 Safer 1332 (20 January 1914).
93 The director of the museum at that time, Halil Ethem moved to the museum with his family during the war. See, Ayşe Özdemir, 'A History of Turkish Archaeology from the 19th Century to the End of the Single Party Period' (Unpublished master's thesis, Boğaziçi University, İstanbul, 2001), p. 62; Gerçek, *Türk Müzeciliği*, pp. 331–2.
94 Özdoğan, 'Ideology and Archaeology in Turkey', pp. 115–16.
95 Semavi Eyice, 'Türkiye'de Bizans Sanatı Araştırmaları ve İstanbul Üniversitesinde Bizans Sanatı' (Byzantine Art Studies in Turkey and Byzantine Art in İstanbul University), *Cumhuriyetin 50. Yılına Armağan* (50th Anniversary of the Republic Memory Book) (İstanbul: İstanbul Üniversitesi Edebiyat Fakültesi, 1973), p. 378.
96 Şule Kılıç Yıldız, 'A Review of Byzantine Studies and Architectural Historiography in Turkey Today', p. 64; Michael Ursinus, 'From Süleyman Pasha to Mehmet Fuat Köprülü: Roman and Byzantine History in Late Ottoman Historiography', *Byzantine and Modern Greek Studies*, Vol. 12 (1988): pp. 306–7; Michael Ursinus, 'Byzantine History in Late Ottoman Turkish Historiography', *Byzantine and Modern Greek Studies*, Vol. 10 (1986): pp. 214–15.
97 Claire Norton, 'Blurring the Boundaries: Intellectual and Cultural Interactions between the Eastern and Western; Christian and Muslim Worlds', in *The Renaissance and the Ottoman World*, ed. Anna Contadini, Claire Norton (Burlington: Ashgate, 2013), p. 18.
98 Michael Angold, *The Fall of Constantinople to the Ottomans: Context and Consequences* (London: Routledge, 2014), p. 67.
99 Ursinus, 'From Süleyman Pasha to Mehmet Fuat Köprülü: Roman and Byzantine History in Late Ottoman Historiography', pp. 307–9.
100 Ursinus, 'Byzantine History in Late Ottoman Turkish Historiography', pp. 215–18.
101 Ibid., pp. 221–2.

102 Celal Esad Arseven (Djelal Essad), *Constantinople de Byzance a Stamboul* (Paris: Librairie Renouard, 1909) (traduit du turc par l'auteur, preface de M. Charles Diehl), pp. II–III.

103 Ibid., pp. 151–3.

104 Ibid., p. 10.

105 Ibid., pp. 33–6.

106 Ibid., pp. 169, 176.

107 Despite its relatively late publication (1920), in the aftermath of the First World War, this book was considered as belonging to the pre-Republican literature. It was published before the proclamation of the Republic and when the Sultan was still the official head of the state. Therefore, the author could not have been influenced by Republican ideology.

108 İhtifalci Mehmed Ziya, *İstanbul ve Boğaziçi: Bizans ve Türk Medeniyetinin Eserleri* (Istanbul and the Bosphorus: The Monuments of Byzantine and Turkish Civilisations) (İstanbul, 1937), p. 133.

109 Ibid., p. 135.

110 Ibid., p. 9.

111 Ibid., p. 17.

112 Shaw, 'Islamic Arts in the Ottoman Imperial Museum, 1889–1923', p. 58.

113 Ayşe Özdemir, 'A History of Turkish Archaeology from the 19th Century to the End of the Single Party Period' (Unpublished master's thesis, Boğaziçi University, Istanbul, 2001), p. 68.

114 Makdisi, 'Ottoman Orientalism', p. 783.

115 Mehmet Özdoğan, 'Ideology and Archaeology in Turkey', p. 115; Tuğba Tanyeri-Erdemir, 'Archaeology as a Source of National Pride in the Early Years of the Turkish Republic', *Journal of Field Archaeology*, Vol. 31, No. 4 (Winter 2006): p. 382.

3 At the intersection of science and politics: Russian Archaeological Institute in the Ottoman Empire

1 M. S. Anderson's monograph, which is in fact a chronological overview of diplomatic events of the late 19th century, was the most cited work on the Eastern Question until recently: M. S. Anderson, *The Eastern Question, 1774–1923: A Study in International Relations* (London: St Martin's Press, 1970), pp. 225–60. Recent studies present a more multifaceted view of international politics in the late 19th century. Most notably, Nazan Çiçek challenged the previous Euro-centric assumptions by arguing that what was regarded as the Eastern Question by European powers was interpreted as the 'Western Question' by Ottoman intellectuals: Nazan Çiçek, *The Young Ottomans: Turkish Critics of the Eastern Question in the Late 19th Century* (London: I.B. Tauris, 2010), pp. 1–12. For further theoretical

discussion on the Eastern Question, see Lucien J. Frary and Mara Kozelsky, 'Introduction: The Eastern Question Reconsidered', in *Russian-Ottoman Borderlands: The Eastern Question Reconsidered*, ed. Lucien J. Frary and Mara Kozelsky (Madison: University of Wisconsin Press, 2014), pp. 3–18.

2 David Saunders, *Russia in the Age of Reaction and Reform, 1801–1881* (London: Longman, 1992), p. 169.

3 Simon Dixon, 'Nationalism versus Internationalism: Russian Orthodoxy in Nineteenth-Century Palestine', in *Religious International in the Modern World: Globalization and Faith Communities since 1750*, ed. Abigail Green and Vincent Viaene (London: Palgrave Macmillan, 2012), p. 148.

4 K. A. Vakh, '"İyerusalimskii Proyekt" Rossii: B. P. Mansurov i Russkie Postroiki', *Velikii Knyaz' Konstantin Nikolayevich i Russkii Iyerusalim: K 150-Letiyu Osnovaniya* (Moskva: Indrik, 2012), p. 16.

5 A. A. Dmitrievskii, *Imperatorskoe Pravoslavnoe Palestinskoe Obshchestvo i Ego Deyatelnost' za Istekshuyu Chervert' Veka, 1882–1907* (St Petersburg: V. O. Kirshbauma, 1907), pp. 18–24.

6 Dixon, 'Nationalism versus Internationalism', p. 148.

7 Tatiana V. Chumakova, Marianna Shakhnovich and Ekaterina Terukova, 'Collections of the Imperial Orthodox Palestine Society in the State Museum of the History of Religion (Saint-Petersburg, Russia)', *European Researcher*, Series A, Vol. 107 (2016): p. 319.

8 Theofanis George Stavrou, *Russian Interests in Palestine, 1882–1914: A Study of Religious and Educational Enterprise* (Thessaloniki: Institute for Balkan Studies, 1963), pp. 57–8.

9 Stavrou, *Russian Interests in Palestine*, pp. 61–2.

10 Ibid., pp. 68–9.

11 Dmitrievskii, *Imperatorskoe*, p. 196.

12 M. V. Pervushin, 'Palomnichestvo na Sviatuiu Zemliu v XIX Vee', in *Khristiyanstvo: Vek za Vekom*, ed. Archbishop Mark Golovkov Yegoryevsk (Moskva: Dar, 2011), p. 508.

13 A. A. Spasskii, 'Noveyshii Vizantinizm i Ego Znachenie', p. 49.

14 M. V. Pervushin, 'Russkaia Dukhovnaia Missiia v Iyerusalime', in *Khristiyanstvo: Vek za Vekom*, ed. Archbishop Mark Golovkov Yegoryevsk (Moskva: Dar, 2011), pp. 505–6.

15 Archbishop Arsenii Volokolamskii, 'V Strane Svyashchennykh Vospominanii', *Bogoslovskii Vestnik*, T. 2, Nos 7/8 (1901): pp. 586–7.

16 Elena Astafieva, 'The Russian Empire in Palestine, 1847–1917: A Look Back at the Origins of Russia's Near Eastern Policy', *Tepsis Papers*, No. 10, Version Anglophone (February 2016), p. 4, <hal-01293323v2>, accessed 10 December 2016.

17 N. N. Lisovoi, 'Russkoe Dukhovnoe i Politicheskoe Prisutstvie v Sviatoi Zemle i na Blizhnem Vostoke v XIX – nachale XX v' (Unpublished Ph.D. dissertation, Institut Vseobshchei Istorii RAN, Moskva, 2007), pp. 63–4.

18 Lora Gerd, *Russian Policy in the Orthodox East: The Patriarchate of Constantinople (1878–1914)* (Warsaw: De Gruyter Open, 2014), p. 54, e-book available at https://www.degruyter.com/view/product/209761?format=EBOK. Accessed 20 March 2017.

19 Dmitrievskii, *Imperatorskoe*, p. 190.

20 Stavrou, *Russian Interests in Palestine*, pp. 205–6.

21 Ibid., p. 209.

22 'O Svyatoi Zemle i Imperatorskom Pravoslavnom Palestinskom Obshchestve', *Bogoslovskii Vestnik*, T. 1, No. 3 (1914): pp. 620, 625–6.

23 Dominique Trimbur, 'A French Presence in Palestine: Notre-Dame de France', *Bulletin du Centre de Recherche Français à Jérusalem* [Online], No. 3 (1998): pp. 127–8.

24 Stavrou, *Russian Interests in Palestine*, p. 211.

25 Ibid., p. 213.

26 S. A. Ershov, IU. A. Piatnitskii, K. N. Iuzbashian, 'Russkii Arkheologicheskii Institut v Konstantinopole'. *Palestinskii Sbornik*, Vol. 29, No. 92 (1987): p. 9.

27 Stavrou, *Russian Interests in Palestine*, p. 137.

28 Basargina, *Russkii Arkheologicheskii Institut v Konstantinopole*, p. 20.

29 Basargina, 'Proekty Sozdaniia Russkikh Arkheologicheskikh Institutov za Rubezhom', *Vestnik Drevnei Istorii*, Vol. 267, No. 4 (2008): pp. 206–8.

30 *Sankt-Peterburgskii filial Arkhiva Rossiiskoi Akademii Nauk* (henceforth cited as PFA RAN), f. 127, op. 1, d. 1, l. 4–5 (Uspenskii to Ambassador Nelidov, October 1890).

31 Anderson, *The Eastern Question*, pp. 256–8.

32 Charles and Barbara Jelavich, *The Establishment of the Balkan National States, 1804–1920* (Seattle: University of Washington Press, 1986), pp. 208–9.

33 İpek Yosmaoğlu, 'Counting Bodies, Shaping Souls: The 1903 Census and National Identity in Ottoman Macedonia', *International Journal of Middle East Studies*, Vol. 38, No. 1 (February 2006): p. 60.

34 Denis Vladimirovich Vovchenko, 'Containing Balkan Nationalism: Imperial Russia and Ottoman Christians (1856–1912)' (Unpublished Ph.D. Dissertation, University of Minnesota, August 2008), pp. 136–40.

35 Yosmaoğlu, 'Counting Bodies, Shaping Souls: The 1903 Census and National Identity in Ottoman Macedonia', pp. 59–60.

36 Andrew Rossos, 'Serbian-Bulgarian Relations, 1903–1914', *Canadian Slavonic Papers / Revue Canadienne des Slavistes*, Vol. 23, No. 4 (December 1981): pp. 398–9.

37 Jelavich and Jelavich, *The Establishment of the Balkan National States*, pp. 164–9.

38 Duncan M. Perry, *Stefan Stamboulov and the Emergence of Modern Bulgaria, 1870–1895* (Durham: Duke University Press, 1993), pp. 121–2.

39 Dominic Lieven, *Towards the Flame: Empire, War and the End of Tsarist Russia* (London: Penguin Books, 2015), p. 5.

40 Gerd, *Russian Policy in the Orthodox East: The Patriarchate of Constantinople (1878-1914)*, p. 117.

41 Basargina, *Russkii Arkheologicheskii Institut v Konstantinopole*, pp. 21-2.

42 *Izvestiia Russkogo Arkheologicheskogo Instituta v Konstantinopole* (henceforth cited as IRAIK), 'Otkrytie Russkogo Arkheologicheskogo Instituta v Konstantinopole 26-go Fevralia 1895 goda', Vol. 1 (1896): p. 3.

43 *Rossiiskii Gosudarstvennyi Istoricheskii Arkhiv* (henceforth cited as RGIA), f. 757, op. 1, d. 1, l. 2-14 (P. B. Mansurov to the Embassy in Istanbul, 30 March 1887).

44 RGIA, f. 757, op. 1, d. 1, l. 3 (P. B. Mansurov to the Embassy in Istanbul, 30 March 1887).

45 Michael Boro Petrovich, *A History of Modern Serbia, 1804-1918*, Vol. 2 (New York: Harcourt Brace Jovanovich, 1976), pp. 511-15.

46 Suzanne L. Marchand, 'The Rhetoric of Artifacts and the Decline of Classical Humanism: The Case of Josef Strzygowski', *History and Theory*, Vol. 33, No. 4, Theme Issue 33: Proof and Persuasion in History (December 1994): p. 110.

47 Suzanne L. Marchand, 'The View from the Land: Austrian Art Historians and the Interpretation of Croatian Art', in *Dalmatia and the Mediterranean: Portable Archaeology and the Poetics of Influence*, ed. Alina Payne (Leiden: Brill, 2014), pp. 41-5.

48 RGIA, f. 757, op. 1, d. 1, l. 14 (P. B. Mansurov to the Embassy in Istanbul, 30 March 1887).

49 Anderson, *The Eastern Question*, pp. 256-7.

50 Barbara Jelavich, *Russia's Balkan Entanglements, 1806-1914* (Cambridge: Cambridge University Press, 2004), pp. 205-6.

51 N. I. Komandorova, *Russkii Stambul* (Moskva: Veche, 2009), p. 263.

52 PFA RAN, f. 1, op. 1a, d. 175, l. 133-134 (from the Meeting Protocol of the USSR Academy of Sciences, 1926).

53 PFA RAN, f. 1, op. 1a, d. 175, l. 132-143 (from the Meeting Protocol of the USSR Academy of Sciences, 1926).

54 PFA RAN, f. 1, op. 1a, d. 175, l. 137 (from the Meeting Protocol of the USSR Academy of Sciences, 1926).

55 PFA RAN, f. 1, op. 1a, d. 175, l. 137 (from the Meeting Protocol of the USSR Academy of Sciences, 1926).

56 IRAIK, 'Otkrytie Russkogo Arkheologicheskogo Instituta v Konstantinopole 26-go Fevralia 1895 goda', p. 4.

57 Uspenskii, 'Iz Istorii Vizantinovedeniia v Rossii', p. 119.

58 Ibid., pp. 124-5.

59 Ibid., pp. 119-20.

60 Musin, *Imperatorskaia Arkheologicheskaia Komissiia, 1859-1917*, p. 204.

61 Uspenskii, 'Iz Istorii Vizantinovedeniia v Rossii', pp. 119-20.

62 Ibid., pp. 121-2.

63 IRAIK, 'Otchet v 1909 godu', Vol. 15 (1911): p. 246.

64 PFA RAN, f. 127, op. 1, d. 1, l. 50 (Ministry of Public Education to the State Council, 25 October 1893).

65 PFA RAN, f. 127, op. 1, d. 1, l. 50 (Ministry of Public Education to the State Council, 25 October 1893).

66 PFA RAN, f. 127, op. 1, d. 1, l. 50–50.5 (Ministry of Public Education to the State Council, 25 October 1893).

67 Komandorova, *Russkii Stambul*, p. 262.

68 PFA RAN, f. 127, op. 1, d. 1, l. 1–3 (Uspenskii to Ambassador Nelidov, 4 July 1889).

69 Musin, *Imperatorskaia Arkheologicheskaia Komissiia*, p. 203.

70 PFA RAN, f. 127, op. 1, d. 1, l. 5–5.5 (Ministry of Public Education to the Ambassador in Istanbul, 12 December 1890).

71 PFA RAN, f. 127, op. 1, d. 1, l. 6–7 (Ministry of Finance to the Ambassador in Istanbul, 9 January 1891).

72 J. Y. Simms, 'The Economic Impact of the Russian Famine of 1891–92', *The Slavonic and East European Review*, Vol. 60, No. 1 (January 1982): p. 63.

73 PFA RAN, f. 127, op. 1, d. 1, l. 52–52.5 (Ministry of Public Education to the State Council, 25 October 1893).

74 Vovchenko, 'Containing Balkan Nationalism', p. 261.

75 PFA RAN, f. 127, op. 1, d. 1, l. 8 (P. B. Mansurov to Uspenskii, 20 September 1893).

76 Komandorova, *Russkii Stambul*, p. 264.

77 O. L. Fetisenko, *Proroki Vizantizma: Perepiska K. N. Leont'eva i T. I. Filippova, 1875–1891* (St Petersburg: Izd-vo Pushkinskii Dom, 2012), pp. 6–7.

78 Basargina, *Russkii Arkheologicheskii Institut v Konstantinopole*, p. 91.

79 Unfortunately, the closure of AVPRI during the research phase of this study made it impossible to track the documents from the Ministry of Foreign Affairs. Therefore, we are unable to know the exact nature of discussions within the Ministry. Especially, the exchange of letters between Nelidov and the Foreign Minister Nikolai Girs, who was in office from 1882 to 1895, would be interesting in this respect.

80 PFA RAN, f. 127, op. 1, d. 1, l. 54–54.5 (Ministry of Public Education to the State Council, 25 October 1893).

81 Musin, *Imperatorskaia Arkheologicheskaia Komissiia*, p. 204.

82 PFA RAN, f. 127, op. 1, d. 1, l. 24–24.5 (Vorontsov-Dashkov to the State Council, 15 March 1894).

83 PFA RAN, f. 127, op. 1, d. 1, l. 66–66.5 (Report by Ministry of Public Education to the State Council, 24 February 1894).

84 PFA RAN, f. 127, op. 1, d. 1, l. 16–17 (P. B. Mansurov to Uspenskii, 20 September 1893).

85 PFA RAN, f. 127, op. 1, d. 1, l. 66.5–67 (Report by Ministry of Public Education to the State Council, 24 February 1894).

86 PFA RAN, f. 127, op. 1, d. 1, l. 67.5–70 (Report by Ministry of Public Education to the State Council, 24 February 1894).

87 PFA RAN, f. 127, op. 1, d. 1, l. 90–91 (Uspenskii to Delianov, 29 September 1894).
88 PFA RAN, f. 127, op. 1, d. 1, l. 27 (Delianov to Uspenskii, 1894).
89 PFA RAN, f. 127, op. 1, d. 1, l. 8.5 (P. B. Mansurov to Uspenskii, 20 September 1893).
90 IRAIK, 'Otchet v 1909 godu', p. 246.
91 PFA RAN, f. 127, op. 1, d. 1, l. 162–163 (Uspenskii to Department of Science in the People's Commissariat for Education, 13 August 1918).
92 PFA RAN, f. 127, op. 1, d. 1, l. 272–275 (Charter of RAIK, 1894).
93 IRAIK, 'Otkrytie Russkogo Arkheologicheskogo Instituta v Konstantinopole 26-go Fevralia 1895 goda', p. 3.
94 PFA RAN, f. 127, op. 1, d. 1, l. 26 (Delianov to Uspenskii, 1894).
95 PFA RAN, f. 127, op. 1, d. 1, l. 36, l. 46–47 (Delianov to Uspenskii, 1894; Uspenskii to Delianov, 1894).
96 IRAIK, 'Otkrytie Russkogo Arkheologicheskogo Instituta v Konstantinopole 26-go Fevralia 1895 goda', Vol. 1 (1896): p. 1.
97 PFA RAN, f. 127, op. 1, d. 1, l. 14 (P. B. Mansurov to Uspenskii, 20 September 1893).
98 IRAIK, 'Otkrytie Russkogo Arkheologicheskogo Instituta v Konstantinopole 26-go Fevralia 1895 goda', pp. 5–6.
99 Ibid., pp. 7–9.
100 PFA RAN, f. 127, op. 1, d. 1, l. 162–163 (Uspenskii to Department of Science in the People's Commissariat for Education, 13 august 1918).
101 PFA RAN, f. 127, op. 1, d. 3, l. 2–3.5 (Uspenskii to Ambassador Zinoviev, 1905).
102 PFA RAN, f. 116, op. 2, d. 40, l. 9–11 (Uspenskii to Ministry of Public Education, 20 March 1915).
103 Basargina, *Russkii Arkheologicheskii Institut v Konstantinopole*, p. 109.
104 IRAIK, 'Otchet v 1909 godu', p. 247.
105 Dominic Lieven, *Nicholas II: Twilight of the Empire* (New York: St Martin's Press, 1994), p. 34.
106 PFA RAN, f. 116, op. 1, d. 269 (Uspenskii to Ministry of Public Education, 26 September 1897).
107 PFA RAN, f. 127, op. 1, d. 32, l. 4–5 (RAIK to Russian diplomatic corpus in the Ottoman Empire, June 1895).
108 PFA RAN, f. 127, op. 1, d. 32, l. 9 (Russian General Consulate in Beirut to Uspenskii, 3 April 1895); PFA RAN, f. 127, op. 1, d. 32, l. 11 (Russian General Consulate in Jerusalem to Uspenskii, 6 September 1895); PFA RAN, f. 127, op. 1, d. 32, l.8 (Imperial Mission in Greece to Uspenskii, 18 March 1895).
109 PFA RAN, f. 127, op. 1, d. 2, l. 56 (Uspenskii to Greek Ambassador in Istanbul, 30 December 1895); PFA RAN, f. 127, op. 1, d. 2, l. 61 (Serbian Ambassador in Istanbul to Uspenskii, December 1895).

110 Harold N. Fowler, 'Archaeological News', *American Journal of Archaeology*, Vol. 5, No. 1 (January – March 1901): p. 94; Harold N. Fowler, 'Archaeological News', *American Journal of Archaeology*, Vol. 6, No. 1 (January–March 1902): p. 66.

111 Arkhimandit Avgustin, 'Russkii Arkheologicheskii Institut v Konstantinopole', *Bogoslovskie Trudy*, Vol. 27 (1986): p. 273.

112 PFA RAN, f. 116, op. 2, d. 40, l. 14 (Uspenskii to Ministry of Public Education, 20 March 1915).

113 IRAIK, 'Otchet v 1905 godu', Vol. 13 (1908): p. 333.

114 PFA RAN, f. 116, op. 2, d. 86, l. 1–3, 7–8 (Paul Gaudin to Uspenskii, 1902 and 31 January 1905).

115 Ludwik Biskupski, 'L'Historique de L'Institut Français d'Études Byzantines', *Slavic and East European Studies*, Vol. 4, Nos 1–2 (Spring-Summer 1959): p. 89.

116 PFA RAN, f. 127, op. 1, d. 148, l. 6–7 (RAIK Report to Ministry of Public Education, 1907).

117 A. L. Frothingham, Jr, 'Archaeological News', *The American Journal of Archaeology and of the History of the Fine Arts*, Vol. 10, Nos. 1 (January–March 1895): p. 132.

4 Expeditions of the Russian Archaeological Institute and contacts with Ottoman authorities

1 BOA, Yıldız Perakende Evrakı Askeri Maruzat (Y. PRK. ASK.), 56/20, 13 Zilkade 1306 (11 July 1889).

2 BOA, Y. PRK. ASK., 91/105, 09 Zilhicce 1310 (24 June 1893).

3 BOA, Meclis-i Vükelâ (MV.), 66/65, 30 Zilhicce 1308 (6 August 1891).

4 BOA, Yıldız Hususi Maruzat (Y. A. HUS.), 307/84, 27 Safer 1312 (30 August 1894).

5 PFA RAN, f. 127, op. 1, d. 147, l. 3 (RAIK Report to Ministry of Public Education, 1900).

6 BOA, BEO., 1006/75417, 09 Rebiülahir 1315 (7 September 1897); PFA RAN, f. 127, op. 1, d. 1, l. 128 (Delianov to Uspenskii, October 1897).

7 PFA RAN, f. 127, op. 1, d. 32, l. 48 (Tevfik Pasha to M. Jadovski, 29 September 1897).

8 PFA RAN, f. 127, op. 1, d. 3, l. 7–8 (Uspenskii to Ambassador Zinoviev, 1905).

9 BOA, İ. HUS., 57/1315-Ca-004, 01 Cemâziyelevvel 1315 (28 September 1897).

10 BOA, İrade, Taltifat (İ. TAL.), 121/1315-Ca-066, 19 Cemâziyelevvel 1315 (16 October 1897).

11 RGIA, f. 757, op. 1, d. 27, l. 1–3 (Uspenskii to Ambassador Zinoviev, 1906).

12 PFA RAN, f. 127, op. 1, d. 3, l. 2 (Uspenskii to Ambassador Nelidov, 4 July 1889).

13 RGIA, f. 757, op. 1, d. 40, l. 3–4 (Uspenskii to Ministry of Public Education, 9 December 1914).

14 PFA RAN, f. 127, op. 1, d. 1, l. 100 (Uspenskii to Ministry of Public Education, 1914).

15 Popruzhenko, *Sorokaletie*, p. 25.

16 All three cities are important ports on the Turkish coasts of the Black Sea. BOA, BEO., 628/47089, 29 Zilkade 1312 (24 May 1895).

17 BOA, Dahiliye Mektubî Kalemi (DH. MKT.), 379/80, 04 Zilhicce 1312 (29 May 1895).

18 BOA, DH. MKT., 428/21, 24 Rebiülevvel 1313 (14 September 1895).

19 IRAIK, 'Otchet v 1895 godu', Vol. 1 (1896): pp. 24–8.

20 IRAIK, 'Vnov Naydenny Purpurovy Kodeks Evangeliya', Vol. 1 (1896): pp. 138–9.

21 PFA RAN, f. 127, op. 1, d. 139, l. 20–25 (Brochure, '33 Days in Asia Minor' by secretary of Russian Consulate in Konya, T. Nikolaev, 1896).

22 IRAIK, 'Otchet v 1897 godu', Vol. 3 (1898): p. 197.

23 RGIA, f. 757, op. 1, d. 5, l. 7 (Uspenskii to Ministry of Public Education, 26 August 1898).

24 IRAIK, 'Otchet v 1898 godu', Vol. 4, No. 3 (1899): p. 109.

25 Archbishop Arsenii Volokolamskii, 'V Strane Svyashchennykh Vospominanii', *Bogoslovskii Vestnik*, T. 1, No. 3 (1902): p. 559.

26 Today, Sorovich is in Greece, known as Amyntiao.

27 PFA RAN, f. 127, op. 1, d. 147, l. 3 (RAIK Report to Ministry of Public Education, 1900).

28 PFA RAN, f. 127, op. 1, d. 150, l. 3–5 (RAIK Report to Ministry of Public Education, 1899).

29 BOA, İ. HUS., 67/1316-R-103, 27 Rebiülahir 1316 (14 September 1898).

30 BOA, DH. MKT., 2147/110, 29 Recep 1316 (13 December 1898).

31 For Miliukov's career as a historian, see Thomas Riha, *A Russian European: Paul Miliukov in Russian Politics* (Notre Dame: Notre Dame University Press, 1969), pp. 20–8; Melissa Kirschke Stockdale, *Paul Miliukov and the Quest for a Liberal Russia, 1880–1918* (Ithaca: Cornell University Press, 1996), pp. 81–5.

32 Leo Wiener, 'A Victim of Autocracy: Prof. Milyukov, Lowell Lecturer 'The Russian Crisis', *Boston Evening Transcript*, 29 November 1904, p. 9.

33 IRAIK, 'Otchet v 1898 godu', Vol. 4, Issue 3 (1898), pp. 150–1.

34 Stockdale, *Paul Miliukov and the Quest for a Liberal Russia*, p. 83.

35 PFA RAN, f. 127, op. 1, d. 147, l. 10–10.5 (RAIK Report to Ministry of Public Education, 1900).

36 RGIA, f. 757, op. 1, d. 11, l. 5 (Russian Embassy in Istanbul to Uspenskii, 5 April 1899).

37 BOA, DH. MKT., 2210/21, 3 Safer 1317 (13 June 1899); DH.MKT., 2191/63, 06 Zilhicce 1316 (17 April 1899).

38 PFA RAN, f. 127, op. 1, d. 147, l. 7 (RAIK Report to Ministry of Public Education, 1900).

39 PFA RAN, f. 127, op. 1, d. 147, l. 7–9, 10.5–11 (RAIK Report to Ministry of Public Education, 1900).

40 PFA RAN, f. 127, op. 1, d. 147, l. 10–15 (RAIK Report to Ministry of Public Education, 1900).

41 PFA RAN, f. 127, op. 1, d. 147, l. 11.5–12 (RAIK Report to Ministry of Public Education, 1900).

42 PFA RAN, f. 127, op. 1, d. 147, l. 13.5–14 (RAIK Report to Ministry of Public Education, 1900).

43 PFA RAN, f. 127, op. 1, d. 150, l. 5–7 (RAIK Report to Ministry of Public Education, 1899).

44 BOA, DH. MKT., 2264/88, 27 Cemaziyelahir 1317 (2 November 1899).

45 BOA, DH. MKT., 2273/76, 16 Recep 1317 (20 November 1899).

46 BOA, DH. MKT., 2288/87, 21 Şaban 1317 (25 December 1899).

47 PFA RAN, f. 127, op. 1, d. 147, l. 15 (RAIK Report to Ministry of Public Education, 1900).

48 RGIA, f. 757, op. 1, d. 34, l. 6–7 (Uspenskii to Ambassador Girs, 19 June 1913).

49 IRAIK, P. N. Miliukov, 'Khristiyanskaia Drevnosti Zapadnoi Makedonii', Vol. 4, No. 1 (1899): pp. 21–2.

50 Mikhail Ivanovich Rostovtsev (1870–1952) was an important historian of the ancient world, whose career stretched from pre-Revolutionary Russia to the 20th-century United States. In 1918, Rostovtsev emigrated first to Europe, and then to the United States. He taught at the University of Wisconsin-Madison (1920–5) and later at Yale (1925–44) and continued to lecture on Roman and ancient Greek history. Most of his academic works are available in English. For biographical information, see C. Bradford Welles, 'Michael Ivanovich Rostovtzeff (1870–1952)', *Russian Review*, Vol. 12, No. 2 (April 1953): pp. 128–33.

51 IRAIK, M. I. Rostovtsev, 'Nadpisi iz Makedonii', Vol. 4, No. 3 (1899): p. 166.

52 IRAIK, 'Otchet v 1898 godu', Vol. 4, No. 3 (1899): p. 125.

53 For further information on the Macedonian conflict, see İpek Yosmaoğlu, *Blood Ties: Religion, Violence, and the Politics of Nationhood in Ottoman Macedonia, 1878–1908* (Ithaca, NY: Cornell University Press, 2013), pp. 19–47.

54 IRAIK, 'Otchet v 1898 godu', Vol. 4, No. 3 (1899): pp. 124–5.

55 Ibid., p. 125.

56 Lieven, *Towards the Flame: Empire, War, and the End of Tsarist Russia*, p. 3.

57 Jelavich and Jelavich, *The Establishment of the Balkan National States*, p. 208.

58 Riha, *A Russian European: Paul Miliukov in Russian Politics*, pp. 35–6.

59 Paul N. Miliukov, *Political Memoirs, 1905–1917* (Ann Arbor: University of Michigan Press, 1967), pp. 174–5.

60 Ibid., p. 181.

61 Ibid., p. 184.

62 Riha, *A Russian European,* p. 250.

63 Aboba is today known as Pliska.

64 IRAIK, Uspenskii, 'Istoriko-Arkheologicheskoe Znachenie Aboby i ee Okrestnostei. Raskopki. Naimenovanie Drevnogo Poseleniia', Vol. 10 (1905): pp. 1–9.

65 PFA RAN, f. 127, op. 1, d. 151, l. 6–7 (RAIK Report to Ministry of Public Education, 1898).

66 PFA RAN, f. 127, op. 1, d. 151, l. 14–15 (RAIK Report to Ministry of Public Education, 1898).

67 PFA RAN, f. 127, op. 1, d. 151, l. 8–9 (RAIK Report to Ministry of Public Education, 1898).

68 PFA RAN, f. 127, op. 1, d. 151, l. 17 (RAIK Report to Ministry of Public Education, 1898).

69 PFA RAN, f. 127, op. 1, d. 151, l. 19–24 (RAIK Report to Ministry of Public Education, 1898).

70 IRAIK, 'Otchet v 1900 godu', Vol. 7, Nos 2–3 (1902): p. 246.

71 PFA RAN, f. 127, op. 1, d. 151, l. 26–27 (RAIK Report to Ministry of Public Education, 1898).

72 IRAIK, 'Otchet v 1899 godu', Vol. 6, Nos 2–3 (1901): p. 449.

73 Perry, *Stefan Stamboulov,* p. 45.

74 IRAIK, 'Otchet v 1899 godu', Vol. 6, Nos 2–3 (1901): pp. 437–9.

75 B. T. Gorianov, 'F. I. Uspenskii i Ego Znachenie v Vizantinovedenii', *Vizantiiskii Vremennik,* Vol. 1, No. 26 (1947): pp. 91–2.

76 IRAIK, 'Otchet v 1900 godu', Vol. 7, Nos 2–3 (1902): pp. 232–6.

77 IRAIK, Uspenskii, 'Arkheologicheskie Pamyatniki Sirii', Vol. 7, Nos 2–3 (1902): p. 94.

78 IRAIK, Uspenskii, 'O Perevozke iz Palmiry v S. Peterburg Plity s Nadpisiu', Vol. 13 (1908): p. 363.

79 BOA, BEO., 1731/129825, 27 Cemaziyelahir 1319 (11 October 1901).

80 IRAIK, Uspenskii, 'O Perevozke iz Palmiry v S. Peterburg Plity s Nadpisiu', Vol. 13 (1908): pp. 369–70.

81 Ibid., p. 366.

82 IRAIK, P. K. Kokovtsev, 'Novaia Arameiskaia Nadpisi iz Palmiry', Vol. 8, No. 3 (1903): pp. 302–3.

83 IRAIK, A. A. Pavlovskii and N. K. Kluge, 'Madeba', Vol. 8, Nos. 1–2 (1902): pp. 82–3, 114.

84 PFA RAN, f. 116, op. 2, d. 152, l. 1–1.5 (Viktor F. Kal' to Uspenskii, 26 November 1902).

85 PFA RAN, f. 116, op. 2, d. 152, l. 5–6 (Viktor F. Kal' to Uspenskii, 22 December 1902).

86 PFA RAN, f. 116, op. 2, d. 152, l. 11–12 (Viktor F. Kal' to Uspenskii, 15 February 1903).
87 PFA RAN, f. 116, op. 2, d. 152, l. 13–14.5 (Viktor F. Kal' to Uspenskii, 17 June 1903).
88 IRAIK, 'Otchet v 1904 godu', Vol. 13 (1908), pp. 312–14.
89 PFA RAN, f. 127, op. 1, d. 3, l. 9–10 (RAIK Report to Ministry of Public Education, 1905).
90 PFA RAN, f. 127, op. 1, d. 3, l. 10.5–11 (RAIK Report to Ministry of Public Education, 1905).
91 PFA RAN, f. 127, op. 1, d. 3, l. 11–16 (RAIK Report to Ministry of Public Education, 1905).
92 BOA, BEO., 2885/216333, 15 Cemâziyelahir 1324 (06 August 1906).
93 RGIA, f. 757, op. 1, d. 34, l. 17–18 (Uspenskii to Ambassador Girs, 19 June 1913).
94 Nurettin Can, *Eski Eserler ve Müzelerle İlgili Kanun Nizamname ve Emirler* (Ankara: Milli Eğitim Basımevi, 1948), p. 77.
95 RGIA, f. 757, op. 1, d. 34, l. 7 (Uspenskii to Ambassador Girs, 19 June 1913).
96 RGIA, f. 757, op. 1, d. 34, l. 4–5 (Uspenskii to Ambassador Girs, 19 June 1913).
97 RGIA, f. 757, op. 1, d. 34, l. 7 (Uspenskii to Ambassador Girs, 19 June 1913).
98 Marchand, *Down from Olympus*, p. 214.
99 PFA RAN, f. 116, op. 2, d. 254, l. 8, 14 (Arkadii A. Orlov to Uspenskii, 14 February 1911 and 22 December 1911).
100 BOA, DH. MKT., 2641/39, 03 Şevval 1326 (29 October 1908).
101 BOA, MF. MKT., 1158/47, 05 Şevval 1328 (10 October 1910); Dahiliye İdari, (DH.İD.), 28–2/9, 19 Şevval 1330 (01 October 1912).
102 BOA, BEO., 2868/215062, 18 Cemâziyelevvel 1324 (10 July 1906).
103 BOA, Yıldız Perakende Evrakı Mabeyn Başkitabeti (Y. PRK. BŞK.), 76/28, 03 Cemâziyelevvel 1324 (25 June 1906); BEO., 2879/215895, 04 Cemâziyelahir 1324 (26 July 1906).
104 PFA RAN, f. 116, op. 2, d. 173, l. 1 (Nikolay V. Kokhmanskii to Uspenskii, 29 January 1908).
105 PFA RAN, f. 116, op. 2, d. 173, l. 2 (Nikolay V. Kokhmanskii to Uspenskii, 27 March 1908).
106 IRAIK, Uspenskii, 'O Vnov Otkrytykh Mozaikah v Tserkvi Sv. Dmitriya v Soluni', Vol. 14 (1909): p. 1.
107 Ibid., p. 2.
108 This was discussed earlier in Chapter 2.
109 PFA RAN, f. 127, op. 1, d. 149, l. 1–2 (Uspenskii to IPPO, 1905).
110 PFA RAN, f. 127, op. 1, d. 1, l. 105.5 (Uspenskii to Ministry of Public Education, 1914).

111 In the Ottoman Empire, functioning mosques, even if they had a historical and artistic value, were under the jurisdiction of the Ministry of Religious Foundations. Therefore, the study permit for Chora or Kariye was not requested from the Ottoman Museum.

112 PFA RAN, f. 127, op. 1, d. 149, l. 4–5 (Uspenskii to IPPO, 1905).

113 PFA RAN, f. 127, op. 1, d. 1, l. 110 (Uspenskii to Ministry of Public Education, 1914).

114 BOA, DH. MKT., 564/73, 19 Cemâziyelevvel 1320 (24 August 1902).

115 PFA RAN f. 127, op. 1, d. 1, l. 104–105 (Uspenskii to Ministry of Public Education, 1914).

116 John Lowden, 'Illustrated Octateuch Manuscripts: A Byzantine Phenomenon', in *The Old Testament in Byzantium*, ed. Paul Magdalino and Robert Nelson, (Washington, D.C.: Harvard University Press, 2010), pp. 111–15.

117 IRAIK, Uspenskii, 'Seral'skii Kodeks', Vol. 12 (1907), pp. 1, 19–21.

118 Popruzhenko, *Sorokaletie*, p. 27.

119 IRAIK, 'Otchet v 1909 godu', Vol. 15 (1911): p. 248.

120 IRAIK, 'Otchet v 1907 godu', Vol. 14 (1909): p. 155.

121 PFA RAN, f. 127, op. 1, d. 148, l. 3–4 (RAIK Report to Ministry of Public Education, 1907).

122 PFA RAN, f. 127, op. 1, d. 1, l. 105–106 (Uspenskii to Ministry of Public Education, 1914).

123 Ousterhout, 'The Rediscovery of Constantinople and the Beginning of Byzantine Archaeology: A Historiographical Survey', p. 191.

124 IRAIK, 'Otchet v 1909 godu', Vol. 15 (1911): p. 250.

125 IRAIK, 'Otchet v 1906 godu', Vol. 14 (1909): p. 132.

126 PFA RAN, f. 127, op. 1, d. 1, l. 107–108 (Uspenskii to Ministry of Public Education, 1914).

127 Konstantin Papoulidis, 'The Russian Archaeological Institute of Constantinople (1894–1914): From Its Establishment until Today', in *Perceptions of the Past in the Turkish Republic: Classical and Byzantine Periods*, ed. Scott Redford and Nina Ergin (Leuven: Peeters, 2010), p. 188.

5 On the eve of the Balkan Wars: Archaeology in the midst of political unrest

1 PFA RAN, f. 116, op. 2, d. 427, l. 5 (F. I. Shmit to Uspenskii, 29 July 1903).

2 L. S. Stavrianos, *The Balkans, 1815–1914* (New York: Holt, Rinehart, and Winston, 1963), pp. 103–4; Yosmaoğlu, 'Counting Bodies, Shaping Souls: The 1903 Census and National Identity in Ottoman Macedonia', pp. 69–72.

3 Mark Mazower, *The Balkans: A Short History* (New York: Modern Library, 2000), p. 100.

4 Ibid., pp. 97–8.

5 PFA RAN, f. 116, op. 2, d. 427, l. 5 (F. I. Shmit to Uspenskii, 29 July 1903).

6 Duncan M. Perry, 'Death of a Russian Consul: Macedonia 1903', *Russian History*, Vol. 7, No. 1 (1980): pp. 201–12.

7 IRAIK, 'Otchet v 1908 godu', Vol. 14 (1909): p. 179.

8 PFA RAN, f. 116, op. 2, d. 427, l. 5 (F. I. Shmit to Uspenskii, 29 July 1903).

9 Mazower, *The Balkans*, p. 99.

10 Miliukov, *Political Memoirs, 1905–1917*, p. 181; Rossos, 'Serbian-Bulgarian Relations', pp. 399–400.

11 William M. Hale, *Turkish Foreign Policy since 1774* (New York: Routledge, 2013), pp. 24–6; Hasan Ünal, 'Young Turk Assessments of International Politics, 1906–9', in *Turkey: Identity, Democracy, Politics*, ed. Sylvia Kedourie (New York: Routledge, 2013), p. 40.

12 Rossos, 'Serbian-Bulgarian Relations', p. 403.

13 George F. Kennan, *The Fateful Alliance: France, Russia, and the Coming of the First World War* (New York: Pantheon Books, 1984), pp. 249–58.

14 Ronald Bobroff, 'Behind the Balkan Wars: Russian Policy toward Bulgaria and the Turkish Straits, 1912–1913', *Russian Review*, Vol. 59, No. 1 (January 2000): p. 81.

15 Edward C. Thaden, *Russia and the Balkan Alliance of 1912* (University Park, PA: Pennsylvania State University Press, 1965), p. 17.

16 Owen Pearson, *Albania and King Zog: Independence, Republic and Monarchy, 1908–1939,* Vol. 1 of *Albania in the Twentieth Century Series* (London: I. B. Tauris, 2004), pp. 1–3.

17 Nicola Guy, *The Birth of Albania: Ethnic Nationalism, the Great Powers of World War I, and the Emergence of Albanian Independence* (London: I. B. Tauris, 2012), pp. 28–38.

18 Jelavich and Jelavich, pp. 219–20.

19 Gerd, *Russian Policy in the Orthodox East: The Patriarchate of Constantinople (1878–1914)*, p. 100.

20 PFA RAN, f. 116, op. 2, d. 247, l. 1 (Dragoman Nusret Efendi to Uspenskii, 16 February 1909).

21 IRAIK, 'Otchet v 1908 godu', Vol. 14 (1909), p. 172.

22 PFA RAN, f. 116, op. 2, d. 254, l. 1–2 (Arkadii A. Orlov to Uspenskii, 8 June 1908).

23 Gerd, *Konstantinopolskii Patriarkhat i Rossiia: 1901–1914*, pp. 240–1.

24 PFA RAN, f. 6, op. 1, d. 37, l. 2–3 (Uspenskii to President of the Imperial Academy of Sciences, 1914).

25 PFA RAN, f. 116, op. 2, d. 40, l. 12–13 (Uspenskii to Ministry of Public Education, 20 March 1915).

26 IRAIK, 'Otchet v 1900 godu', Vol. 7, Nos 2–3 (1902), p. 232.

27 IRAIK, 'Otchet v 1911 godu', Vol. 16 (1912), p. 366.

28 Ibid., p. 367.

29 Gerd, *Konstantinopolskii Patriarkhat i Rossiia: 1901–1914*, p. 136.

30 IRAIK, 'Otchet v 1911 godu', Vol. 16 (1912), pp. 368–9.
31 Ibid., p. 369.
32 Thaden, *Russia and the Balkan Alliance of 1912*, p. 28.
33 PFA RAN, f. 127, op. 1, d. 1, l. 132–132.5 (Charter of the Slavic Department, 2 March 1911).
34 Nadia Abu El-Haj, *Facts on the Ground: Archaeological Practice and Territorial Self-Fashioning in Israeli Society* (Chicago, IL: University of Chicago Press, 2001), p. 3.
35 PFA RAN, f. 127, op. 1, d. 1, l. 139 (Charter of the Slavic Department, 2 March 1911).
36 PFA RAN, f. 127, op. 1, d. 1, l. 130–131 (Charter of the Slavic Department, 2 March 1911).
37 IRAIK, 'Otchet v 1911 godu', Vol. 16 (1912), p. 371.
38 Mazower, *The Balkans*, p. 105.
39 Bobroff, 'Behind the Balkan Wars', pp. 80–3.
40 Gerd, *Russian Policy in the Orthodox East: The Patriarchate of Constantinople (1878–1914)*, p. 36.

6 The doom of empires: The fate of the Russian Archaeological Institute after 1914

1 PFA RAN, f. 127, op. 1, d. 1, l. 146–149 (Uspenskii to Ministry of Public Education, 22 February 1916).
2 Gerd, *Russian Policy in the Orthodox East: The Patriarchate of Constantinople (1878–1914)*, p. 38.
3 RGIA, f. 757, op. 1, d. 40, l. 1–4 (Uspenskii to Ministry of Public Education, 9 December 1914).
4 RGIA, f. 757, op. 1, d. 40, l. 9 (Uspenskii to Ministry of Public Education, 9 December 1914).
5 Riha, *A Russian European*, p. 249.
6 Sean McMeekin, *The Russian Origins of the First World War* (Cambridge, MA: Harvard University Press, 2011), pp. 194–6.
7 Basargina, 'Proekty Sozdaniia Russkikh Arkheologicheskikh Institutov za Rubezhom', pp. 210–11.
8 S. A. Ershov, IU. A. Piatnitskii, K. N. Iuzbashian, 'Russkii Arkheologicheskii Institut v Konstantinopole', pp. 8–9.
9 RGIA, f. 757, op. 1, d. 38, l. 2–4 (Uspenskii to Ministry of Public Education, 11 December 1914).
10 PFA RAN, f. 116, op. 2, d. 40, l. 3–8 (Uspenskii to Ministry of Public Education, 20 March 1915).
11 PFA RAN, f. 127, op. 1, d. 1, l. 163–164 (Uspenskii to Department of Science in the People's Commisariat for Education, 13 August 1918).
12 IRAIK, 'Otchet v 1901 godu', Vol. 8, No. 3 (1903): p. 338.

13 PFA RAN, f. 127, op. 1, d. 1, l. 146–149 (Uspenskii to Ministry of Public Education, 22 February 1916).

14 RGIA, f. 757, op. 1, d. 38, l. 6 (Uspenskii to Ministry of Public Education, 11 December 1914).

15 PFA RAN, f. 127, op. 1, d. 1, l. 170–171 (Uspenskii to Commissariat of National Education, 20 May 1918). There were some rumours that the archives were plundered in Odessa, but in 1926, the archive of RAIK was reclaimed by Byzantine Commission from the Odessa Central Scientific Library.
   PFA RAN, f. 127, op. 1, d. 1, l. 268 (Uspenskii to the Russian Academy of the History of Material Culture); PFA RAN, f. 127, op. 1, d. 1, l. 218, 235 (Odessa Central Scientific Library to Uspenskii, 23 September 1926 and 6 October 1926).

16 PFA RAN, f. 127, op. 1, d. 1, l. 163–164 (Uspenskii to Department of Science in the People's Commissariat for Education, 13 August 1918).

17 The National Archives, Public Records Office, FO 608/277/8, pp. 305–6, 1920.

18 Halil Etem, *İstanbul'da İki İrfan Evi: Alman ve Fransız Arkeoloji Enstitüleri ve Bunların Neşriyatı* (İstanbul: İstanbul Müzeleri Neşriyatı, 1937), pp. 7–8.

19 For a more detailed account of the Trabzon expedition, see Pınar Üre, 'Byzantine Past, Russian Present: Russian Archaeological Institute's Trabzon Expedition during the First World War', *Byzantium's Other Empire: Hagia Sophia in Trebizond*, ed. Antony Eastmond (İstanbul: Koç University Press, 2016), pp. 215–36.

20 Bernhardsson, *Reclaiming a Plundered Past*, p. 7.

21 Nikolai Yakovlevich Marr and Josif Abgarovich Orbeli, *Arkheologicheskaya Ekspeditsiya 1916 goda v Van: Doklady* (St Petersburg: Russkoe Arkheologicheskoe Obshchestvo, 1922).

22 PFA RAN, f. 169, op. 1, d. 1, l. 2–45 (I. Y. Stelletskii to Military General Governorate of Occupied Territories, 6 May 1917).

23 Jersild, *Orientalism and Empire*, p. 6. Russians were not alone in conducting wartime archaeological activities. For instance, in the parts of Macedonia claimed by Greece, French archaeologists carried out excavations. Not to be left behind in the competition with the French, the British army also commanded their men to report archaeological findings to headquarters. Despite the disappointment of Greeks, these artefacts were transported to the British Museum and the Louvre after the war. Mark Mazower, *Salonica: City of Ghosts, Christians, Muslims and Jews, 1430–1950* (New York: Alfred A. Knopf, 2005), pp. 296–7.

24 PFA RAN, f. 169, op. 1, d. 4, l. 1 (Decree by commander-in-chief of the Caucasian Armies, 17 March 1916).

25 William Miller, *Trebizond: The Last Greek Empire* (London: S.P.C.K., 1926), pp. 14–19; Antony Eastmond, *Art and Identity in 13th Century Byzantium: Hagia Sophia and the Empire of Trebizond* (Burlington, VT: Ashgate, 2003), pp. 1–3.

26 Papoulidis, 'The Russian Archaeological Institute of Constantinople (1894–1914): From Its Establishment until Today', p. 190.

27 Uspenskii, 'Soobsheniya i otchet akademika F. I. Uspenskogo o Komandirovke v Trapezunt', Izvestiia Imperatorskoi Akademii Nauk, Serial 6, Vol. 10, Nos 11–18 (June–December 1916): pp. 1464–5.

28 Ibid., p. 1468.

29 PFA RAN, f. 169, op. 1, d. 4, l. 21 (Decree by Commander in Chief of the Caucasian Armies, 17 March 1916).

30 PFA RAN, f. 169, op. 1, d. 4, l. 24–25 (Decree by Commander in Chief of the Caucasian Armies, 17 March 1916).

31 Avgustin, 'Russkii Arkheologicheskii Institut v Konstantinopole', pp. 274–5.

32 PFA RAN, f. 169, op. 1, d. 4, l. 20 (Decree by Commander in Chief of the Caucasian Armies, 17 March 1916).

33 Uspenskii, 'Soobsheniya i otchet akademika F. I. Uspenskogo o Komandirovke v Trapezunt', p. 1466.

34 Ibid.

35 Ibid., p. 1480.

36 PFA RAN, f. 169, op. 1, d. 4, l. 23 (Decree by Commander in Chief of the Caucasian Armies, 17 March 1916).

37 PFA RAN, f. 127, op. 1, d. 1, l. 164–165 (Uspenskii to Department of Science in the People's Commissariat for Education, 13 August 1918).

38 PFA RAN, f. 169, op. 1, d. 4, l. 22 (Decree by Commander in Chief of the Caucasian Armies, 17 March 1916).

39 PFA RAN, f. 127, op. 1, d. 1, l. 164–165 (Uspenskii to Department of Science in the People's Commissariat for Education, 13 August 1918).

40 Papoulidis, 'The Russian Archaeological Institute of Constantinople (1894–1914): From Its Establishment until Today', p. 190.

41 PFA RAN, f. 127, op. 1, d. 1, l. 180–181, 210 (Uspenskii to the Bureau for RAIK's Affairs, 1 September 1920).

42 PFA RAN, f. 127, op. 1, d. 1, l. 165–166 (Uspenskii to Department of Science in the People's Commissariat for Education, 13 August 1918).

43 Alexander A. Vasiliev, 'Byzantine Studies in Russia, Past and Present', pp. 543–5.

44 PFA RAN, f. 127, op. 1, d. 1, l. 209 (Meeting Resolution of the Board of the Russian Academy for the History of Material Culture, 11 August 1924).

45 PFA RAN, f. 127, op. 1, d. 1, l. 140–141 (Uspenskii to the Presidium of the Academy of USSR, 21 December 1925).

46 PFA RAN, f. 127, op. 1, d. 1, l. 213–214 (permanent secretary of Academy of Sciences to Glavnauk, 15 December 1926).

47 PFA RAN, f. 127, op. 1, d. 1, l. 250–250.5 (Unidentified newspaper, 17 July 1927).

48 PFA RAN, f. 127, op. 1, d. 1, l. 253–255 (Uspenskii to USSR Academy of Sciences, 15 August 1927).

49 PFA RAN, f. 127, op. 1, d. 1, l.256–256.5 (Administrative Department of the People's Commissars to the USSR Academy of Sciences, 6 April 1928).

50 PFA RAN, f. 127, op. 1, d. 1, l. 259 (Uspenskii, Beneshevich, Zhebelev, Bartold to USSR Academy of Sciences, May 1928).

51 PFA RAN, f. 127, op. 1, d. 1, l. 248 (USSR Academy of Sciences to Uspenskii, 19 July 1927).

52 PFA RAN, f. 127, op. 1, d. 1, l. 251 (USSR Academy of Sciences to Uspenskii, 27 July 1927).

53 PFA RAN, f. 127, op. 1, d. 1, l. 266 (USSR Academy of Sciences to Uspenskii, 4 September 1928).

54 Ershov, Piatnitskii, Iuzbashian, 'Russkii Arkheologicheskii Institut v Konstantinopole', p. 7.

55 *Dokumenty Vneshnei Politiki SSSR*, Vol. XI (Moskva: Izd-vo Polit. Lit-ry,1966), pp. 617–18.

56 Etem, *İstanbul'da İki İrfan Evi*, p. 8.

57 E. V. Stepanova, 'Iubileinoe Zaselenie, Posviashchennoe Deiatel'nosti Russkogo Arkheologicheskogo Instituta v Konstantinopole (23 Ianvaria 1985 g.)', *Vizantiiskii Vremennik*, Vol. 46 (1985): p. 276.

58 Geraldine Norman, *The Hermitage: The Biography of a Great Museum* (London: Jonathan Cape, 1997), pp. 168–9.

59 Avgustin, 'Russkii Arkheologicheskii Institut v Konstantinopole', p. 288.

60 PFA RAN, f. 116, op. 2, d. 164, l. 11–12 (N. K. Kluge to Uspenskii, 12 April 1923).

61 Medvedev, *Peterburgskoe Vizantinovedenie*, p. 192.

62 Ibid., pp. 194–203.

63 PFA RAN, f. 127, op. 1, d. 1, l. 260 (USSR Academy of Sciences to Uspenskii, 22 June 1928).

64 PFA RAN, f. 127, op. 1, d. 1, l. 265 (Uspenskii to USSR Academy of Sciences, August 1928).

65 Basargina, *Russkii Arkheologicheskii Institut v Konstantinopole*, pp. 97, 100, 108, 118.

66 Medvedev, *Peterburgskoe Vizantinovedenie*, pp. 201–2.

67 Vernadsky, *Russian Historiography*, pp. 450–5, 225–8.

68 Obolensky, *Byzantium and the Slavs*, pp. 70–1.

69 Tuğba Tanyeri-Erdemir, 'Archaeology as a Source of National Pride in the Early Years of the Turkish Republic', *Journal of Field Archaeology*, Vol. 31, No. 4 (Winter 2006): pp. 382–3.

70 Matthew Elliot, 'European Archaeological and Historical Institutes in Turkey: An Italian Ambassador's View in 1925', in *Archaeology, Anthropology, and Heritage in the Balkans and Anatolia: The Life and Times of F. W. Hasluck, 1878–1920*, ed. David Shankland, Vol. 1 (Istanbul: Isis Press, 2004), p. 284.

71 Ibid., p. 281.

72 Ibid., p. 286.

73 Samuel J. Hirst, 'Anti-Westernism on the European Periphery: The Meaning of Soviet-Turkish Convergence in the 1930s', *Slavic Review*, Vol. 72, No. 1 (Spring 2013): pp. 37–8.
74 'Sessiya Otdeleniya Istorii i Filosofii Akademii Nauk SSSR, Posvyashchennaya Pamyati F. I. Uspenskogo', *Vizantiiskii Vremennik*, Vol. 1, No. 26 (1947): pp. 370–1.

Conclusion

1 David C. Harvey, 'National Identities and the Politics of Ancient Heritage: Continuity and Change at Ancient Monuments in Britain and Ireland, c. 1675–1850', *Transactions of the Institute of British Geographers*, New Series, Vol. 28, No. 4 (December 2013): p. 475.
2 Cornelius J. Holtorf, 'The Life-Histories of Megaliths in Mecklenburg-Vorpommern (Germany)', *World Archaeology*, Vol. 30, No. 1, The Past in the Past: The Reuse of Ancient Monuments (June 1998): p. 24.
3 Pierre Nora, 'Between Memory and History: Les Lieux de Mémoire', *Representations*, No. 26, Special Issue: Memory and Counter-Memory (Spring 1989): p. 19.
4 Robert Ousterhout, 'Ethnic Identity and Cultural Appropriation in Early Ottoman Architecture', *Muqarnas*, Vol. 12 (1995): p. 60.

Suggestions for further reading

The following bibliographical survey brings together some of the most
important works that inspired the theoretical framework of this study. It
is far from being complete, and there are many more books and articles
on these subjects than this brief survey can highlight. This section is only
designed as an introductory guide for readers who want to delve deeper
into the history of archaeology in Russia, Ottoman Empire or elsewhere in
the world.

Politics, identity and archaeology

Historians as well as archaeologists have long scrutinized the use of archaeology
in nation-building and empire-building processes in different historical and
geographical settings, as Bruce Trigger (1984) does in his pioneering article
'Alternative Archaeologies: Nationalist, Colonialist, Imperialist', *Man,* Vol. 19,
No. 3, pp. 355–70. An invaluable contribution to literature is the collection
of articles edited by Philip L. Kohl and Clare Fawcett (1995), *Nationalism,
Politics, and the Practice of Archaeology* (Cambridge: Cambridge University
Press). Another similar book was edited by Philip L. Kohl, Mara Kozelsky
and Nachman Ben-Yehuda (2007): *Selective Remembrances: Archaeology
in the Construction, Commemoration, and Consecration of National Past*
(Chicago, IL: University of Chicago Press).
The volume edited by Tim Murray and Christopher Evans (2008), *Histories
of Archaeology: A Reader in the History of Archaeology* (New York: Oxford
University Press) contains articles on the social and political functions of
archaeology in different geographical and temporal settings.
R. Alexander Bentley, Herbert D. G. Maschner and Christopher Chippindale's
(2008) edited volume *Handbook of Archaeological Theories* (Lanham,
MD: AltaMira Press) is one of the most comprehensive sources for anyone
interested in the theoretical evolution of archaeological scholarship. Another
very useful study that highlights how modern archaeologists tackle with the
question of objectivity is Michael Rowlands's article (1998) 'Objectivity and
Subjectivity in Archaeology' in *Social Transformations in Archaeology: Global
and Local Perspectives,* edited by Kristian Kristiansen and Michael Rowlands
(London: Routledge).
The political use of ancient history was not only a top–down process that was
engineered by the state, but different segments of the society participated
in the production of archaeological knowledge. Don Fowler (1987) focuses
on the generation, control and allocation of the past as a symbolic resource,

both officially by bureaucrats and unofficially by nationalist citizens in his article 'Uses of the Past: Archaeology in the Service of the State', *American Antiquity*, Vol. 52, No. 2 (April 1987): pp. 229–48.

Philip Kohl (1998) draws attention to archaeology's role in 'inventing traditions' and constructing collective memories and a shared past in his article 'Nationalism and Archaeology: On the Constructions of Nations and the Reconstructions of the Remote Past', *Annual Review of Anthropology*, Vol. 27 (1998): pp. 223–46.

The volume edited by Lynn Meskell (2002) provides insight about how archaeology is intrinsically linked to politics in the Middle East and the Balkans: *Archaeology under Fire: Nationalism, Politics and Heritage in the Eastern Mediterranean and Middle East* (London: Routledge).

Israeli-Palestinian conflict offers an obvious example to a case in which ancient history became a platform where contested political and territorial designs come to the surface. In *Facts on the Ground: Archaeological Practice and Territorial Self-Fashioning in Israeli Society* (Chicago, IL: University of Chicago Press), Nadia Abu El-Haj (2001) examines how archaeology became a political and touchy subject in Israel, shaping national and cultural imagination.

Egypt has been yet another setting, where archaeology became instrumental in the construction of imperial, colonial and national identities. This issue is covered by Donald Malcolm Reid (2002) in *Whose Pharaohs? Archaeology, Museums, and Egyptian National Identity from Napoleon to World War I* (Berkeley: University of California Press). On the one hand, acquisition of Egyptian antiquities showcased Franco-British rivalry over the country. On the other hand, Reid discusses the training of local Egyptian archaeologists, most notably, Rifaa al-Tahtawi (1801–1873), who popularized ancient Egypt among his fellow countrymen.

Kamyar Abdi (2001) analyses the beginnings of archaeological interest among Iran's ruling elite in the late 19th century as a reaction to increasing foreign archaeological involvement in his article 'Nationalism, Politics, and the Development of Archaeology in Iran', *American Journal of Archaeology*, Vol. 105, No. 1: pp. 51–76.

The congruence of archaeology and diplomacy in Mesopotamia is examined by Magnus Bernhardsson (2005) in *Reclaiming a Plundered Past: Archaeology and Nation Building in Modern Iraq* (Austin: University of Texas Press).

Yannis Hamiliakis (2007) examines the simultaneous development of the nation-state and archaeology as an organized discipline in the 19th-century Greece in *The Nation and Its Ruins: Antiquity, Archaeology, and National Imagination in Greece* (Oxford: Oxford University Press). His focus is not only on the nationalist use of archaeology by the state, but more broadly, on how antiquity is incorporated as a part of social life, daily practices, touristic activities, literature and theatre plays.

Robert Shannan Peckham (2001) also discusses the spatial dimensions of the Greek nation-building process in the 19th century, while briefly referring to the German and French archaeological institutes in Greece, as their activities reflected the bitter imperial rivalry between these two powers after the 1870s: *National Histories, Natural States: Nationalism and the Politics of Place in Greece* (New York: I.B. Tauris).

The collection of articles edited by Roderick Beaton and David Ricks (2009), *The Making of Modern Greece: Nationalism, Romanticism, and the Uses of the Past*, (Farnham: Ashgate), discusses how ancient history was used to create the illusion that a distinctive Hellenic cultural community that existed continuously for more than a millennium.

Acquisitions of artefacts for European museums reflected the imperial competition between the major powers of Europe. Thomas Gaehtgens's (1996) article 'The Museum Island in Berlin' in the volume edited by Gwendolyn Wright, *The Formation of National Collections of Art and Archaeology* (Washington, DC: National Gallery of Art) shows how the acquisition of Pergamon antiquities from the Ottoman Empire in 1879 reiterated the rise of Germany as an imperial power on a symbolic level, as Bismarck personally participated in the negotiations with the Ottoman Empire over the transfer of archaeological findings. The other articles in this collection give insight about the educative and political functions of museums in modern urban centres around the world.

For a discussion of British archaeological activities in the Ottoman Empire, one can consult Debbie Challis's (2008) work, *From the Harpy Tomb to the Wonders of Ephesus: British Archaeologists in the Ottoman Empire, 1840–1880* (London: Duckworth).

Suzanne Marchand (2003) examines the development of classical archaeology and philhellenism in Germany in *Down from Olympus: Archaeology and Philhellenism in Germany, 1750–1970* (Princeton, NJ: Princeton University Press). Athena Leoussi (1998) undertakes a similar task for Britain and France in *Nationalism and Classicism: The Classical Body as National Symbol in Nineteenth-Century England and France* (New York: St Martin's Press).

In his monograph *From Paris to Pompeii: French Romanticism and the Cultural Politics of Archaeology* (Philadelphia: University of Pennsylvania Press), Göran Blix (2009) discusses how ancient history served as an inspiration for aesthetic, social and political revival in 19th-century France.

History of archaeology in Russia

Unfortunately, there is little literature in English on the history of archaeology in Imperial Russia. There are articles and monographs dealing with certain aspects of the question, but there is not a comprehensive monograph explaining the development of archaeological scholarship in the Russian Empire from the 18th century to 1917. In Russian, most monographs focus on the history of Soviet archaeology and refer to the imperial period only in passing. Such examples include Mikhail Miller, *Archaeology in the USSR* (New York: Praeger, 1956); Aleksandr Mongait, *Archaeology in the USSR* (Moscow: Foreign Languages Publishing House, 1959); *Ocherki Istorii Russkoi i Sovetskoi Arkheologii,* edited by A. A. Formozov (Moskva: Akademiia Nauk SSSR, 1991); Lev S. Klejn, *Fenomen Sovetskii Arkheologii* (St Petersburg: FARN, 1993); A. D. Priakhin, *Istoriia Otechestvennoi Arkheologii* (Voronezh: Voronezhskii Gosudarstvenny Universitet, 2005).

The study edited by A. E. Musin (2009) is a comprehensive work on the institutional structure of the Imperial Archaeological Commission: *Imperatorskaia Arkheologicheskaia Komissiia, 1859–1917: U Istokov Otechestvennoi Arkheologii i Okhrany Kul'turnogo Naslediia: K 150-letiiu so Dnia Osnovaniia* (St Petersburg: DB).

With regard to RAIK, there are only two monographs. The first monograph was written by Konstantinos Papoulidis (1987) in Greek as his doctoral dissertation: *To Rosiko Arkheologiko Institouto Konstantinoupoleos (1894–1914)* (Thessaloniki: Idrima Meleton Hersonisu tu Emu). Ye. Yu. Basargina (1999) is the author of the other monograph, *Russkii Arkheologicheskii Institut v Konstantinopole* (St Petersburg: DB). Basargina particularly deals with the organizational structure of the Institute, its legal status and relationship to the Russian Embassy in Istanbul. She also gives a detailed account of the biographies and academic achievements of individual archaeologists affiliated with the Institute.

Mara Kozelsky (2010) examines the relationship between archaeological knowledge and empire-building in her *Christianizing Crimea: Shaping Sacred Space in the Russian Empire and Beyond* (DeKalb: Northern Illinois University Press). Vera Tolz (2011) briefly touches upon the role of archaeology in empire-building in her *Russia's Own Orient: The Politics of Identity and Oriental Studies in the Late Imperial and Early Soviet Periods* (Oxford: Oxford University Press). Lora Gerd (2006) refers to archaeological practices as they related to Russian religious policy in the Ottoman Empire in her *Konstantinopol' i Peterburg: Tserkovnaia Politika Rossii na Pravoslavnom Vostoke* (Moskva: Indrik).

Ekaterina Pravilova's (2014) *A Public Empire: Property and the Quest for the Common Good in Imperial Russia* (Princeton, NJ: Princeton University Press) discusses how archaeological objects acquired a new meaning as public property and as markers of a common national past beginning with the late 19th century.

History of archaeology in the Ottoman Empire

In recent years, history of archaeology in the Ottoman Empire is becoming a popular subject for Ottomanist with an interest in cultural history. As a result of this growing interest, there are several very comprehensive studies on the subject. Wendy Meryem Kural Shaw (2003) was one of the first scholars who opened the field for inquiry. She recounts the development of Ottoman archaeology as a reflection of Ottoman modernization in her *Possessors and Possessed: Museums, Archaeology, and the Visualization of History in the Late Ottoman Empire* (Berkeley: University of California Press). More recently, Zeynep Çelik (2016) uses new sources to scrutinize the agency of (until now) unheard people such as Ottoman museum officials, labourers who took part in archaeological excavations, and museum visitors in *About Antiquities: Politics of Archaeoogy in the Ottoman Empire* (Austin: University of Texas Press).

Ottoman perceptions of foreign archaeologists also attracted scholarly attention in recent years, which culminated in the publication of two valuable collection of essays. The first one was edited by Scott Redford and Nina Ergin (2010): *Perceptions of the Past in the Turkish Republic: Classical and Byzantine Periods* (Leuven: Peeters). This volume, which was the outcome of a symposium, is a collection of articles discussing the use of ancient past in national narratives and the context in which archaeological knowledge was produced. This edited volume was followed by *Scramble for the Past: A Story of Archaeology in the Ottoman Empire, 1753–1914*, edited by Zainab Bahrani, Zeynep Çelik and Edhem Eldem (İstanbul: SALT, 2011). The latter study brings together articles dealing with European archaeological activities in the Ottoman Empire and Ottoman responses to them in a time span that stretches from the establishment of the British Museum to the First World War, but unfortunately left out Russian archaeologists among other European scholars.

Bibliography

ARCHIVAL SOURCES

Başbakanlık Osmanlı Arşivleri (BOA), **Prime Ministerial Ottoman Archives,**
İstanbul.

Bab-ı Âli Evrak Odası (BEO):
95/7104, 628/47089, 1006/75417, 1726/129384, 1731/129825, 2868/215062,
2879/215895, 2885/216333.

Dahiliye Nezâreti:
Dahiliye Hukuk Müşavirliği (DH. HMŞ.): 9/8.
Dahiliye, İdari (DH. İD.): 28–2/9.
Dahiliye Mektubî Kalemi (DH. MKT.): 379/80, 428/21, 555/16, 564/73,
2147/110, 2150/4, 2191/63, 2210/21, 2264/88, 2273/76, 2288/87, 2563/22,
2641/39.
Dahiliye Nezareti Muhaberât ve Tensîkât Müdüriyeti Belgeleri (DH. EUM.
MTK.): 13/12.

Hariciye Mektubî Kalemi (HR. MKT.):
190/98, 198/64, 238/35, 243/68, 251/78, 287/24, 293/92, 300/90, 301/48.

İradeler:
İradeler, Hususi (İ. HUS.): 1/1310-M-074, 57/1315-Ca-004, 67/1316-R-103.
İradeler, Meclis-i Mahsus (İ. MMS.): 78/3401.
İradeler, Mesail-i Mühimme (İ. MSM.): 17/387.
İradeler, Şura-yı Devlet (İ. ŞD.): 11/547.
İradeler, Taltifat (İ. TAL.): 121/1315-Ca-066.

Maarif Mektubî Kalemi (MF. MKT.): 18/97, 18/147, 1158/47.

Meclis-i Vükelâ (MV.): 66/65.

Sadaret:
Sadaret Mektubî Kalemi (A. MKT.): 51/75.
Sadaret Mektubî Kalemi – Nezaret ve Devâir (A. MKT. NZD.): 223/73.

Yıldız Evrakı:
Yıldız Hususi Maruzat (Y. A. HUS.): 307/84.
Yıldız Perakende Evrakı Askeri Maruzat (Y. PRK. ASK.): 56/20, 91/105.
Yıldız Perakende Evrakı Mabeyn Başkitabeti (Y. PRK. BŞK.): 76/28.

Sankt-Peterburgskii Filial Arkhiva Rossiiskoi Akademii Nauk (PFA RAN), **St.**
Petersburg Branch of the Archive of the Russian Academy of Sciences, St.
Petersburg.

f. 1, op. 1a, d. 175: 'F. I. Uspenskii v Akademiyu Nauk SSSR: Osnovanie Russkogo Arkheologicheskogo Instituta v Konstantinopole, 1926'.

f. 6, op. 1, d. 37: 'F. I. Uspenskii k Konstantinu Konstantinovichu (Prezident Akademii Nauk), 1914'.

Fond 116: Fond Uspenskogo (Fyodor Ivanovich).
f. 116, op. 2, d. 40 / f. 116, op. 2, d. 152 / f. 116, op. 2, d. 164 / f. 116, op. 2, d. 173 / f. 116, op. 2, d. 247 / f. 116, op. 2, d. 254 / f. 116, op. 2, d. 427.

Fond 127: Fond Russkogo Arkheologicheskogo Instituta v Konstantinopole.
f. 127, op. 1, d. 1 / f. 127, op. 1, d. 3 / f. 127, op. 1, d. 32 / f. 127, op. 1, d. 139 / f. 127, op. 1, d. 147 / f. 127, op. 1, d. 148 / f. 127, op. 1, d. 149 / f. 127, op. 1, d. 150 / f. 127, op. 1, d. 151.

Fond 169: Fond Trapezundskoi Voenno-Arkheologicheskoi Ekspeditsii.
f. 169, op. 1, d. 1 / f. 169, op. 1, d. 4.

***Rossiiskii Gosudarstvenny Istoricheskii Arkhiv* (RGIA), Russian State Historical Archives, St. Petersburg.**

Fond 757: Fond Russkogo Arkheologicheskogo Instituta v Konstantinopole.

f. 757, op. 1, d. 1 / f. 757, op. 1, d. 5 / f. 757, op. 1, d. 11 / f. 757, op. 1, d. 27 / f. 757, op. 1, d. 34 / f. 757, op. 1, d. 38 / f. 757, op. 1, d. 40.

Other Archival Documents

Dokumenty Vneshnei Politiki SSSR, Vol. XI. Moskva: Izd-vo Polit. Lit-ry, 1966.
The National Archives, Public Records Office, London. FO 608/277/8.

PUBLISHED PRIMARY SOURCES

IRAIK – Izvestiia Russkogo Arkheologicheskogo Instituta v Konstantinopole (Bulletin of the Russian Archaeological Institute in Constantinople)

'Otkrytye Russkogo Arkheologicheskogo Instituta v Konstantinopole 26-go Fevralya 1895 goda', Vol. 1 (1896): pp. 1–21.
'Otchet v 1895 godu,"' Vol. 1 (1896): pp. 23–53.
'Vnov Naydenny Purpurovy Kodeks Evangeliya', Vol. 1 (1896): pp. 138–72.
'Otchet v 1897 godu', Vol. 3 (1898): pp. 195–230.
P. N. Miliukov, 'Khristiyanskaia Drevnosti Zapadnoi Makedonii', Vol. 4, No. 1 (1899): pp. 21–151.
'Otchet v 1898 godu', Vol. 4, No. 3 (1899): pp. 109–55.
M. I. Rostovtsev, 'Nadpisi iz Makedonii', Vol. 4, No. 3 (1899): pp. 166–88.
'Otchet v 1899 godu', Vol. 6, No. 2–3 (1901): pp. 397–481.

F. I. Uspenskii, 'Arkheologicheskie Pamyatniki Sirii', Vol. 7, Nos 2–3 (1902): pp. 94–212.

'Otchet v 1900 godu', Vol. 7, Nos 2–3 (1902): pp. 213–44.

A. A. Pavlovskii and N. K. Kluge, 'Madeba', Vol. 8, Nos 1–2 (1902): pp. 79–115.

'Otchet v 1901 godu', Vol. 8, No. 3 (1903): pp. 330–41.

P. K. Kokovtsev, 'Novaia Arameiskaia Nadpisi iz Palmiry', Vol. 8, No. 3 (1903): pp. 302–29.

F. I. Uspenskii, 'Istoriko-Arkheologicheskoe Znachenie Aboby i ee Okrestnostei. Raskopki. Naimenovanie Drevnogo Poseleniia', Vol. 10 (1905): pp. 1–15.

F. I. Uspenskii, 'Konstantinopol'skii Seral'skii Kodeks Vosmiknizhiia', Vol. 12 (1907): pp. 1–36.

'Otchet v 1904 godu', Vol. 13 (1908): pp. 303–22.

'Otchet v 1905 godu', Vol. 13 (1908): pp. 323–47.

F. I. Uspenskii, 'O Perevozke iz Palmiry v S. Peterburg Plity s Nadpisiu', Vol. 13 (1908): pp. 363–71.

'Otchet v 1906 godu', Vol. 14 (1909): pp. 127–35.

'Otchet v 1907 godu', Vol. 14 (1909): pp. 136–65.

'Otchet v 1908 godu', Vol. 14 (1909): pp. 166–84.

F. I. Uspenskii, O Vnov Otkrytykh Mozaikah v Tserkvi Sv. Dmitriya v Soluni, Vol. 14 (1909): pp. 1–61.

'Otchet v 1909 godu', Vol. 15 (1911): pp. 240–58.

'Otchet v 1911 godu', Vol. 16 (1912): pp. 360–98.

Uspenskii, F. I. 'Soobshcheniia i otchet akademika F. I. Uspenskogo o Komandirovke v Trapezunte'. *Izvestiia Imperatorskoi Akademii Nauk*, Ser. 6, Vol. 10, Nos 11–18 (1916): pp. 1464–80.

BOOKS AND ARTICLES

'Layard and the Discoveries at Nimroud'. *The Illustrated Magazine of Art*, Vol. 1, No. 4 (1853): pp. 206–22.

'O Svyatoi Zemle i Imperatorskom Pravoslavnom Palestinskom Obshchestve'. *Bogoslovskii Vestnik*, T. 1, No. 3 (1914): pp. 618–28.

'Sessiya Otdeleniya Istorii i Filosofii Akademii Nauk SSSR, Posvyashchennaya Pamyati F. I. Uspenskogo'. *Vizantiiskii Vremennik*, Vol. 1, No. 26 (1947): pp. 370–4.

Abu El-Haj, Nadia. *Facts on the Ground: Archaeological Practice and Territorial Self-Fashioning in Israeli Society*. Chicago, IL: University of Chicago Press, 2001.

Ahibay, Banu. 'Theoretical Approaches in Turkish Archaeology'. Unpublished master's thesis, Bilkent University, Ankara, 2007.

Ahmad, Feroz. *The Making of Modern Turkey*. New York: Routledge, 1993.

Akın, Nur. 'Osman Hamdi Bey, Asar-ı Atika Nizamnamesi ve Dönemin Koruma Anlayışı Üzerine' (Osman Hamdi Bey, Antiquities Regulations, and the Preservation of Antiquities in His Period). In *Osman Hamdi Bey ve Dönemi, 17–18 Aralık 1992*, edited by Zeynep Rona, pp. 233–9. İstanbul: Tarih Vakfı Yurt Yayınları, 1993.

Anderson, Benedict. *Imagined Communities*. New York: Verso, 1991.

Anderson, M. S. *The Eastern Question, 1774–1923: A Study in International Relations*. London: St Martin's Press, 1970.

Angold, Michael. *The Fall of Constantinople to the Ottomans: Context and Consequences*. London: Routledge, 2014.

Arkhimandit Avgustin, 'Russkii Arkheologicheskii Institut v Konstantinopole' (Russian Archaeological Institute in Constantinople). *Bogoslovskie Trudy*, Vol. 27 (1986): pp. 266–93.

Arseven, Celal Esad (Djelal Essad). *Constantinople de Byzance a Stamboul*. Paris: Librairie Renouard, 1909.

Artun, Ali. 'İmkansız Müze' (The Impossible Museum). http://www.aliartun.com/content/detail/1. Accessed 21 November, 2016.

Astafieva, Elena. 'The Russian Empire in Palestine, 1847–1917: A Look Back at the Origins of Russia's Near Eastern Policy'. *Tepsis Papers*, No. 10, Version Anglophone (February 2016). <hal-01293323v2>. Accessed 10 December 2016.

Atlıman, Selin Adile. 'Museological and Archaeological Studies in the Ottoman Empire during the Westernization Process in the 19th Century'. Unpublished master's thesis, Middle East Technical University, Ankara, 2008.

Baehr, Stephen L. 'From History to National Myth: Translatio Imperii in Eighteenth Century Russia'. *Russian Review*, Vol. 37, No. 1 (January 1978): pp. 1–13.

Baron, Nick. 'New Spatial Histories of 20th-Century Russia and the Soviet Union: Exploring the Terrain'. *Kritika: Explorations in Russian and Eurasian History*, Vol. 9, No. 2 (Spring 2008): pp. 433–47.

Basargina, Ye. Yu. *Russkii Arkheologicheskii Institut v Konstantinopole* (Russian Archaeological Institute in Constantinople). St Petersburg: DB, 1999.

Basargina, Ye. Yu. 'Proekty Sozdaniia Russkikh Arkheologicheskikh Institutov za Rubezhom' (Projects for the Creation of Russian Archaeological Insitutes Abroad). *Vestnik Drevnei Istorii*, Vol. 267, No. 4 (2008): pp. 206–8.

Başgelen, Nezih. *Ölümünün 100. Yılında Osman Hamdi Bey: Yaptığı Kazılar – Bulduğu Eserler* (Osman Hamdi Bey on the 100th Anniversary of His Death: His Excavations and Findings). İstanbul: Arkeoloji ve Sanat Yayınları, 2010.

Berkes, Niyazi. *Türkiye'de çağdaşlaşma* (Modernisation in Turkey). İstanbul: Yapı Kredi Yayınları, 2003.

Bernhardsson, Magnus. *Reclaiming a Plundered Past: Archaeology and Nation Building in Modern Iraq*. Austin: University of Texas Press, 2005.

Biskupski, Ludwik. 'L'Historique de L'Institut Français d'Études Byzantines'. *Slavic and East European Studies*, Vol. 4, Nos 1–2 (Spring–Summer 1959): pp. 88–94.

Bobroff, Ronald. 'Behind the Balkan Wars: Russian Policy toward Bulgaria and the Turkish Straits, 1912–1913'. *Russian Review*, Vol. 59, No. 1 (January 2000): pp. 76–95.

Bray, Warwick, and Ian C. Glover. 'Scientific Investigation or Cultural Imperialism: British Archaeology in the Third World'. *Institute of Archaeology Bulletin*, Vol. 24 (1987): pp. 109–25.

Chaadaev, Peter. 'Letters on the Philosophy of History'. In *Readings in Russian Civilization*, Vol. 2, edited by Thomas Riha, pp. 304–8. Chicago: University of Chicago Press, 1969.

Campbell, Elena. 'K voprosu ob Orientalizme v Rossii (vo vtoroi polovine XIX veka – nachale XX veka)'. *Ab Imperio*, 1 (2002): pp. 311–22.

Can, Nurettin. *Eski Eserler ve Müzelerle İlgili Kanun, Nizamname ve Emirler* (Laws, Regulations, and Acts about Ancient Objects and Museums). Ankara: Milli Eğitim Bakanlığı, 1948.

Cezar, Mustafa. *Müzeci ve Ressam Osman Hamdi Bey*. İstanbul: Türk Kültürüne Hizmet Vakfı Sanat Yayınları, 1987.

Cezar, Mustafa. *Sanatta Batı'ya Açılış ve Osman Hamdi*. İstanbul: Türkiye İş Bankası Kültür Yayınları, 1971.

Cherniavsky, Michael. 'Khan on Basileus: An Aspect of Russian Mediaeval Political Theory'. *Journal of the History of the Ideas*, Vol. 20, No. 4 (October–December 1959): pp. 459–76.

Chumakova, Tatiana, and Marianna Shakhnovich, Ekaterina Terukova. 'Collections of the Imperial Orthodox Palestine Society in the State Museum of the History of Religion (Saint-Petersburg, Russia)'. *European Researcher*, Series A, Vol. 107 (2016): pp. 318–23.

Çal, Halil. 'Osmanlı Devletinde Asar-ı Atika Nizamnameleri' (Antiquities Regulations in the Ottoman Empire). *Vakıflar Dergisi*, Vol. 26 (1997): pp. 391–400.

Çelik, Zeynep. *The Remaking of İstanbul: Portrait of an Ottoman City in the Nineteenth Century*. Seattle: University of California Press, 1986.

Çelik, Zeynep. *Asar-ı Atika: Osmanlı İmparatorluğu'nda Arkeoloji Siyaseti* (About Antiquities: Politics of Archaeology in the Ottoman Empire). Istanbul: Koç University Press, 2016.

Çiçek, Nazan. *The Young Ottomans: Turkish Critics of the Eastern Question in the Late 19th Century*. London: I.B. Tauris, 2010.

Daniel, Glyn E. *150 Years of Archaeology*. London: Duckworth, 1975.

Deringil, Selim. '"They Live in a State of Nomadism and Savagery": The Late Ottoman Empire and the Post-Colonial Debate'. *Comparative Studies in Society and History*, Vol. 45, No. 2 (April 2003): pp. 311–42.

Derzhavin, G. R. *Sochineniia*. Moskva: Pravda, 1985.

194   *Bibliography*

Díaz-Andreu García, Margarita. *A World History of Nineteenth-Century Archaeology: Nationalism, Colonialism, and the Past.* New York: Oxford University Press, 2007.

Dixon, Simon. 'Nationalism versus Internationalism: Russian Orthodoxy in Nineteenth-Century Palestine'. In *Religious International in the Modern World: Globalization and Faith Communities since 1750,* edited by Abigail Green and Vincent Viaene, pp. 139–62. London: Palgrave Macmillan, 2012.

Dmitrievskii, A. A. *Imperatorskoe Pravoslavnoe Palestinskoe Obshchestvo i Ego Deyatelnost' za Istekshuyu Chervert' Veka, 1882–1907.* St Petersburg: V. O. Kirshbauma, 1907.

Dolukhanov, Pavel M. 'Archaeology in Russia and Its Impact on Archaeological Theory'. In *Theory in Archaeology: A World Perspective,* edited by Peter J. Ucko, pp. 327–42. London: Routledge, 1995.

Dostoievsky, F. M. *The Diary of a Writer.* Translated by Boris Brasol. Santa Barbara: P. Smith, 1979.

Dyson, Stephen L. *In Pursuit of Ancient Past: A History of Classical Archaeology in the Nineteenth and Twentieth Centuries.* New Haven, CT: Yale University Press, 2006.

Eastmond, Antony. *Art and Identity in Thirteenth Century Byzantium: Hagia Sophia and the Empire of Trebizond.* Burlington, VT: Ashgate, 2003.

Eldem, Edhem. 'An Ottoman Archaeologist Caught between Two Worlds: Osman Hamdi Bey (1842–1910)'. In *Archaeology, Anthropology, and Heritage in the Balkans and Anatolia: The Life and Times of F. W. Hasluck, 1878–1920,* Vol. 1, edited by David Shankland, pp. 121–49. İstanbul: Isis Press, 2004.

Elliot, Matthew. 'European Archaeological and Historical Institutes in Turkey: An Italian Ambassador's View in 1925'. In *Archaeology, Anthropology, and Heritage in the Balkans and Anatolia: The Life and Times of F. W. Hasluck, 1878–1920,* Vol. 1, edited by David Shankland, pp. 281–93. Istanbul: Isis Press, 2004.

Epikman, Refik. *Osman Hamdi.* İstanbul: Milli Eğitim Basımevi, 1967.

Ershov, S. A., IU. A. Piatnitskii and K. N. Iuzbashian. 'Russkii Arkheologicheskii Institut v Konstantinopole' (Russian Archaeological Institute in Constantinople). *Palestinskii Sbornik,* Vol. 29, No. 92 (1987): pp. 3–12.

Etem, Halil. *İstanbul'da İki İrfan Evi: Alman ve Fransız Arkeoloji Enstitüleri ve Bunların Neşriyatı* (Two Houses of Wisdom in Istanbul: German and French Archaeology Institutes and Their Publications). İstanbul: İstanbul Müzeleri Neşriyatı, 1937.

Eyice, Semavi. 'Arkeoloji Müzesi ve Kuruluşu' (The Establishment of the Archaeology Museum). In *Tanzimat'tan Cumhuriyet'e Türkiye Ansiklopedisi* 6 (Encyclopedia of Turkey from Tanzimat to the Republic), edited by Feroz Ahmad, pp. 1596–9. İstanbul: İletişim Yayınları, 1985.

Eyice, Semavi. 'Türkiye'de Bizans Sanatı Araştırmaları ve İstanbul Üniversitesinde Bizans Sanatı' (Byzantine Art Studies in Turkey and Byzantine Art in İstanbul University). In *Cumhuriyetin 50. Yılına*

Armağan (50th Anniversary of the Republic Memory Book), pp. 375–428. İstanbul: İstanbul Üniversitesi Edebiyat Fakültesi, 1973.

Fadieev, Rostislav A. 'What Should Be the Policy of Russia?' In *Readings in Russian Foreign Policy*, edited by Robert A. Goldwin, pp. 67–73. New York: Oxford University Press, 1959.

Fetisenko, O. L. *Proroki Vizantizma: Perepiska K. N. Leont'eva i T. I. Filippova, 1875–1891*. St Petersburg: Izd-vo Pushkinskii Dom, 2012.

Florinsky, Michael. *Russia: A History and an Interpretation*. New York: Macmillan, 1953.

Fowler, Harold N. 'Archaeological News'. *American Journal of Archaeology*, Vol. 6, No. 1 (January–March 1902): pp. 55–100.

Frary, Lucien J., and Mara Kozelsky, 'Introduction: The Eastern Question Reconsidered'. In *Russian-Ottoman Borderlands: The Eastern Question Reconsidered*, edited by Lucien J. Frary and Mara Kozelsky, pp. 3–33. Madison: University of Wisconsin Press, 2014.

Frothingham, Jr., A. L. 'Archaeological News'. *The American Journal of Archaeology and of the History of the Fine Arts*, Vol. 10, No. 1 (January–March 1895): pp. 65–136.

Gautier, Théophile. *Constantinople*. Paris: 1856.

Gerçek, Ferruh. *Türk Müzeciliği* (Turkish Museology). Ankara: Kültür Bakanlığı, 1999.

Gerd, Lora A. *Konstantinopolskii Patriarkhat i Rossiia: 1901–1914*. Moskva: Indrik, 2012.

Gerd, Lora. *Russian Policy in the Orthodox East: The Patriarchate of Constantinople (1878–1914)*. Warsaw: De Gruyter Open, 2014. E-book available at https://www.degruyter.com/view/product/209761?format=EBOK. Accessed 20 March 2017.

Goode, James. *Negotiating for the Past: Archaeology, Nationalism and Diplomacy in the Middle East, 1919–1941*. Austin: University of Texas Press, 2007.

Gorianov, B. T. 'F. I. Uspenskii i Ego Znachenie v Vizantinovedenii'. *Vizantiiskii Vremennik*, Vol. 1, No. 26 (1947): pp. 29–108.

Gunning, Lucia Patrizio. *The British Consular Service in the Aegean and the Collection of Antiquities for the British Museum*. Farnham: Ashgate, 2009.

Guy, Nicola. *The Birth of Albania: Ethnic Nationalism, the Great Powers of World War I, and the Emergence of Albanian Independence*. London: I.B. Tauris, 2012.

Hale, William M. *Turkish Foreign Policy Since 1774*. New York: Routledge, 2013.

Hanioğlu, Şükrü. *A Brief History of the Late Ottoman Empire*. Princeton, NJ: Princeton University Press, 2008.

Hanioğlu, Şükrü. *The Young Turks in Opposition*. New York: Oxford University Press, 1995.

Harlan, Deborah. 'Travel, Pictures, and a Victorian Gentleman in Greece'. *Hesperia: The Journal of the American School of Classical Studies at Athens*, Vol. 78, No. 3 (July–September 2009): pp. 421–53.

Harvey, David C. 'National Identities and the Politics of Ancient Heritage: Continuity and Change at Ancient Monuments in Britain and Ireland, c. 1675–1850'. *Transactions of the Institute of British Geographers*, New Series, Vol. 28, No. 4 (December 2013): pp. 473–87.

Hirst, Samuel J. 'Anti-Westernism on the European Periphery: The Meaning of Soviet-Turkish Convergence in the 1930s'. *Slavic Review*, Vol. 72, No. 1 (Spring 2013): pp. 32–53.

Holtorf, Cornelius J. 'The Life-Histories of Megaliths in Mecklenburg-Vorpommern (Germany)'. *World Archaeology*, The Past in the Past: The Reuse of Ancient Monuments, Vol. 30, No. 1 (June 1998): pp. 23–38.

İhtifalci Mehmed Ziya Bey. *İstanbul ve Boğaziçi: Bizans ve Türk Medeniyetinin Eserleri* (Istanbul and the Bosphorus: The Monuments of Byzantine and Turkish Civilisations). İstanbul: 1937.

Innokentii, Archbishop of Kherson and Tauride. *Izbrannye Sochineniia*. St Petersburg: Russkaia Simfoniia, 2006.

Ivask, George [Yuri]. 'North and South: Some Reflections on Russian Culture'. *Russian Review*, Vol. 24, No. 3 (July 1965): pp. 235–44.

Jelavich, Barbara. *Russia's Balkan Entanglements, 1806–1914*. Cambridge: Cambridge University Press, 2004.

Jelavich, Charles, and Barbara Jelavich. *The Establishment of the Balkan National States, 1804–1920*. Seattle: University of Washington Press, 1986.

Jersild, Austin. *Orientalism and Empire: North Caucasus Mountain Peoples and the Georgian Frontier, 1845–1917*. Montreal: McGill-Queen's University Press, 2002.

Karamzin, Nikolay Mikhailovich. *Istoriia Gosudarstva Rossiiskogo, Tom:1*. Moskva: Olma-Press, 2004.

Kazhdan, Alexander. 'Russian Pre-Revolutionary Studies on Eleventh-Century Byzantium'. In *Byzantine Studies: Essays on the Slavic World and the Eleventh Century*, Vol. 9, edited by Speros Vryonis, Jr., pp. 111–24. New Rochelle, NY: Aristide D. Caratzas, 1992.

Kennan, George F. *The Fateful Alliance: France, Russia, and the Coming of the First World War*. New York: Pantheon Books, 1984.

Khatchadourian, Lori. 'Making Nations from the Ground up: Traditions of Classical Archaeology in the South Caucasus'. *American Journal of Archaeology*, Vol. 112, No. 2 (April 2008): pp. 247–78.

Klejn, Lev S. *Fenomen Sovetskii Arkheologii*. St Petersburg: FARN, 1993.

Klejn, Lev S., and Igor L. Tikhonov. 'The Beginnings of University Archaeology in Russia'. In *The Beginnings of Academic Pre- and Protohistoric Archaeology (1890–1930) in a European Perspective: International Meeting at the Humboldt University of Berlin, March 2003, 13–16*, edited by Johan Callmer, pp. 197–207. Rahden: Verlag Marie Leidorf, 2006.

Kocabaş, Rezan. 'Müzecilik Hareketi ve İlk Müze Okulunun Açılışı' (Opening of the First School of Museology). *Belgelerle Türk Tarihi Dergisi*, Vol. 21 (1969): pp. 74–8.

Kohl, Philip L. 'Introduction.' In *Selective Remembrances: Archaeology in the Construction, Commemoration, and Consecration of National Past*, edited by Philip L. Kohl, Mara Kozelsky and Nachman Ben-Yehuda, pp. 1–28. Chicago, IL: University of Chicago Press, 2007.

Komandorova, N. I. *Russkii Stambul*. Moskva: Veche, 2009.

Korenevskiy, A. V. 'Russia's Byzantine Heritage: The Anatomy of Myth'. *Novoe Proshloe / The New Past*, No. 1 (2016): pp. 62–79.

Kozelski, Mara. 'Ruins into Relics: The Monument to Saint Vladimir on the Excavations of Chersonessos, 1827–57'. *Russian Review*, Vol. 63, No. 4 (October 2004): pp. 655–72.

Kozelsky, Mara. *Christianizing Crimea: Shaping Sacred Space in the Russian Empire and Beyond*. DeKalb: Northern Illinois University Press, 2010.

Lapteva, L. P. *Istoriia Slavianovedeniia v Rossii v XIX Veke*. Moskva: Indrik, 2005.

Lieven, Dominic. *Nicholas II: Twilight of the Empire*. New York: St Martin's Press, 1994.

Lieven, Dominic. *Towards the Flame: Empire, War and the End of Tsarist Russia*. London: Penguin Books, 2015.

Lisovoi, N. N. 'Russkoe Dukhovnoe i Politicheskoe Prisutstvie v Sviatoi Zemle i na Blizhnem Vostoke v XIX – nachale XX v'. Unpublished Ph.D. dissertation, Institut Vseobshchei Istorii RAN, Moskva, 2007.

Lowden, John. 'Illustrated Octateuch Manuscripts: A Byzantine Phenomenon'. In *The Old Testament in Byzantium*, edited by Paul Magdalino and Robert Nelson, pp. 107–52. 2010. Washington, DC: Harvard University Press, 2010.

Lowenthal, David. *The Past Is a Foreign Country*. New York: Cambridge University Press, 1985.

Makdisi, Ussama. 'Ottoman Orientalism'. *The American Historical Review*, Vol. 107, No. 3 (June 2002): pp. 768–96.

Malley, Shawn. 'Layard Enterprise: Victorian Archaeology and Informal Imperialism in Mesopotamia'. *International Journal of Middle East Studies*, Vol. 40, No. 4 (November 2008): pp. 623–46.

Mansel, Arif Müfid. *Osman Hamdi Bey*. Ankara: Ankara Üniversitesi, 1959.

Marchand, Suzanne. *Down from Olympus: Archaeology and Philhellenism in Germany, 1750–1970*. Princeton, NJ: Princeton University Press, 2003.

Marchand, Suzanne L. 'The Rhetoric of Artifacts and the Decline of Classical Humanism: The Case of Josef Strzygowski'. *History and Theory*, Vol. 33, No. 4, Theme Issue 33: Proof and Persuasion in History (December 1994): pp. 106–130.

Marchand, Suzanne. 'The View from the Land: Austrian Art Historians and the Interpretation of Croatian Art'. In *Dalmatia and the Mediterranean: Portable Archaeology and the Poetics of Influence*, edited by Alina Payne, pp. 21–58. Leiden: Brill, 2014.

Mardin, Şerif. *Türk Modernleşmesi: Makaleler IV* (Essays on Turkish Modernisation)]. İstanbul: İletişim, 1991.

Marr, Nikolai Yakovlevich, and Josif Abgarovich Orbeli. *Arkheologicheskaya Ekspeditsiya 1916 goda v Van: Doklady.* St Petersburg: Russkoe Arkheologicheskoe Obshchestvo, 1922.

Mazour, Anatole G. *Modern Russian Historiography: A Revised Edition.* Westport, CT: Greenwood Press, 1975.

Mazower, Mark. *Salonica: City of Ghosts, Christians, Muslims and Jews, 1430–1950.* New York: Alfred A. Knopf, 2005.

Mazower, Mark. *The Balkans: A Short History.* New York: Modern Library, 2000.

McMeekin, Sean. *The Russian Origins of the First World War.* Cambridge: Harvard University Press, 2011.

Medvedev, Igor Pavlovich. *Peterburgskoe Vizantinovedenie.* St Petersburg: Aleteiia, 2006.

Meyendorff, John. *Byzantium and the Rise of Russia: A Study of Byzantino-Russian Relations in the Fourteenth Century.* Crestwood, NY: St Vladimir's Seminary Press, 1989.

Miliukov, Paul. *Political Memoirs: 1905–1917.* Ann Arbor: University of Michigan Press, 1967.

Miller, William. *Trebizond: The Last Greek Empire.* London: S.P.C.K., 1926.

Mongait, Aleksandr. *Archaeology in the USSR.* Moscow: Foreign Languages Publishing House, 1959.

Musin, A. E. *Imperatorskaia Arkheologicheskaia Komissiia, 1859–1917: U Istokov Otechestvennoi Arkheologii i Okhrany Kul'turnogo Naslediia: K 150-letiiu so Dnia Osnovaniia.* St Petersburg: DB, 2009.

Nora, Pierre. 'Between Memory and History: Les Lieux de Mémoire'. *Representations.* No. 26, Special Issue: Memory and Counter-Memory (Spring 1989): pp. 7–24.

Norman, Geraldine. *The Hermitage: The Biography of a Great Museum.* London: Jonathan Cape, 1997.

Norton, Claire. 'Blurring the Boundaries: Intellectual and Cultural Interactions between the Eastern and Western; Christian and Muslim Worlds'. In *The Renaissance and the Ottoman World*, edited by Anna Contadini, Claire Norton, pp. 3–22. Burlington: Ashgate, 2013.

Obolensky, Dimitri. *Byzantium and the Slavs.* London: Variorum Reprints, 1971.

O'Neill, Kelly. *Claiming Crimea: A History of Catherine the Great's Southern Empire.* New Haven, CT: Yale University Press, 2017.

Ortaylı, İlber. *İmparatorluğun En Uzun Yüzyılı* (The Longest Century of the Empire). İstanbul: Alkım Yayınevi, 2006.

Ortaylı, İlber. 'Tanzimat'ta Vilayetlerde Eski Eser Taraması' (Antiquities Survey in Provinces during Tanzimat). In *Tanzimat'tan Cumhuriyet'e Türkiye Ansiklopedisi* 6 (Encyclopedia of Turkey from Tanzimat to the Republic), edited by Feroz Ahmad, pp. 1599–603. İstanbul: İletişim Yayınları, 1985.

Osman Hamdi Bey, and Marie de Launay. *1873 Yılında Türkiye'de Halk Giysileri: Elbise-i Osmaniyye* (The Popular Costumes of Turkey in 1873). İstanbul: Sabancı Üniversitesi, 1999.

Osman Hamdi Bey, and Osgan Efendi. *Le Tumulus de Nemroud-Dagh* (The Tumulus of Mount Nemrud). İstanbul: Archaeology and Art Publications, 1987.

Osman Hamdi Bey, and Osgan Efendi. *Le Voyage à Nemrud Dağı d'Osman Hamdi Bey et Osgan Efendi (1883): Récit de voyage et photographies*. Paris: Institut français d'études anatoliennes-Georges Dumézil, 2010.

Osman Hamdi Bey, and Theodore Reinach. *Une Nécropole Royale à Sidon: Fouilles de Hamdy Bey* (A Royal Necropolis in Sidon: Excavations of Hamdi Bey). Paris: Ernest Leroux, 1892.

Ousterhout, Robert. 'Ethnic Identity and Cultural Appropriation in Early Ottoman Architecture'. *Muqarnas*, Vol. 12 (1995): pp. 48–62.

Ousterhout, Robert. 'The Rediscovery of Constantinople and the Beginning of Byzantine Archaeology: A Historiographical Survey'. In *Scramble for the Past: A Story of Archaeology in the Ottoman Empire, 1753-1914*, edited by Zainab Bahrani, Zeynep Çelik and Edhem Eldem, pp. 181–211. İstanbul: SALT, 2011.

Özdemir, Ayşe. 'A History of Turkish Archaeology from the 19th Century to the End of the Single Party Period'. Unpublished master's thesis, Boğaziçi University, İstanbul, 2001.

Özdoğan, Mehmet. 'Ideology and Archaeology in Turkey'. In *Archaeology Under Fire: Nationalism, Politics and Heritage in the Eastern Mediterranean and Middle East*, edited by Lynn Meskell, pp. 111–23. London: Routledge, 2002.

Paksoy, İsmail Günay. 'Bazı Belgeler Işığında Osmanlı Devleti'nin Kültür Mirası Üzerine Düşünceler' (Opinions on the Cultural Legacy of the Ottoman Empire in the Light of Documents). In *Osman Hamdi Bey ve Dönemi, 17-18 Aralık 1922*, pp. 202–9. İstanbul: Tarih Vakfı Yurt Yayınları, 1993.

Papoulidis, Konstantinos K. *To Rosiko Arheologiko Institouto Konstantinoupoleos (1894-1914)* (Russian Archaeological Institute in Constantinople, 1894–1914). Thessaloniki: Idrima Meleton Hersonisu tu Emu, 1987.

Papoulidis, Konstantin. 'The Russian Archaeological Institute of Constantinople (1894-1914): From Its Establishment until Today'. In *Perceptions of the Past in the Turkish Republic: Classical and Byzantine Periods*, edited by Scott Redford and Nina Ergin, pp. 187–92. Leuven: Peeters, 2010.

Pearson, Owen. *Albania and King Zog: Independence, Republic and Monarchy, 1908-1939*. Vol. 1 of *Albania in the Twentieth Century Series*. London: I.B. Tauris, 2004.

Perry, Duncan M. 'Death of a Russian Consul: Macedonia 1903'. *Russian History*, Vol. 7, No. 1 (1980): pp. 201–12.

Perry, Duncan M. *Stefan Stamboulov and the Emergence of Modern Bulgaria, 1870-1895*. Durham: Duke University Press, 1993.

Pervushin, M. V. 'Russkaia Dukhovnaia Missiia v Iyerusalime'. In *Khristiyanstvo: Vek za Vekom*, edited by Archbishop Mark Golovkov Yegoryevsk, pp. 499–506. Moskva: Dar, 2011.

Pervushin, M. V. 'Palomnichestvo na Sviatuiu Zemliu v XIX Veke'. In
    Khristiyanstvo: Vek za Vekom, edited by Archbishop Mark Golovkov
    Yegoryevsk, pp. 507–10. Moskva: Dar, 2011.

Petrovich, Michael Boro. *The Emergence of Russian Panslavism, 1856–1870*.
    Westport: Greenwood Press, 1985.

Petrovich, Michael Boro. *A History of Modern Serbia, 1804–1918*, Vol.
    2. New York: Harcourt Brace Jovanovich, 1976.

Pokrovskii, N. V. 'Zhelatel'naia Postanovka Tserkovnoi Arkheologii v
    Dukhovnykh Akademiiakh'. *Khristiyanskoe Chtenie*, No. 3 (1906): pp.
    333–49.

Pokrovskii, N. V. 'O Merakh k Sokhraneniiu Pamiatnikov Tserkovnoi Stariny'.
    Khristiyanskoe Chtenie, No. 4 (1906): pp. 471–98.

Popruzhenko, M. G. *Sorokaletie Uchenoi Deiatel'nosti Akademika Feodora
    Ivanovicha Uspenskogo (rech', skazannaia v zasdanii Istoriko-Filologicheskogo
    Obshchestva pri Imperatorskom Novorossiiskom Universitet v den iubileia – 3
    Noiabria 1911 g.)*. Odessa: Ekonomicheskaia Tipografiia, 1912.

Priakhin, A. D. *Istoriia Otechestvennoi Arkheologii*. Voronezh: Voronezhskii
    Gosudarstvenny Universitet, 2005.

Prousis, Theophilus C. *Russian Society and the Greek Revolution*.
    DeKalb: Northern Illinois University Press, 1994.

Ragsdale, Hugh. 'Evaluating the Tradition of Russian Aggression: Catherine II
    and the Greek Project'. *Slavonic and East European Review*, No. 66 (1988):
    pp. 91–117.

Riha, Thomas. *A Russian European: Paul Miliukov in Russian Politics*. Notre
    Dame: Notre Dame University Press, 1969.

Rossos, Andrew. 'Serbian-Bulgarian Relations, 1903–1914'. *Canadian Slavonic
    Papers / Revue Canadienne des Slavistes*, Vol. 23, No. 4 (December 1981):
    pp. 394–408.

Saunders, David. *Russia in the Age of Reaction and Reform, 1801–1881*.
    London: Longman, 1992.

Schimmelpenninck van der Oye, David. 'Orientalizm – delo tonkoe'. *Ab Imperio*,
    Vol. 1 (2002): pp. 249–64.

Shaw, Stanford, and Ezel Kural Shaw. *History of the Ottoman Empire and
    Modern Turkey*. New York: Cambridge University Press, 1976.

Shaw, Wendy M. K. 'Islamic Arts in the Ottoman Imperial Museum, 1889–
    1923'. *Ars Orientalis*, Vol. 30, Exhibiting the Middle East: Collections and
    Perceptions of Islamic Art (2000): pp. 55–68.

Shaw, Wendy M. K. *Osmanlı Müzeciliği: Müzeler, Arkeoloji ve Tarihin
    Görselleşmesi* (Possessors and Possessed: Museums, Archaeology,
    and the Visualization of History in the Late Ottoman Empire).
    İstanbul: İletişim, 2004.

Shnirelman, Victor A. 'The Faces of Nationalist Archaeology in Russia'. In
    Nationalism and Archaeology in Europe, edited by Margarita Díaz-Andreu
    García and T. C. Champion, pp. 218–42. Boulder: Westview Press, 1996.

Silberman, Neil Asher. 'Promised Lands and Chosen Peoples: The Politics and Poetics of Archaeological Narrative'. In *Nationalism, Politics, and the Practice of Archaeology*, edited by Philip L. Kohl and Clare Fawcett, pp. 249–62. Cambridge: Cambridge University Press, 1995.

Simms, J. Y. 'The Economic Impact of the Russian Famine of 1891–92'. *The Slavonic and East European Review*, Vol. 60, No. 1 (January 1982): pp. 63–74.

Sokolov, I. I. 'Vizantologicheskaia Traditsiia v S.-Peterburgskoi Dukhovnoi Akademii'. *Khristiyanskoe Chtenie*, Vol. 1 (1904): pp. 143–56.

Spasskii, A. A. 'Noveyshii Vizantinizm i Ego Znachenie', *Bogoslovskii Vestnik*, T. 2, Vol. 4 (1894): pp. 34–62.

Stavrianos, L. S. *The Balkans, 1815–1914*. New York: Holt, Rinehart, and Winston, 1963.

Stavrou, Theofanis George. *Russian Interests in Palestine, 1882–1914: A Study of Religious and Educational Enterprise*. Thessaloniki: Institute for Balkan Studies, 1963.

Stepanova, E. V. 'Iubileinoe Zaselenie, Posviashchennoe Deiatel'nosti Russkogo Arkheologicheskogo Instituta v Konstantinopole (23 Ianvaria 1985 g.), *Vizantiiskii Vremennik*, Vol. 46 (1985): pp. 276–7.

Stockdale, Melissa Kirschke. *Paul Miliukov and the Quest for a Liberal Russia, 1880–1918*. Ithaca: Cornell University Press, 1996.

Strizhova, N. B. 'Moskovskii Arkheologicheskii Institut po Materialam Otdela Pis'mennykh Istochnikov Gosudarstvennogo Istoricheskogo Muzeia'. In *Ocherki Istorii Russkoi i Sovetskoi Arkheologii*, edited by A. A. Formozov, pp. 102–20. Moskva: Akademiia Nauk SSSR, 1991.

Tan, Ahmet Cemil. 'Osman Hamdi Bey'. *Ankara Sanat*, Vol. 10 (1 February 1967): pp. 8–9.

Tanyeri-Erdemir, Tuğba. 'Archaeology as a Source of National Pride in the Early Years of the Turkish Republic'. *Journal of Field Archaeology*, Vol. 31, No. 4 (Winter 2006): pp. 381–93.

Thaden, Edward C. *Russia and the Balkan Alliance of 1912*. University Park: Pennsylvania State University Press, 1965.

The Moscow Times. 'Russian Orchestra Holds Concert in Ruined City of Palmyra'. Last modified 5 May 2016, http://www.themoscowtimes.com/arts_n_ideas/news/article/russian-orchestra-holds-concert-in-ruined-city-of-palmyra/568161.html. Accessed 15 June 2016.

Tikhonov, Igor. 'Russia'. In *The History of Archaeology: An Introduction*, edited by Paul Bahn, pp. 155–76. New York: Routledge, 2014.

Tikhonov, Igor L. 'Archaeology at St. Petersburg University (From 1724 Until Today)'. *Antiquity*, Vol. 81, No. 312 (2007): pp. 446–56.

Tikhonov, Igor L. 'Deiatel'nost' Akademika A. S. Lappo-Danilevskogo v Arkheologii'. In *Ocherki Istorii Otechestvennoi Arkheologii*, Vyp. 2. Moskva: Gosudarstvenny Istoricheskii Muzei Institut Arkheologii RAN, 1998.

Trigger, Bruce G. 'Alternative Archaeologies: Nationalist, Colonialist, Imperialist'. *Man*, Vol. 19, No. 3 (1984): pp. 355–70.

Trigger, Bruce G. 'Romanticism, Nationalism, and Archaeology'. In *Nationalism, Politics, and the Practice of Archaeology*, edited by Philip L. Kohl and Clare Fawcett, pp. 263–79. Cambridge: Cambridge University Press, 1995.

Trigger, Bruce G. *A History of Archaeological Thought*. Cambridge: Cambridge University Press, 1989.

Trimbur, Dominique. 'A French Presence in Palestine: Notre-Dame de France'. *Bulletin du Centre de Recherche Français à Jérusalem* [Online], No. 3 (1998): pp. 117–40.

Tsetskhladze, Gocha R. *North Pontic Archaeology: Recent Discoveries and Studies*. Leiden: Brill, 2001.

Tunkina, I. V. *Russkaia Nauka o Klassicheskikh Drevnostiakh Iuga Rossii (XVIII-seredina XIX v.)*. St Petersburg: Nauka, 2002.

Tunkina, I.V. 'Kabinet Redkostei Chernomorskogo Depo Kart'. In *Ocherki Istorii Russkoi i Sovetskoi Arkheologii*, edited by A. A. Formozov, pp. 9–24. Moskva: Akademiia Nauk SSSR, 1991.

Ursinus, Michael. 'Byzantine History in Late Ottoman Turkish Historiography'. *Byzantine and Modern Greek Studies*, Vol. 10 (1986): pp. 211–22.

Ursinus, Michael. 'From Süleyman Pasha to Mehmet Fuat Köprülü: Roman and Byzantine History in Late Ottoman Historiography'. *Byzantine and Modern Greek Studies*, Vol. 12 (1988): pp. 305–14.

Uspenskii, F. I. *Ocherki Po Istorii Vizantiiskoi Obrazovannosti: Istoriia Krestovykh Pokhodov*. Moskva: Mysl', 2001.

Uspenskii, F. I. *Vizantiiskii Pisatel' Nikita Akominat iz Khon*. 1874.

Uspenskii, F. I. 'Iz Istorii Vizantinovedeniia v Rossii'. *Annaly*, Vol. 1 (1922), pp. 110–26.

Ünal, Hasan. 'Young Turk Assessments of International Politics, 1906–9'. In *Turkey: Identity, Democracy, Politics*, edited by Sylvia Kedourie, pp. 30–44. New York: Routledge, 2013.

Üre, Pınar. 'Byzantine Past, Russian Present: Russian Archaeological Institute's Trabzon Expedition during the First World War'. In *Byzantium's Other Empire: Hagia Sophia in Trebizond*, edited by Antony Eastmond, pp. 215–36. İstanbul: Koç University Press, 2016.

Vakh, K. A. '"İyerusalimskii Proyekt" Rossii: B. P. Mansurov i Russkie Postroiki'. In *Velikii Knyaz' Konstantin Nikolayevich i Russkii Iyerusalim: K 150-Letiyu Osnovaniya*, edited by K. A. Vakh, pp. 16–25. Moskva: Indrik, 2012.

Vasiliev, Alexander A. 'Byzantine Studies in Russia, Past and Present'. *The American Historical Review*, Vol. 32, No. 3 (April 1927): pp. 539–45.

Vasiliev, Alexander A. 'Was Old Russia a Vassal State of Byzantium?' *Speculum*, Vol. 7, No. 3 (July 1932): pp. 350–60.

Vernadsky, George. *Russian Historiography: A History*. Belmont, MA: Nordland Publishing, 1978.

Volokolamskii, Archbishop Arsenii. 'V Strane Svyashchennykh Vospominanii'. *Bogoslovskii Vestnik*, T. 2, Nos 7/8 (1901): pp. 542–92.

Volokolamskii, Archbishop Arsenii. 'V Strane Svyashchennykh Vospominanii'. *Bogoslovskii Vestnik*, T. 1, No. 3 (1902): pp. 532–61.

Vovchenko, Denis Vladimirovich. 'Containing Balkan Nationalism: Imperial Russia and Ottoman Christians (1856–1912)'. Unpublished Ph.D. Dissertation, University of Minnesota, August 2008.

Welles, C. Bradford. 'Michael Ivanovich Rostovtzeff (1870–1952)'. *Russian Review*, Vol. 12, No. 2 (April 1953): pp. 128–33.

Wiener, Leo. 'A Victim of Autocracy: Prof. Milyukov, Lowell Lecturer 'The Russian Crisis'. *Boston Evening Transcript*, 29 November 1904.

Winterer, Caroline. *The Culture of Classicism: Ancient Greece and Rome in American Intellectual Life, 1780–1910*. Baltimore: Johns Hopkins University Press, 2002.

Yıldız, Şule Kılıç. 'A Review of Byzantine Studies and Architectural Historiography in Turkey Today (1)'. *METU Journal of the Faculty of Architecture*, Vol. 28, No. 2 (2011/12): pp. 63–80.

Yosmaoğlu, İpek. *Blood Ties: Religion, Violence, and the Politics of Nationhood in Ottoman Macedonia, 1878–1908*. Ithaca, NY: Cornell University Press, 2013.

Yosmaoğlu, İpek. 'Counting Bodies, Shaping Souls: The 1903 Census and National Identity in Ottoman Macedonia'. *International Journal of Middle East Studies*, Vol. 38, No. 1 (February 2006): pp. 55–77.

Zenkovsky, Vasily V. 'The Spirit of Russian Orthodoxy'. *Russian Review*, Vol. 22, No. 1 (January 1963): pp. 38–55.

Zorin, Andrey. *Kormya Dvuglavogo Orla: Literatura i Gosudarstvennaia Ideologiia v Rossii v Posledney Tretii XVIII – Pervoy Tretii XIX Veka*. Moskva: Novoe Literaturnoe Obozrenie, 2001.

Zürcher, Erik Jan. *Modernleşen Türkiye'nin Tarihi* [Turkey, A Modern History]. İstanbul: İletişim, 2007.

Index

With a Prayer from Palmyra: Music
    Revives the Ancient Walls'
    (concert) 1
Witte, Sergei 72, 74

Yasebelev, S. A. 136
Yıldız Evrâkı 8
Yosmaoğlu, İpek 172 n.53

Young Turk Revolution 43, 117, 118
Young Turks 44, 117
Yudenich, Nikolai 133

Zinoviev, Ivan Alekseevich 90, 95,
    102, 104–5, 108, 116
Zlatarskii, V. N. 99
Zürcher, Erik Jan 158 n.1